LADY UNVEILED

Piñata Publishing
626 Old Plantation Road
Jekyll Island, GA 31527
(912) 635-9402
www.pinatapub.com

Library of Congress Cataloging-in-Publication Data
Bauer Mueller, Pamela.
Lady Unveiled : Catharine Greene Miller, 1755-1814 / Pamela
Bauer Mueller.
     pages cm
ISBN 978-0-9809163-3-1
1. Greene, Catharine Littlefield—Fiction. 2. United States—
History—Revolution, 1775-1783—Fiction. I. Title.
PS3602.A93566L33 2014   813'.6--DC23   2013027565

Cover art by Gini Steele
Typeset by Vancouver Desktop Publishing Centre
Printed and bound in the United States by Cushing-Malloy, Inc.

To Miss Bellie —
Happy Birthday 2014

Lady Unveiled

Catharine Greene Miller
1755-1814

Enjoy this true story
Of amazing Kitty —

Warm Wishes,
Pamela Bauer Mueller
Pamela Bauer Mueller
06/28/14

PIÑATA PUBLISHING

For Michael Mueller—my dearest friend, my loving husband, my best critic and my partner in life. Thank you for making the journey easier, more intense, more interesting and more fun.

"I Can Do All Things Through Christ Who Strengthens Me"
—*Philippians 4:13*

AUTHOR'S NOTE

It is a true blessing to have a career that I love—even when words aren't flowing smoothly—and the company of many caring, creative supporters. Writing is a solitary pursuit, yet constantly enriched with love given and received.

Although my writing practice can be irregular, I am not satisfied for long if I'm not creating. I have a busy family life and follow numerous pursuits. I'm involved in church and community service, enjoy traveling and learning new things, and have friends and family spread around the globe. Returning to a story formulated in my mind, then transformed into written words, brings me a sense of deep personal peace.

After moving to the South thirteen years ago, I quickly discovered a passion for its past. The region's rich history and vibrant characters captivated my attention as it proclaimed its singular spirit. In my historical novels, I choose protagonists whose stories "need to be told," relating their tales through the novel format. Because I write about real people and true events, I have discovered that by utilizing dialogue I am able to bring the narrative to life and enhance the character development.

My newest character, Catharine Littlefield Greene Miller, certainly broke the bonds of tradition. She attracted me from the moment I heard her story from a naturalist on Cumberland Island. This sensational, controversial, almost mythical figure happily bent the rules of propriety, ultimately expanding the role of the eighteenth-century woman. Like two of my other female protagonists, Mary Musgrove and Eliza Lucas Pinckney, she was certainly "ahead of her time." But she had a unique difference—Kitty assisted in an epochal invention.

Kitty Littlefield, like her husband General Nathanael

Greene, was born and raised in Rhode Island. To gain a personal feel for their natural environment and background, I visited the jagged cliffs and craggy hills of Block Island, where Kitty Littlefield lived as a child. Additional research in Potowomut, Coventry, Providence and Newport, Rhode Island, helped to fill in the facts about their time together as a young couple.

I unexpectedly discovered that both Georgia and her little sister Rhode Island continue to vie in rendering honor and tribute to the greatness of General Nathanael Greene. Claiming the brilliant strategist and capable warrior as its most illustrious hero, each state also reveres his memorable, intelligent and charming wife Lady Greene.

I visited Nathanael Greene's vault in Savannah and Kitty Littlefield Greene Miller's gravesite on Cumberland Island, and prayed over the two new "friends" who had so deeply touched my life.

I am thankful to my Savior for granting me His presence as I tackled this undertaking. I also thank Him for showing me that I am not special, simply blessed, to chronicle their lives.

Enjoy Kitty's story.

PROLOGUE

1793

Eli had given up. Turning slowly to face Phineas and Kitty, he no longer hid his frustration and embarrassment and mumbled dejectedly, "I have reached the end of my road; I am prepared to abandon this machine altogether."

All three of them stared at Eli's invention, willing it to spring into action.

"It is not such a difficult task," Eli said to the cotton engine, as if to a lazy child. "The teeth I have set into the wooden cylinder pull the cotton fibers away from the seeds, and the seeds drop away..."

Feeding a handful of fluffy cotton into the machine, he turned the crank. Wheels studded with wire teeth caught the lint and ripped it from the seeds. The seeds fell to the bottom of the machine. Up to this point the engine worked perfectly. But Eli had found no way to remove the accumulated lint from the teeth, which impeded its passage between the slats. It took only a few moments before the machine bogged down. Again.

With the mood as somber as a wake Phineas studied his friend, trying to find encouraging words.

But Kitty's thoughts were elsewhere, her blue-green eyes darkening with concentration. Finally she spoke.

"Eli, do you remember on the vessel coming to Savannah when we talked about the giant? How if we let him, he'll take away our peace?"

Eli nodded reluctantly, wondering what she would say next. She seemed to have a way of getting him out of a rut.

"Please retain your focus," she continued. "You are so close. Just keep the giant at bay."

Phineas' hand was firm on Eli's shoulder as he agreed. "You are almost there, my friend."

Seeking a solution, Kitty continued. "Eli, have you considered replacing the wooden pegs with different wire hooks?"

Her question was met with silence. After a long moment Eli responded. "I have drawn my own wire, but I will take another look at it." His words came out splintered.

Rising slowly, he reclaimed the model and headed for the door. Kitty watched him solemnly.

Just as he grasped the door latch, Kitty's eyes widened with an insight. She startled her companions by throwing back her head and laughing delightedly.

Dashing to the door, she stood before Eli. "What! Would you allow such a trifling problem to change your resolve? Trust it to a woman's wit to find the cure—prepare to turn the cylinder once again!" Her eyes filled with mischief.

Hurrying across to the fireplace, she picked up the hearth brush and came back to wave it over his model, now sitting on the table. "Perhaps this brush's stiff bristles would help you remove the lint from the teeth!" She flicked the hearth brush at the cylinder, still clogged with cotton fibers.

After a few flicks of her wrist, the cotton fibers lay in a pile on the table top.

Eli stared at her in shock and amazement, struggling to understand how such an elegant solution could be so simple.

Then he cried out, "Kitty, thank you for the cue! I do believe that's it!" Brown eyes ignited with inspiration, he rushed out of the room with his model.

Alone in the basement, hands trembling in anticipation, Eli went back to work. He painstakingly added another cylinder that turned in the opposite direction of the picker and forced it to move faster. As the short stiff hog's bristles combed and removed the cotton, the fibers were thrown off away from the gin, making them easier to retrieve. The cotton filaments fell in small, white, downy clouds.

Sinking into a chair, Eli wearily massaged his shadowed eye sockets and pushed back his disheveled hair. He sat quietly, rubbing his palms against the tops of his thighs. Time passed, and he looked down at his hands, pressed together in front of him as if in prayer. Staring vacantly at the floor, he kept trying to sort it all out.

Eli felt his fingers wiping away a slow stream of tears trickling down his cheeks.

"Kitty has solved the puzzle. We have done it. My machine is complete." A small smile gradually blossomed into a joyful grin.

Pulling himself together, he staggered upstairs to inform his friends, who waited anxiously for him by a window. Eli's face radiated triumph as his fragile voice shared his news.

"If my calculations are accurate, this machine will turn out in one hour what several workers cleaning cotton by hand now do in a day." His grin spread.

Kitty was startled by her overflowing sense of pride in this news.

Her lower lip quivered as she reached up to hug Eli. She turned to Phineas, flinging her arms around his neck and kissing him soundly. She let out a whoop of delight.

Thunderstruck, they could only stare at each other as the room became wrapped in peaceful silence. Outside, a night bird cooed to its mate, who answered with a seductive warble. Palm fronds rattled in the rising wind.

The world had just changed forever.

Part 1

ONE

1764

She gazed out over the craggy cliffs, searching for the mainland almost twelve miles away. For the moment she felt content with the silence and the gathering light. Rugged hills held the early morning mist and enshrouded the landscape. The air was filled with the scent of honeysuckle and the tang of sea-spray while distant birds heralded the morning with a melodic chorus. She inhaled long breaths of sea air, clearing her head. Gathering her knees to her chest, Kitty tipped her face toward the sun. The light strengthened effortlessly as the cloudless sky opened to depths of gentle blue. As she watched, the sun rose majestically over the Atlantic.

She sat quietly and let the sunbeams warm her face. Her horse foraged through a field of young dandelions and other dew-soaked weeds, unaware of the air of mystery settling over the azure waters below. Kitty squinted as she discerned movement near the water. Playful harbor seals appeared on the enormous rocks, splashing themselves and each other as they welcomed the sunshine. Kitty laughed softly and looked around for her favorite bird: the great egret. Her eyes wandered over the medley of stone colors on the sandy beach below while shorebirds skipped to the water's edge. Not an egret in sight. Too early perhaps.

This was Kitty's first return visit since leaving Block Island several years after her mother's death. Only six years old at the time of her mother's passing, she stayed on the island with her father, John Littlefield, and her four siblings. Kitty vividly remembered standing by her mother Phebe's gravesite as they lowered her coffin into the ground. She held her older brother's hand and thought about her young mother flying up into the Heavens and meeting Jesus. But she could not remember who told her about that. Probably her father, since he loved to read.

For the next two and a half years, Kitty stayed close to her family, creating precious memories as she rode her horse over the meadows, across the trails and into the dunes. Her schooling consisted of listening to the adults at the Meeting Hall, where the conversations were generally political or religious. Her father, an educated man and a deputy to the General Assembly of Rhode Island, spent his evenings with the children recounting stories of their kinsmen and their island, asking them questions to help them understand cause and effect. They begged him for pirate stories, and he obliged them with true accounts of French privateers who invaded and seized Block Island.

"Hear me now. Your great-grandfather Ray on your Mama's side was the patriarch of the settlement and was as just and as firm as a leader can be. Well, he hid his family's treasures when he saw the French marauders coming onto the island. They searched his dwelling and found nothing. Then they demanded that he show them where the goods were." At this point John Littlefield paused for effect, searching the faces of his speechless children.

"Well, that brave man told them 'Nay' and for that he was beaten, tied to a tree, and left for dead."

Kitty gasped and scurried over to his lap. "Papa, did he die?" she whispered.

John reached out and squeezed her hand. "No, my little one. The pirates eventually gave up and left the island, and the other settlers cut him down from the tree. He was mighty weak and ailin' for some time, but he pulled through it."

"Did my mama know him?" asked the inquisitive six-year-old, now warmly accommodated in his arms.

"Aye, she did, my Kitty," he smiled warmly. "Now, let us prepare for sleep. Johnny, would you say prayers for us this evening?"

John had seen great potential in Kitty and wanted her to get an education, but there were no schools on the island. There was also no sense of time or urgency and no need to quicken the pace of life. The children rode horses everywhere, straddling them bareback and racing over fields and trails until they reached the edge of the cliffs, where the entire breadth of the ocean was revealed—extravagantly blue and glittering with sunshine. They became familiar with every stone fence, road and wooden dwelling and the interwoven paths leading between them. Listening to the adults speak at the Meeting Hall, they developed good vocabularies, but were atrocious writers and spellers.

John wanted more for his sons and for Kitty. He recognized Kitty's high intelligence and jumped at the opportunity when it presented itself. His wife Phebe's sister Catharine, the spouse of William Greene Jr.—a Rhode Island political leader—reached out to him and offered to take Kitty into her home on the mainland. Because she lived in East Greenwich, there were excellent tutors available, so John selflessly accepted her generous proposal, although it nearly broke his heart to let her go.

So at the tender age of eight, Kitty Littlefield gathered her belongings and went to live in the fine home of her namesake, Aunt Catharine. In order to get there, she had to travel to Newport in a "double-ender": a sailing vessel launched from the beach with the ability to sail or be rowed. Although these boats were considered seaworthy, they terrified Kitty, because she knew first-hand how the shrieking winds could abruptly toss them into channels of huge waves. She had traveled through storms that savagely lashed the little boats and sent torrents of windswept rain across the bay's narrow, sandy width. Her fear of the winds and currents kept her in East Greenwich for nearly a year, but her desire to spend time with her family finally overcame her dread of the journey, and she returned home.

Her mare Eve whinnied and gently nudged her, lifting her out of her reverie. Swinging onto Eve's broad back, she dug her heels in as they galloped through the lush meadows and around the sea-green ponds. Kitty's emerald eyes sparkled and her glossy black hair streamed behind her, like an extension of her companion's mane.

TWO

1765-1766

Kitty looked forward to her study periods with the tutors provided by her Aunt Catharine and Uncle William. She became an avid reader and enjoyed the well-stocked library in the Greene's East Greenwich home. The world began to open up to her. Only one subject frustrated her—spelling. Although she enjoyed writing, it troubled her that neither she nor her aunt were proper spellers.

"Auntie, I've just added a note in the letter to your friend, Mr. Benjamin Franklin, but I fear it is completely misspelled. Will you have a look at it, please?" requested the ten-year-old child.

"Oh Kitty, you know my spelling deficiency is worse than yours, and I should know better by now," laughed Catharine. "Why, even my husband tells me to take advantage of your tutor."

"But Mr. Franklin is such a learned man. What must he think of your letters?"

"I've known Benjamin for some time now, and he's never mentioned my spelling. I think he's more interested in our lives and your education than my usage of the proper letters. Let me see what you've written," she added, gently lifting the letter from her niece's fingers.

Kitty once asked her aunt if she had been engaged to marry Ben Franklin before she met Uncle Greene.

Surprised by the question, Catharine hesitated before responding. Her eyes softened as she stared into the fire, choosing her words carefully. "No dear, we were never engaged. But we were quite fond of each other. He was a friend of my sister Judith, who is married to Ben's nephew. I met him in their home and was fascinated by his way with words. We have been friends over the years, but he was married, and I was about to be. Now we simply exchange letters."

"Do you think I shall meet him one day?" Kitty had included that suggestion in her note to him.

"I certainly hope so. You two will like each other; of that I am certain," her aunt said with a gracious laugh.

Beautiful gardens surrounded the spacious home of William and Catharine Greene. The house sat near the top of a ridge, offering a lovely view of the emerald valley below. Kitty, along with her young friends, often took picnic lunches to the ridge's summit, where they could enjoy the vistas as well as the warmth of the summer sun. They liked to ride horseback to the opposite slope and descend to the water in Warwick, where the afternoon sunlight pierced holes in the evergreen canopy. They learned to swim in tidal pools among the mats of olive-green seaweed, and played in the lower rocks and crevasses where mussels and starfish lived. Sometimes her aunt and uncle accompanied her and made it a special family event.

Shortly after her arrival, the Greenes bought Kitty an older mare called Bella. She bonded quickly with her new horse, although she missed Eve. Working hard to overcome her fear of the rolling waves, she yearned to return to Block Island more frequently and spend time with Eve and her younger siblings. Her father and older brothers sometimes came to East Greenwich to visit her.

Kitty's Uncle Greene was a leader of the Rhode Island Whig Party. Kitty loved to listen in on the conversations at gatherings taking place around the parlor's inviting fireplace. Her active mind soaked up ideas and new vocabulary words, giving her fodder for more probing queries.

"Uncle Greene, you spoke of the Stamp Act this evening. What exactly is that?"

William turned to her with a warm smile. "In simple terms,

let us say it is an unfair law that the British have placed on our business transactions here in the colonies. They want everything we do to be recorded, printed on paper, stamped and then taxed by the Crown."

She looked surprised. "Why would they do that?" Kitty needed to make sense of this.

"Some say so they can finance their debts from the French and Indian War. But the real problem is that they never allowed contribution from our colonial legislatures."

"And we colonists feel that our rights as English citizens were violated because we were not represented in the decision," interjected Catharine.

These get-togethers were beginning to shape Kitty's character. With a ready tact and her speed of comprehension, she enjoyed the political banter and even the grumbling that accompanied it. She joined in the impulsive dancing around the parlor when they learned that Parliament had repealed the Stamp Act the following year. Listening closely, she found out that the guests predicted more political unrest.

At one of these gatherings Kitty was reunited with her cousin, Sammy Ward. He and his family had visited Kitty's family on Block Island but it had been some time since she'd seen Sammy, the son of Aunt Anna—Phebe's sister—and her husband Samuel from Westerly. Both Sammy and Kitty resembled their beautiful mothers: dark curly hair, a dramatic pair of blue-green eyes and a lively vocabulary. Sammy was several years older than Kitty, good-looking, bright, volatile, and very mischievous. He found out how to make Kitty laugh and basked in her steadfast admiration.

"Sammy, I don't know much about our mothers' family history. Do you?" asked Kitty as they rode the path down to the water. She led him across a rough-planked bridge and on through a fragrant eucalyptus grove to an open meadow. The day was perfect. The sky was an inverted bowl of cerulean blue. The path trickled on, now turning into a precipitous and dangerous-looking descent into a secret cove.

"I know our great-grandfather Simon Ray was blind. Mama told me he could recite a great deal of the Old Testament from memory, though."

"So how did he learn it if he couldn't read?" she asked him.

"Probably the same way you learn things...listening and memorizing." Sammy watched as the expression in Kitty's large eyes changed from confusion to comprehension.

"I see," she said. "My mama told me that his family was one of the first families to come to Plymouth and settle. And my papa says that our grandfather was really old when he died."

"Around 101 or 102, they tell me. Did you know they came to Block Island because they were tired of the people of Massachusetts telling them how to live, how to worship, and they felt they'd lost their liberties? On Block Island, they were isolated and independent. They cleared the land, worked the soil, fished and lived freely."

Cautiously, their horses guided them back to the trail. "That freedom talk is what I keep hearing at the gatherings at my Aunt Catharine's house. They are saying Mother England is not allowing us to govern ourselves as we wish. Is that true?"

"Ah lassie, that conversation is too complicated for you to worry over. Let's enjoy the beauty of the bay and...

"Sammy, what do you mean it's too complicated for me? I want to know," she scowled.

Laughing, he rode up beside her. "I challenge you to a race. First one to reach the sand gets the choice of the sweeties in the basket."

Before he had finished announcing the dare, Kitty's horse Bella shot forward. Turning back to gloat over her lead, she watched in disbelief as he galloped past her, laughter brimming in his eyes. Sammy tossed her a wave and a roguish smile over his shoulder.

THREE

1771-1772

"Uncle Greene, some of the gentlemen who come to the gatherings here are saying the Loyalists are keeping watch over our house. Are we in any danger?" asked Kitty, concern filling her eyes.

"Danger no, but we are under observation. Because I am a leader of the Rhode Island Whig party and a sympathizer to the Patriots, this small group of party supporters makes some Loyalists nervous. But they will not bother you or Catharine."

"Do they also monitor the movements of my cousin Sammy and his family? And what about Sammy's sister Nancy, who is romancing that outspoken Patriot, Nathanael Greene? Are they in danger?" Kitty's anxiety was transparent.

Nathanael Greene, the son of a Quaker farmer and blacksmith, was a frequent visitor and William Greene's distant relative. Born and reared at Potowomut, a tiny community near East Greenwich, he was the second son of Mary Mott, his father Nathanael's second wife. The first wife Phoebe had two sons, making young Nathanael the fourth son. He grew up with seven brothers, and tragically lost his two half-brothers the year he turned nineteen. He and his brother Jacob were then chosen as their father's chief heirs in the forge and mill businesses.

In 1770, Nathanael moved to Coventry to take charge of the family-owned forge built there. Jacob and the younger boys worked with their father at the parent forge at Potowomut. At the age of twenty-eight, Nathanael had the means to build his own home at Coventry on the banks of the Pawtuxet River. It was here that he hoped to bring his bride one day and raise a family.

Subsequently, he was chosen to be a member of the Rhode Island General Assembly and spent considerable time at the gatherings in William Greene's home. He, along with the other young male visitors, had become aware that William's niece Kitty was blossoming into a beautiful young woman.

"Fear not, my child," answered her discerning uncle. "If there were any peril to my family, I would be the first to know." His smile spread slowly across his face.

As the spirit of uprising grew among the Patriots, Nathanel found himself frequently riding the ten miles to Greenwich for political conversation. William Greene's lovely niece Kitty—a teenager but enchanting and comfortable in the society of men—was often in his thoughts. Her ringing laughter was infectious and her lively wit was irresistible to him. He sensed that Kitty was not unaware of her charm. At sixteen, she could already discern that her power of fascination was unique. Her clear-cut features, her white translucent skin and her brilliant blue-green eyes blended together to form a pleasing young lady. If she were not such a kind and considerate girl, one might say she was pampered.

"Kitty, are you interested in any of the gentlemen who come to the gatherings?" asked her aunt as they sat together cross-stitching before the glowing fire.

Kitty lifted her eyes warily, a faint wrinkle of puzzlement at the side of her eyes. "Why do you ask, Auntie?"

Catharine smiled softly. "You are my ward, and my beloved niece. Your Uncle Greene and I have watched you grow up. We love you. The young men who visit our home for the political gatherings are all vying for your attention, which is normal. However, we want you to be selective in your choices. Tell me truly, do any of them interest you?"

Kitty grinned. "Only one, Auntie. And he is not the most handsome of them, but his thoughtfulness and love of the written word are endearing to me."

Catharine knew the answer, but she asked the question nevertheless. "And who would that be, my dear?" Her smile was full of tenderness as she reached over to squeeze Kitty's hand.

Kitty tilted her head to one side and gave a small shrug. "Nathanael Greene. I know he's betrothed to Nancy Ward, but Sammy told me she no longer loves him. I know not if he knows that yet, but when he finds out, I hope to help ease his sadness. He's already just suffered the death of his father." After a thoughtful pause she continued. "Auntie, I wonder why he limps. Do you know?"

One of Catharine's thin eyebrows rose imperceptibly at the sudden twist of the conversation. "Yes dear, I believe I do. William told me he's always had a stiff knee, of unknown origin, since his childhood. Although it makes his gait a bit uneven, it certainly hasn't interfered in his dancing or riding or other boyhood sports. Does it bother you?"

Kitty was quick to reply. "Oh no Auntie! 'Tis only my curiosity rearing up." She laughed lightly. "How would something physical make any difference in my opinion of him? Not when I see such goodness and kindness in his eyes."

Catharine Greene looked at her niece with a renewed respect. She heard the gaiety in her young voice. She knew that her appeal and magnetism were absolutely enticing to men. Yet she possessed maturity and insight as well. She felt a deep satisfaction in this woman-child. Setting down her embroidery, she stood and wrapped Kitty in a heartfelt embrace.

⋐☉◈☉⋑

Nathanael regretted that he did not have a formal education, but at least his father taught him to read and spent many evenings discussing the Bible with him and his siblings. As the fourth son of a Quaker preacher, he and his brothers were needed on the farm and in the forges and grist mills. With eight children to raise, Nathanael Sr. realized his namesake would be the best one to carry the load of the businesses. He begrudgingly gave in to Nathanael's requests and hired an itinerant teacher during the winter months for him and his brothers. He knew his son needed to have a better understanding of mathematics, law and Latin. No longer was his reading confined to the Scriptures.

When Nathanael turned fourteen, he was allowed to attend a little school in East Greenwich where a Scot named Maxwell introduced him to geometry. His understanding of Latin improved quickly and he read Caesar, Euclid and Horace, often while attending the forge fires and the hopper at the grist mill. As he grew older, he chose to spend his evenings after supper in an unheated little room above the kitchen, reading and studying without interruption. The rest of the family settled before the fire on the first floor, warming their bodies and conversing. Nathanael realized how much he enjoyed philosophy and debate, especially now that he had become a firm believer in the Patriots' cause.

Kitty liked the challenge of arguing with Nathanael and his friends. At first he seemed so worldly and mature, yet passionate in his convictions and gentle with his words. His clear hazel eyes fascinated her and she told him that his face radiated smoke and fire. He was a tall, large-boned, wide-shouldered young man, with rich brown hair and high cheekbones. She found him very attractive.

After several years of friendship, their twelve-year age difference was of no great concern to either of them. They shared political beliefs and principles.

Kitty was a typical teenager who enjoyed dancing and quickly included Nathanael and his brothers in her evenings at the dance socials. The Greenes were amused and encouraged her lighthearted pursuits. On the other hand, Nathanael's self-righteous Quaker father forbade his sons to engage in this frivolous pastime, and on more than one occasion Nathanael received thrashings when he returned home after a night of dancing.

"Oh my, Nathanael, how horrid! Why even in the Bible they danced," gasped Kitty when she heard about the beating.

"Ay lassie, the beating was for breaking curfew and sneaking out an upper window for an evening with my friends." Nathanael's face broke into a slow grin. "T'was not so bad. My Pa did nothing to us the last time we danced at a neighbor's farm." He laughed gaily.

"What is so humorous? What happened?"

"He told me and the brothers to plow to a certain stone before quitting for the day, knowing that it would take hours to reach it and keep us from going to the dance. Well, the four of us muscled that stone halfway across the field, plowed to it without problems, and cleaned up for the dance. He just watched us without a word, knowing he had been beat."

Kitty's merry laughter filled the room, and the story quickly became the topic at many socials.

On another occasion, she questioned him about privateering—a system by which small privately-owned vessels were armed and preyed on foreign cargo ships, taking the goods to sell at a profit in the home ports.

"Nat, how can this be legitimate?" she asked.

"According to the governor, it is. And we give the government its percentage, so no one loses."

Yet when the tables were turned, and British vessels detained their vessels to tax these "smuggled" goods, the atmosphere became volatile.

Nathanael and his brothers owned a merchant vessel that they employed in Caribbean trade. They heard the stories about other ships that had been boarded and taxed by the Royal schooners patrolling the Rhode Island waters. The Patriots were furious over this enforcement of the revenue acts. When Nathanael's ship was seized by the *Gaspee*, commanded by Lieutenant William Duddington, the Greene brothers quietly made plans.

One evening in June the *Gaspee* was chasing another merchant vessel when it was lured into shallow water and ran aground. Under the cover of darkness, a small group rowed out to the schooner and burned her to the water-line, wounding Commander Duddington during the attack. The Loyalists raised an uproar over this act of rebellion, especially since British blood had been shed.

Many vessel owners were accused, including Nathanael and his brothers, but they claimed their innocence. Indeed, Nathanael was at his home in Coventry that night and privately regretted missing the action. A short time later the Greene brothers presented a countersuit. Nathanael brought a lawsuit against Lieutenant Duddington, alleging illegal seizure of his merchant ship and his goods. He spent a great deal of time preparing for this, and was grateful for his law studies.

"Will you win this judgment, Nathanael?" asked William Greene. "Have you any idea?"

"Yes sir. I fully expect to win. We believe strongly that the law is on our side." Kitty watched this exchange with interest, knowing full well that Nathanael had done thorough preparation in the formalities.

Some time later, at one of the social events they attended, Nathanael looped an arm around Kitty's waist and led her to the corner of the room, away from the others. He was wearing a smile, his voice full of surprise and delight.

"I want you to be the first to know," he said, eyes dancing. "Not even my brothers know as of yet."

"Know what, Nathanael?" She held her breath, mesmerized by the way he was looking into her eyes. She could see flecks of rust in his irises.

"We won, Kitty! We won the lawsuit against the Loyalists. They can no longer bully us and get away with it!" He raised a fist in triumph.

She laughed, and it felt contagious, like unfettered energy. Moonlight drifted through the window as they listened to the steady drone of the water. He took her hand in his as they walked back to share the news with their friends. After that event, all of Rhode Island held young Nathanael Greene in high esteem. No one was more proud of him than Kitty Littlefield.

FOUR

1773-1774

K itty had her opportunity to meet Benjamin Franklin in William Greene's home, and just as her Aunt Catharine had anticipated, he found her to be engaging and intelligent. After she left the room Mr. Franklin made a point of congratulating Catharine and William on the foundation they had given her.

During the warm months of the year Kitty traveled to Block Island to visit her family, now expanded in number since her father's remarriage. It was evident to those close to her that she loved spending time with young children. She hoped that one day Nathanael could see that for himself.

"Oh Nat, you are entirely too busy for your own peace of mind," she pouted with a teasing smile. "I do appreciate it when you include me in your public events, but we simply have no time together these days. You rush from one crisis to another, and even our social events frequently turn into political affairs."

Nathanael turned to her with a puckered brow. "You are correct, Kitty. I promise thee a lovely evening of dancing, and then I feel compelled to rush off to deliberate the best way to protest the tax on tea. And now I am deeply concerned about the people of Boston, whose harbor was just closed by an act of Parliament." Reaching for her hand, he appealed to her sympathetic eyes. "Please forgive me, lass."

It began in December 1773, when Boston citizens disguised as Indians dumped the over-taxed tea into the harbor. They anticipated wrath and reprisals from King George III's Parliament.

The Whigs, little groups of passionate Patriots, prepared for the worst and formed companies of volunteers to practice drill procedures as they had seen the British soldiers do. The beginning of 1774 brought about the Boston Port Bill: a blockade to isolate and starve Boston into submission. A Congress was called to meet in Philadelphia, and Sammy Ward's father was one of two men chosen to participate from Rhode Island.

No one knew what the Philadelphia Congress was expected to accomplish, yet Patrick Henry was already advocating American independence from Britain. If that occurred, they believed England might send an army, and that would mean civil war. East Greenwich formed an independent volunteer company, the Kentish Guards. Nathanael Greene was one of the first volunteers, along with his two close friends—Sammy Ward and James Varnum.

"I have an extremely difficult decision to make, Kitty," he told her one evening. "It will change the very course of my life."

"Oh my, Nat. You are concerning me. What must you decide?"

His expression was filled with sorrow. "If I take up the sword in support of the colonial cause, I will be cast out from the Quaker society in which I've been reared."

She went to him and embraced him, hoping to give him encouragement. Suddenly at a loss for words, he held her gaze, smiling at her compassion.

When Nathanael and his cousin Griffin attended a military rally in Connecticut, the word was spread in East Greenwich. When it was discussed "in Meeting," a committee was formed to look into the conduct of the two Greenes. The consensus was to "put them out from under the care of the Meeting." Nathanael expected nothing less and dolefully stood firm in his decision.

He had enlisted in the Kentish Guards as a private without pay, but his friends wanted him to be a lieutenant. The amateurs who formed the drill team were unsettled by his limp and objected to his presence in the company, a decision that hurt and humiliated Nathanael. Nathanael's friend Varnum, who had already been chosen as a first officer, was furious and threatened to withdraw from the Guards. Nathanael would have no part of that, and wrote him a straightforward letter:

> *Let me entreat you, sir, if you have any regard for me, not to forsake the company at this critical moment. It would be a disgrace upon the country. I feel more mortification than resentment, but I think it would manifest a more generous temper to have given me their opinions of my perceived disability in private than to make a proclamation of it in public; for nobody loves to be the subject of ridicule, however true the cause.*

An arrangement was made: Nathanael remained in the Guards as a private and left for Boston to procure a weapon suitable for military service and smuggle it home. While in Boston he visited his good friend Henry Knox, a bookseller whose shop provided endless reading pleasure to Nathanael. Henry was an elegant man—a lieutenant in the Boston Grenadier Corps—and his bookstore was a favorite gathering for the local high-society ladies and gentlemen. Nathanael discovered Henry and he shared similar convictions and their patriotism intensified.

❧❦❧

Kitty and Nathanael were seeing a great deal of each other, and although Kitty cherished his infrequent moments of undivided attention, she needed more: more time, more commitment, more of him. She devised a plan.

"Nathanael dear, my father would love to meet you. You've never been to Block Island, which is my birthplace and where a great part of my heart remains. Would you like to join me on a visit to see my family?" she asked, eyes twinkling.

"Yes Kitty, I believe I would. You plan our travel and I shall accompany you." He smiled at her. "I think it's a splendid idea, and I do crave the peace and tranquility of an island."

"And we can dance to our hearts' content, for my father approves and your family will never know," she taunted him. Nathanael lifted her hand to his lips, and she knew the pact was sealed.

On a warm October day they sailed over to the island in the double-ender boat. This time, with Nathanael at her side, Kitty felt free from anxiety. She told him the island's history and how it was named after Adriane Block, the Dutch explorer who was fascinated by the isolated isle with the ragged cliffs. Nathanael gasped when he caught sight of the raw rock faces rising vertically from the sea.

"Kitty, this is magnificent!" he declared in amazement. "I have never seen a more beautiful island."

She was pleased. She knew her family would approve of this man she was determined to marry. Perhaps here on her island he would come to realize that they belonged together.

The waves rose with crests decorated in white salty lace. He stared across the high seas with their wind-whipped froth. His eyes flickered over waves painted a scattering of blues and greens and golds by the clouds and sun. Tapping her shoulder, he pointed in the air. White pelicans circled their boat, flying just above the water. They counted fifteen in one single dazzling line moving in synchronized motion, drenched in light, black wingtips gleaming. And then they were gone.

Stepping gingerly off the boat, Kitty threw her arms wide open in a salute of sheer joy. "This is the first time I've not been frightened by the sea," she exclaimed with a wide grin. "You have done that for me, dear Nat!" A steady offshore breeze tousled her raven curls, bringing with it a strong and vaguely unpleasant odor from the kelp beds. Nathanael watched as Kitty skipped over the sand and small rocks. He loved her unabashed enthusiasm. He liked the way her eyes shone and her cheeks flushed as she revived her memories.

Kitty wanted to show Nathanael her island of paradise

before he met the others. They started walking toward her family home. The island was as beautiful as she had remembered. Surrounded on three sides by jagged cliffs, the glen extended before her like a great outdoor cathedral, canopied by a sweep of glorious sky. Birds flitted across the arch of blue calling to one another and welcoming her back. But this time she was not alone to appreciate the flowers and birdsong and lazy clouds drifting high overhead. This time she was with her man.

Her friends and relatives celebrated her homecoming. The tall strongly-built man with the sparkle in his eyes endeared himself to them just as Kitty had expected. He enjoyed being treated like family and felt comfortable and confident with them. She shared him cheerfully and still found times for them to be alone; reading, discussing books and unveiling their dreams. Kitty organized evenings of dancing and fun, steering the conversations away from the dissention on the mainland. Nathanael found himself completely relaxed and content.

"Nat, do you think you've learned a lot from people, as well as from books?" Kitty watched him intently, his nose buried in one of her father's journals.

He looked up, puzzled by the question. "Hmm, I suppose I have. Why do you ask?"

"I believe the only way we can learn from others is by humbling ourselves. And that's not an easy thing to do." Pausing, she continued. "Do you suppose I have taught you anything?"

Nathanael placed the book on the small table beside him. He leaned forward, facing her and looking into her eyes—the exact color of the ocean. "You've taught me the small kindnesses of everyday life. You've shown me how to find beauty in each day." After a long pause, he added,"And Kitty, I'm trying to learn how to correct a wrong when I can, because I very much want to please you."

As the sun made its way toward the horizon, Kitty suggested a walk on the beach. She slipped her hand into his as they made their way over the large rocks down to the sand. The island felt otherworldly, entrancing and seductive with the swish of the surf breaking on the beach and the weight of the heavy salt air on their skin. It was low tide; the water held traces of blue, green, turquoise, and purple, all laced and streaked with white surf. Rock-pools gleamed like jewels, while breakers formed far out, moving in and gathering height and weight before crashing against the jagged granite coastline.

Overhead the gulls wheeled. The loons announced their presence somewhere out on the water with their haunting calls. She stopped abruptly, turning to face him.

"I love those final minutes when the darkness folds us in for the night. The ocean comes alive, the birds settle and the night weather kicks in." She felt his eyes on her, shining brilliantly like the rising sun, and sensed a flicker of trepidation. "Is something wrong, Nat?" she asked gently.

He placed his hands lightly on her shoulders. A quick chill danced up her spine. His gaze was solemn. She held her breath, mesmerized by the way he was looking into her eyes.

"You're a very special person," he said, shifting his fingers momentarily to the soft hollow at the base of her neck. "You make me want things I never thought I could have."

Closing her eyes, she felt his lips brush against hers. She melted against him, moaning his name as his hand curled around the back of her neck. His lips moved to her hair, his breath warm against her skin. "Kitty, I want to fill your life with color and warmth."

With his arms around her, clutching her tightly to him, Nathanael whispered into her ear, "I love you, Kitty. And, dear Lord, how I need you."

Kitty turned slowly and opened her eyes, searching his. She saw a softness and vulnerability she'd never known existed.

Again the soft whisper came. "My darling Kitty, will you be my wife?"

Unexpected tears pooled in her eyes and spilled down her face. He gathered her into his arms, kissing her softly. They rested there in the quiet until he stepped back and released her. Kitty wasn't ready to let go. She pulled him toward her and buried her face against his chest. She nodded, tears still streaming down her cheeks.

He would always remember the way her head silhouetted the moon when she turned to guide him back home. It had been rising behind her, and for maybe two seconds, she appeared like an eclipse, a thin corona around her head and her face cloaked behind a glowing shadow. He chuckled, head tipped back, the sound light and flowing. Then he stopped. Turning to her, he dropped to his knees.

"Did you say yes, my love? I don't seem to remember? Will you marry me?"

"Darling Nat," she whispered, her lips roaming over his face. "I don't think my mouth uttered a single word, but surely my eyes gave you the answer."

FIVE

1774–1775

It was from the city of Boston in July 1774 that Nathanael Greene sent the letter to Sammy Ward with the wedding invitations for his family.

Friend Samuel,

Please deliver the enclosed cards to your sisters. On the 20th of this month I expect to be married to Miss Kitty Littlefield at your Uncle Greene's. As a relative of hers and a friend of mine, your company is desired upon the occasion. The company will be small consisting of only a few choice spirits; since she is not married at her father's house she declined giving invitations to more than a few of her nearest relations and most intimate friends. There will be my brothers and their wives, Mr. James Varnum and his wife, Christopher and Griffin Greene and their wives, and who from Block Island I do not know. Mr. Thomas Arnold will attend, as well as your family.

Believe me to be your sincere friend,
Nathanael Greene

In the parlor where they met, Kitty became Mrs. Nathanael Greene. She was nineteen. He was thirty-two. They were very much in love.

Nathanael proudly drove his young wife to Spell Hall, the home he had built in Coventry, far removed from the nearest neighbor. They traveled through forests of cedar and oak, across creeks and sand and up the high ridges with views of the sparkling waters and jade-colored isles of Narragansett Bay below. Kitty arrived at the small sturdy dwelling and discovered it barren of trees.

"I had hoped we could plant our own verdant gardens and regal trees," he suggested casually as they surveyed the homestead. The house's foundation was of chiseled granite blocks; the large chimneys were made of brick and the house's main structure of clapboard.

"Oh yes! I am so pleased, dear Nathanael. It is our own little piece of glory. Here we will work together, raise little children and grow fat and happy in our older years."

Nathanael threw back his head in laughter. How she amused him, even after a long dreary ride.

He led her through the classical colonial-style entrance. Kitty was pleased that the floors were built of twelve-inch boards, varnished and polished. Paneled blinds trimmed every window.

"It is snug, is it not? You may dress it up as you wish. It already contains three hundred volumes of books I've carefully collected over the years. I am told I have more reading material than the Rhode Island College," he grinned. "I feel certain the books will challenge your inquisitive mind."

They walked together through the unassuming house with low ceilings and small rooms. Kitty was quickly aware of the difference between this house and the elegance of her home in East Greenwich, but she was pleased. There were four rooms on the bottom floor including the parlor, the kitchen, dining room and the library, divided by a wide hall. Between the library and the kitchen was a concealed stairway extending from the cellar to the attic where the servants would room.

The library overlooked the Pawtucket River, where cool waters rushed over stones and shrubs. She could also see the forge from the library: Nat's workplace. He eagerly pointed out the little northeast room that served as a country store. From here he dispensed fishing gear and other goods required by his employees and neighbors. The second floor held the four large bedrooms.

"Oh my darling, we shall be so happy here," she gushed, throwing her arms around his wide chest. "I will learn to cook you the things you love, and I'll make this little house our peaceful sanctuary."

Nathanael offered her his gentle smile as his eyes took inventory of her face. Catharine Greene had warned him that his new wife did not cook or sew well and had never been interested in learning the domestic skills. Her virtues were in entertaining, good humor, stimulating conversation and caring for the needy. Appreciating all of this, he considered himself a blessed man.

⚬⚬⚬

As they settled into married life, Nathanael acquired even more expensive volumes on military tactics and began to teach himself the art of war. He convinced a British deserter to become drillmaster to the Kentish Guards and urged his fellow Patriot volunteers to practice and prepare themselves for war.

Kitty and Nat were getting ready for bed when they heard the approaching sound of a horse's hooves. A lone horseman dismounted and breathlessly relayed the news.

"At dawn today the British marched from Boston to destroy military stores at Concord!" he exclaimed. Nathanael held up a hand.

"Slow down, my friend. Come inside, and share with us the information you have brought."

"The Brits were challenged at Lexington by the Militiamen; shots were fired, and men were killed!"

Nathanael nodded slowly. "The time for armed resistance has come."

"Dear Nat, what will you do?" asked Kitty, her face crumpling with shock.

He reached out for her hand. "Sir, tell me more about the Militiamen," prodded Nathanael.

"On the evening of April 18, 1775, Dr. Joseph Warren sent for Paul Revere and instructed him to ride to Lexington, Massachusetts to warn Samuel Adams and John Hancock that British troops were marching to arrest them. On the way to Lexington he stopped at each house, alarming everyone on his way."

"When did he arrive in Lexington?"

"At midnight, sir. He was joined there by William Dawes and Dr. Sam Prescott, where they were all arrested, and Revere lost his horse to the British."

"Dear Lord," muttered Nathanael. "I must go immediately to the Guards with this report." He rose to escort the rider to the entryway when Kitty grabbed his arm.

"I'm frightened, Nat. What will I do if you leave me? How long will you be away?" She cried softly as he gathered her into his arms, her lovely face glimmering with moonlit tears.

"Not long at all, my angel. I shall return at the first opportunity. Perhaps my brother Jacob and Peggy will come to stay until further notice. The forge will need to be operated in my absence."

Sobbing now, Kitty watched as he gathered his belongings and held him in a tight grip while he attempted to saddle his horse. "This is not what I imagined when I left my home to marry you," she whimpered, her eyes crashing into his.

"Hush, Kitty. You don't mean that, I know. Please let me go to East Greenwich and see what the Guards need to do." Gently wiping away her tears, he added, "I shall do my best to be back tomorrow with news." He held her to his chest until she settled down.

Giving him a sad smile, she slipped her hand in his and squeezed tightly.

"Go now, Nathanael. But return quickly." She tore her eyes from his.

Nathanael knew that war was certain. He knew he would lead his Kentish Guards into Massachusetts to assist the Patriots in Boston. What he didn't know was for how long.

SIX

1775

Two days later Nathanael was home, enfolding Kitty in his arms. Her surprise and joy triggered a new eruption of tears: "happy tears," as she called them.

"Oh my angel, I have missed you greatly. It was a long ride, and for naught."

"What do you mean, Nat?" She released him and searched his weary face.

"We rode from East Greenwich, with Varnum as our colonel up front, to the Massachusetts border and were stopped from entering by a direct order from Rhode Island's Tory governor, Joseph Wanton. My men and I ignored the order, waited it out a short time and rode deep into Massachusetts before we learned the British had retreated back to Boston."

She nodded her head gravely. "My goodness. You have to be exhausted. Yet I am so grateful you're back with me," she said. "How long can you stay this time? Do you know?" Her smile froze suddenly.

"For a very short time, my Kitty. I am summoned in two days to assist the General Assembly in Providence. Because your Uncle Samuel Ward Sr. is in Congress in Philadelphia, they have named me to the committee in his place. We must organize our army into a brigade at that assembly and prepare for war." Kitty could see the excitement shining through his eyes, and she swallowed her objection.

"My brother Jacob and his wife have agreed to move into Spell Hall with you during my absence, if you agree. He can operate the Coventry forge and she can help you with the daily chores and meals. Or, you could move back in with my family at Potowomut. You know how my brothers adore you."

Kitty nodded absently, lost in her thoughts. After a short time they agreed that Peggy and Jacob would move to Coventry. The following morning Nathanael set out to Providence, promising to return in several days.

He returned with the most incredible news. "I've been commissioned as Brigadier General of the Continental Army in command of the Rhode Island Brigade! The date of my commission began on June 22nd. Can you believe this?"

Kitty, Jacob and Peggy were stunned by his words. "Is thou serious, Nathanael? My brother, you left us as a private, and have returned a brigadier general?" Admiration snuck past Jacob's defenses.

They listened astonished as he recounted his incredible jump in rank.

"'Tis a fact. The Assembly authorized us a brigade of 1,500 men to cooperate with other New England colonies for the common defense of the provinces. Two colonels of militia were offered the command, and they both turned it down. When they presented the position to me, I told them, 'Since the Episcopalian and the Congregationalist won't, I suppose the Quaker must.'"

Kitty threw back her head and laughed: a deep, bright, confident laugh—the same laugh that made him fall in love with her. "What about Colonel Varnum of the Kentish Guards?"

"For some inexplicable reason he was passed over," responded Nathanael, handing her his commission papers, authorized by King George III.

Kitty's eyes swept slowly over his family. "It was the direct interposition of Providence," she murmured.

Jacob broke the spell and spoke out loud what the others felt. "How very strange the King assigns this authority to an officer committed to rebellion," he stated. "Yet thee can only perform this duty through the constitutional head of government."

The thrill of Nathanael's commission evaporated with his brother's declaration. Kitty realized how Nat's Quaker family must judge her influence over him. *How unfair*, she thought. *He joined the military without my consent. The choice was his alone.*

She embraced her husband and kissed his cheek. "I'm very proud of you, Nat. You are doing your duty as a soldier to protect the rights of the colonists. They have selected you wisely."

Nathanael responded with a cheerless smile. "The restrictions imposed on the citizens of Boston have already deprived them of their common rights. They cannot leave the city or be out of their homes at night without a pass, and even now the British soldiers are seizing their houses and stores for their comfort. Boston has become a city of hatred."

৩৩৩

Kitty followed her husband's campaign through the *Providence Gazette* and his letters.

> *My dear wife,*
> *I have not so much in my mind that wounds my peace as the separation from you. My bosom is knitted to yours by all the gentle feelings that inspire the softest sentiments of conjugal love. It would have been happy for me if I could live a private life in peace and plenty, enjoying all the happiness resulting from a well-tempered society founded on mutual esteem. But the injury done my country, and the chains of slavery forging for posterity, call me forth to defend our common rights and repel the bold invaders of the sons of freedom. I hope the righteous God that rules the world will bless the armies of America, and receive the spirits of those whose lot it is to fall in action into the paradise of God, and into whose protection I commend you and myself.*
> *I am, with truest regard, your loving husband,*
> *N. Greene*

Kitty understood that Boston was the great testing ground in America. If Boston were made to submit, any place in America could. If Boston broke free of the British, every colony could do so. She now believed that Patriots would fight to their death to free their countrymen.

She had written Nathanael that she was expecting a baby. She wanted to share this blessed news with him face to face, but did not know when she would see him. She needed an outlet for her irrational feelings. In her letters to him she complained she was not appreciated by Jacob and Peggy. She told him she was sure they did not even like her, but remained in Spell Hall because he had asked them to.

Kitty often felt on the verge of tears and loathed being shut up with his family. *I despise the drabness of the ugly, gray Quaker dresses,* she thought. *And hearing them speak to each other and to Nathanael and even to me with their thee's and thou's and not even looking directly at each other when they talk. This is no way to live, and it depresses me. This cannot be good for my child.*

She considered moving over to Potowomut, but realized there would be more people to deal with. Although she liked Nathanael's stepmother, she wondered if she thought highly of her, or just pretended to.

Peggy knocked lightly on her bedroom door and found her wrapped between the quilts.

"Is thou cold?" she asked, her face drawn in concern.

Kitty shook her head. "I'm sad," she answered in a meek voice.

Crossing the room to sit at the foot of her bed, Peggy smiled gently. "I understand how lonely thee must feel," she said in a whisper. "I could not bear it if my Jacob were taken from me."

Kitty felt a soft gasp rise to her throat and hoped she had caught it in time. Peggy appreciated her circumstances, and had come to her in friendship.

Reaching for her hand, Kitty smiled. "Thank you, Peggy. Perhaps in the morning, you can show me how you knead the bread. Yours looks so much nicer than mine," she giggled.

"'Tis not the look, but the taste that counts, sister. I shall be happy to roll the bread with thee in the morning." Kneeling to place several logs over the embers, she stirred them with a poker and slipped quietly from the room.

The following morning, after baking bread with her sister-in-law, Kitty made a trip to Providence to shop for beautiful gowns for herself. She had already made up her mind she would go and spend time with Nathanael at his headquarters in Jamaica Plains, just west of Boston. Now she had to convince him to let her make the journey. She knew she would need to depend on her feminine wiles.

SEVEN

1775

For the first time, Kitty observed her husband as a stern commanding officer who worked endlessly trying to make soldiers of his raw undisciplined men. These boys were completely unprepared for military life, sulking when reprimanded by Nat and threatening to return home when they disliked the orders. She watched the dress parades with disbelief as they arrived without shoes or stockings and made little effort to keep proper formation.

She and Nathanael were housed in a fine home, formerly owned by the Tories, just west of Boston near his brigade's camp. Happy that she now had a purpose as the General's wife, she enjoyed conversing with the officers and Nathanael. She finally felt useful. She was where she belonged—at Nathanael's side.

Kitty's curiosity about the war was encouraged by her husband. When she asked him about their strategy, he eagerly explained the colonial plan to force the enemy from Boston.

"Their base is inside the city of Boston on a peninsula leading to the Boston Harbor. At the southern end a narrow 'neck of land' connects them to the shore. We will occupy the harbor and keep them from bringing artillery and other supplies through. Eventually, we'll starve them out."

"Will that be enough to send them back to England?" she asked hopefully.

He shook his head. "Nay, Kitty. They will continue their strategy elsewhere. At the moment, we have no navy to protect the harbor. They have cannons within the city to foil our plan, so we cannot proceed forthwith."

In mid-June Kitty and Nathanael returned to Coventry to muster supplies. Kitty was happy sharing the peace and beauty of the Coventry countryside, grateful for this short respite from worry. On their second evening at Spell Hall, a messenger came pounding through the outer gates, his horse blowing hard and steaming. He pulled to a dusty halt and delivered his urgent message from Cambridge—fighting had broken out north of Boston. Nathanael hastily kissed his wife, mounted his horse and rode off into the night. Once again, Kitty was left behind.

Kitty, Jacob and Peggy soon received the news that Nat had reached Charlestown village the following morning to discover it "all burnt to ashes." The British forces had fortified the hill of a farmer named Bunker, giving them command of the bay and Charlestown. The Americans, confused in the dark, placed their ammunition on Breed's Hill erroneously. The Brits woke up to see American cannons trained on them. They rowed across the harbor and set fires in Charlestown, after which they attacked the hill. Nathanael wrote them that the Americans held fast until their powder ran out. Both sides suffered losses. Although the British won, they sacrificed more than one thousand men, including ninety-two officers.

We proved that raw provincial recruits would stand their ground and fight the disciplined British regulars, Nat wrote in a letter to Kitty. *And we kept them from following up with an immediate attack on Cambridge.*

In the early afternoon of July 2, Commander-in-Chief George Washington rode into Cambridge to replace General Artemus Ward as the commanding officer. He was conducted to the house built by Harvard University for the use of its presidents, but the courteous Virginian felt awkward staying in the mansion and requested other lodging. The Vassall House on Brattle Street belonged to a wealthy Tory, or Loyalist, whose family had fled into Boston when the colonial forces descended on Cambridge after Concord. This would serve as General Washington's headquarters until the spring of 1776.

Nathanael wrote his wife from Cambridge about the surge of confidence that enveloped the camp once General Washington arrived. He was admired by everyone, and held in high esteem by his subordinates. Nat wrote about the first council of war, held at the headquarters house on Brattle Street on July 9, 1775. Others in attendance were General Artemus Ward, General Horatio Gates, Major General Charles Lee, General Henry Knox, General William Heath, and General Israel Putnam. He told her that everyone was won over by General Washington's quiet authority and good will.

With Nathanael gone, a lonesome and pregnant Kitty fell into a profound state of melancholy. She was convinced that Jacob and Peggy did not understand her so she avoided them as much as possible. Her sense of worth in the cooking department had never been strong, and she was relieved when Peggy suggested taking over the cooking responsibilities.

"Peggy, you have tried with me. I simply am not good at this and I do not enjoy it at all."

"Then let me do the cooking, Kitty. Thou must rest and stay strong for this baby's delivery." Because Peggy was kind and understanding, Kitty knew she should feel appreciative, but found herself becoming distressed with little to occupy her time. Only shopping in Providence for clothing for herself and her child gave her any form of pleasure.

Nathanael, busy as he was, worried about his wife and took the time to comfort her through his letters. He assured her that his family did, indeed, love her and that it was not her fault that her own family had not taught her how to manage a household. He encouraged her to assist Peggy in the few duties she enjoyed in order to occupy her mind and her hands. He smiled indulgently as he read her letters with their grammatical mix-ups and spelling errors, knowing that her education was not as comprehensive as his. He continued to make a huge effort to keep her updated on his life and the war so that she was able to discuss it with the others.

My Dearest Angel,   *July 12, 1775*

General George Washington is as grand as all the tales that have circulated since the French and Indian War claim him to be. You are, no doubt, waiting for me to give you a detailed description of him. His Excellency is a tall man of six feet, with a rugged frame. He is in his mid-forties (about ten years my senior) with keen blue-gray eyes. His face is pleasant to look upon, though scarred by the pox. He grooms himself to perfection, so I cannot report the color of his hair as it is always neatly powdered, though I suspect it to be brown, as are his brows.

As you can imagine, there is no small amount of murmuring from the New Englanders with regard to an outsider being given the command. However, I do not think His Excellency is the least bit offended, for he commented to me that he is not too keen on the New Englanders—present company excepted. (You know the affection I feel for those of New England. Given time, General Washington will come to admire their qualities as well.)

The army is no longer divided into separate militia companies, with confusion as to who commands what. We are now the Continental Army and the Congress in Philadelphia has graciously reaffirmed my commission as brigadier general. I am the junior of Washington's generals. To be truthful, I am in awe of the lot of them.

He ended the letter by saying that he hoped to be with her for the birth of their first child. He mentioned that both he and General Washington were hoping for a quick and peaceful end to this nightmare of war; his prayers for them to be together, living a peaceful life would then be answered.

৶৩৩৶

As Kitty's pregnancy progressed, so did her pessimism. Totally unprepared for and unfamiliar with her condition, she was frightened by the changes in her body and was convinced that everything was going wrong. She decided to move back into Nathanael's family home in Potowomut, where Mother Greene—Nat's stepmother—and the wives of his other brothers could care for her. She also had several doctors at her disposal, who comforted her and assured her that the pregnancy was advancing well. She gradually made peace with this disarranged life inflicted on her by her husband's absence and the war.

When she feuded with her in-laws, she traveled back to Spell Hall and stayed for a short time. In her letters to Nathanael, she explained it was the "other women's fault" that they did not get along. She was fine with the men in the family, she claimed. Nat always acknowledged her viewpoint in his letters to her.

In early November Kitty learned that Mrs. Washington would be arriving at camp to visit her husband George. She sent an immediate request to Nathanael that he allow her to join him as well. His response was to come after the baby's birth, since she was expected to deliver in December. Because he did not say "no," Kitty began planning for the journey to Cambridge. She went on a shopping trip to bolster her morale, packed her carriage with her new wardrobe for after the baby's birth and filled a trunk with baby clothes. She was privately amused at Nathanael's family's shocked faces when she informed them the driver would be by in the morning to take her to his new camp in Prospect Hill.

A messenger reached General Greene to notify him that the carriage was three miles from camp. Nathanael requested permission to ride out to meet her. At full gallop, he and the messenger intercepted the coach as it reached Prospect Heights. Tossing the reins to the messenger, he lifted his long body inside the coach.

Kitty folded him in a tight embrace, a difficult feat because of her oversized stomach. Her eyes misted over but the tears forming in the corners dissolved with her joyful laughter.

"Oh Kitty, how good it is to see you and to hold you again,

my sweet one." His eyes shone on her like the soft heat from a lantern. "And our baby," he whispered, caressing her belly. "I can feel him moving, Kitty!"

She laughed at his delight. Looking him over with her searching gaze, she smiled. "Look at you, General Greene," she murmured. "A thoroughly dashing man you are." She inhaled deeply and touched the epaulets on the shoulders of his dark blue coat. "Is this the sign of a brigadier general?"

Nathanael fingered the bright pink sash across his chest, just beneath his jacket. "This is my symbol," he responded with a crooked smile. "Do you like it?"

Kitty nodded her approval. "I commend you, General Greene. You are even more debonair than when I last saw you. From your powdered hair down to your shiny boots. And you are mine."

His hazel eyes lit up at her words. "Always and forever, my love." The sky groaned and cracked and the cold, shrill needles of rain pierced the sides of the carriage. There wasn't any wind at all and the rain came straight down, spanking the ground in fury.

He grinned at her, leaned down, and kissed her mouth. It was a sweet kiss and she felt it throughout her body. "Now, shall I escort you to my camp?"

EIGHT

1775–1776

The soldiers in Nathanael's camp presented a much better appearance than the ones Kitty had seen in Jamaica Plains. They looked healthy and were well-fed. Their uniforms were made up of homespun shirts, broad-brimmed headgear, coats and waistcoats of various colors, breeches reaching below the knees, long stockings and leather shoes with large buckles. This time Kitty could see the respect in their eyes as they worked with her husband. General Greene's physical presence and charisma helped inspire confidence in this disparate collection of men from different colonies.

Smallpox had broken out in Boston and Nathanael feared his soldiers would be infected. He required that they be inoculated and turned his headquarters into a hospital for many of his staff members who had fallen ill after receiving the live smallpox virus. Kitty had been inoculated in Providence and the doctors assured her and Nat that there would be no problem for her or the baby. Although she wanted to nurse the men, she was unable to attend them because of her pregnancy. However, her cheerful disposition and witty personality propped up the morale of these half-sick, incarcerated officers and gave Nathanael a sense of pride in his young wife.

One of the first social visits Kitty arranged after her arrival was to meet Martha Washington, General Washington's wife, in the John Vassal home. This gracious woman, nearly twice Kitty's age, made her feel welcome.

"My dear Lady Greene, your reputation precedes you," she smiled warmly, seated across from her guest. "The officers have spoken so highly of your kindness to them and also of your beauty." Kitty blushed, taken aback. This gentle woman, tiny in stature yet perceptive and kind, was charming.

"How would you like me to address you, Lady Washington?" asked the ever-respectful Kitty.

Martha beamed with understanding. "Many call me Martha, and some of those who are dearest to me call me Patsy. Which do you prefer?" she answered with a ready smile, displaying beautiful white teeth.

"As I hope this to be the beginning of a long friendship, I shall call you Patsy privately and Lady Washington in public." Kitty paused, and then added, "I have several names as well. I've always been called Kitty, but Nathanael and his family sometimes call me Caty, to distinguish me from a good friend of theirs named Kitty."

"And what about Catharine? Isn't that your proper name?"

Kitty grinned, pleased with the tone of the conversation and quite certain she was making a good impression. "Oh yes, but that is so formal. And I was raised by my Auntie Catharine, so I have become Kitty to make it simpler at home." Kitty noticed Mrs. Washington's tiny hands as they rested on the sides of her easy chair. Never had she seen such delicate hands on a grown woman.

Lady Washington, aware of Kitty's scrutiny, gently broke the silence. "Kitty, would you like to meet the General? Perhaps we could accompany him for a cup of tea."

"Oh yes, I would like that very much. I was hoping to be introduced this afternoon." She smiled and followed her hostess from the room.

The commander-in-chief rose from his chair as they entered. He stood, tall and muscular and straight as an arrow. He had a large straight nose and penetrating widely separated blue-gray eyes. His countenance was commanding, his mouth large and gentle, and his smile warm. Kitty felt awed by his composed and dignified demeanor.

He favored her with an open smile. Looking her fully in the face, he addressed her in a calm, agreeable voice. "So this is the beloved wife of my good friend Nathanael, the 'Quaker preacher'." Kitty was aware of the twinkle in his eyes.

"I am so pleased to meet you, General Washington," she responded demurely. "My Quaker husband thinks so highly of you that we would like to request the honor of naming our son after you."

George Washington threw back his head and laughed out loud. "What makes you think it will be a son?" he countered, already intrigued by this young lady.

"A mother knows," she spoke quietly with lowered eyelids. "And my son will be here in December or January." Kitty lovingly caressed her stomach, captivating them both with her glowing smile.

The Greenes soon became frequent dinner guests of the Washingtons. In their home Kitty became friendly with the other high ranking officers and their wives. She and Lucy Knox were particularly close, as both were newlyweds. Kitty came to know the generals well, and enjoyed her time with most of them. The couples, taking turns entertaining each other for dinner, slowly adopted a social outlook, cleverly organized by the wives. Kitty thrived on these occasions, and was christened by the others as "a joyous, frolicsome creature." Martha Washington was completely taken with her.

"George, I've been meaning to ask you. Do you not think Kitty resembles our Patsy?" she asked him.

George turned to her with a touching smile. "I have thought that, with those eyes and the same dark curls. She's also motherless, did you know?"

Mrs. Washington nodded, thinking about her departed daughter, who had died at age seventeen. The memory of it ruptured her heart once again.

She willed that recollection away. "You know dear, I have become quite fond of them both."

"So have I, Patsy," he added, taking her hand and leading her into the warmth of their bedroom.

ↁↁↁ

During the last month of the year, Kitty experienced severe abdominal pains. Fearful of birth complications, Nathanael wanted Kitty back in Rhode Island, attended by his family and physician. When she recovered enough to travel, he sent her by carriage to Potowomut, where Mother Greene and the others would take care of her.

In early February of 1776, Kitty gave birth to their first son, George Washington Greene. Nathanael's family was at her side and shared in the joy of his arrival.

Mother Greene's face was wreathed in smiles of relief as she held her grandbaby.

"Goodness, he certainly resembles Nathanael, does he not?" she asked the others.

Kitty nodded weakly, eyes brimming with tears. Grateful for Nat's family, she wondered how she would have delivered her child without their loving care. Knowing how Nathanael would want to see his son, she resolved to recover quickly.

Kitty returned to Cambridge just as soon as she was able to travel. Nathanael's eyes glowed with love as he reached out for her and the baby.

Bashfully, she placed their baby in his father's arms.

"Oh my darling, he is so perfect," enthused Nathanael, cradling his small son as he embraced his wife with his other arm. Beaming, he bent down and cautiously kissed his baby's brow.

Martha Washington and the other officers' wives had formed a social circle, similar to the one Kitty had participated in when they were in Virginia. She joined them reluctantly, knowing that her needlework skills were inadequate, but longing for the conversations and social companionship. After a short time Martha recommended they stop embroidery and begin darning, knitting or making shirts. The other women were shamed into joining her. When Kitty learned that dry woolen socks without holes were an infantryman's greatest joy, she set her mind to become skilled at mending.

With baby George Washington Greene sleeping at her side, Kitty sipped her tea and offered up a suggestion.

"Ladies, should we inform our husbands that we wish to remain with them throughout the winter?"

Martha looked up from knitting a new pair of socks. "I feel certain you will get no resistance from Nathanael, or any of the others," she smiled, realizing the men considered Kitty the center of the social group.

"Yes, and with the scarcity of firewood they will surely need us to keep them warm on these cold nights," laughed the irrepressible Lucy Knox. The others agreed and the decision was unanimous.

But Nathanael was extremely concerned for the baby's welfare and immediately sent Kitty and his son back to East Greenwich, where he believed they would be safe. Kitty left reluctantly, hoping to convince him to let her return by spring.

After only two months in the family home, an urgent message reached Kitty that she must return to headquarters—Nathanael was extremely ill with jaundice.

I am yellow as a saffron. My appetite is all gone and my flesh too. I am so weak I can scarcely walk across the room. I am grievously mortified at my confinement as this is the critical period of the American war. Should Boston fall, I intend to be there if I am able to sit on horseback.

Kitty quickly set out with baby George to Prospect Hill, stopping over at Providence to buy some supplies. She nursed Nathanael back to health and soon he was able to lead his troops. Kitty was determined to remain at headquarters until the campaign was over and sought out Lucy Knox.

"Will you be staying on over the winter, Lucy?"

Lucy turned to her in surprise. "Why, that depends on what Henry and the others tell us."

Kitty nodded, looking down at her hands as she picked up her coffee mug. "Lucy, my husband tells me that your father was quite unhappy with your choice of Henry as a husband. Is there truth to that?"

"Oh yes, Kitty. As royal secretary to the province of Massachusetts, he wanted nothing to do with that outspoken Patriot—my Henry," laughed Lucy. "And then many of the books Henry sold in his shop were banned for reading by the Tories, you know." Lucy's eyes held a perpetual glimmer.

"Are you still estranged from the family?" asked her concerned friend, resuming the task of darning socks.

"Sadly, I am. But I have hope that it will all sort out once this campaign is over."

Kitty said nothing. She found Henry to be negative—the opposite of his wife. She could not understand how Lucy found him attractive with his obese body. Henry, in turn, considered Kitty a superficial woman, and did not approve of Lucy's close friendship with her. Henry had returned from an expedition to Ticonderoga, bringing back much-needed artillery pieces found in New York. He and Lucy sat together in the warm parlor, sharing news over a glass of sherry.

"I have been so delighted to have Kitty here again," exclaimed Lucy.

During any conversation in which Kitty Greene's name was mentioned, he generally frowned and shook his head. After a time, Lucy spoke up.

"You do not know her, my dear. To her close friends she gives her heart freely. She is loyal and passionate, and truly loves her husband, as you can see."

Henry snorted, mocking her words. "That is not how she appears at the parties in the other generals' homes. She's flirtatious and outspoken, often breaking into the men's conversations when the other women are in the next room. And she laughs at the double entendres that horrify the women and delight the men."

Lucy walked over to him, encircling her arms around his portly waist. She reached up and kissed his lips. "Darling, you do not realize how little she thinks of her intellect. I do, because I encourage her to overcome that complex. And however charming and vivacious she is around the generals, she does it all in plain view of their wives and her husband."

Lucy Knox understood Kitty. While Kitty enjoyed being the center of attention, she felt most comfortable just being herself—her own woman. If she felt the stilted proprieties were unnatural, she did not participate in them. When she attended social events she wore lovely fashions that accentuated her ample bosom. Kitty laughed, danced, drank Madeira wine and played cards with the women and men alike, married or single. And she did all this with Nathanael and the officers' wives looking on.

"Please do not judge her, Henry. Under all that gaiety, she's still a mere girl. With a baby to raise, no less," said Lucy, laughing softly.

"And when the young aides become smitten, what shall we do?" asked her skeptical spouse.

"Let them. Nathanael is thrilled to see their gloomy faces light up when she enters the room. And she takes the time to smile and converse with each of them. Do you not see that her playfulness is a needed respite from the miserable assignment of fighting a war?"

Henry smiled tenderly at his wife. "Ah, dear Lucy, have you not heard the gossipers? They say many deplore Kitty's indifference to religion. She seldom attends the church services at camp."

"I asked her about that, Henry. She says she believes church is an option, not a requirement. She has her faith and practices it privately." Turning to face him, she continued. "Did you know what the Quaker religion did to Nathanael? He was read out of his own meeting at East Greenwich because he was seen watching a military parade in Connecticut."

Henry remained quiet as Lucy reached for his hand. "She told me she did not wish to be a part of such hypocrisy."

⁂

The American troops occupied Boston Harbor's outer shore, but needed an area to place their batteries for easy artillery range. On March 2, 1776, the Colonials cannonaded Boston from the north and west, attacking Prospect Hill. The British returned the fire. Timbers shook and windows rattled in the Greene home while Kitty kept a worried eye on her son, sleeping peacefully through the night.

Several hours later a message arrived from Lady Washington, worried about Kitty and her son. Kitty assured her she was less concerned now than when she was back in Coventry, pregnant and alone, and consumed by imagined fears. However, she sent a grateful note to Martha that all was well.

A colonial battery slipped undetected to the top of the hill south of the city overlooking Boston's docks to set the final trap. Intelligence was received that the British were preparing to leave the city by water. Indescribable confusion reigned in the city for the next ten days. Troops, stores, loot and Tory refugees were embarked without regard for comfort or conveniences. Nook's Hill was seized by the Americans, and the British prepared to leave. Three days later, Kitty trained her spy glass on Boston, observing dozens of transports loading at the wharves, and a hundred more at anchor in the harbor. She wondered if the British would attack.

The British ships finally left the docks and proceeded due east toward the harbor exit. They were leaving Boston, sailing for the open sea. Boston was again in the hands of its own people. Kitty dropped to her knees and gave thanks to the Lord. She had just lived through a miracle.

NINE

1776

The British left behind a devastated Boston. Houses, buildings and churches had been torn apart to make firewood, and the beautiful Boston Common was disfigured by trenches. Most of the city's Tories had fled with the British fleet; the few who stayed hid behind closed doors.

Nathanael was given new orders: he would lead the command of the Long Island defense in New York. Before reporting for duty, he was allowed to accompany his family back to Coventry while moving his troops to New York. They traveled together over the same muddy roads.

Kitty and her son moved back into their Coventry home with Jacob and Peggy, and once again, Kitty felt restricted. Baby George was the center of her life, and she happily shared him with the family. Yet she felt the pervading tension. Her visits to Potowomut only reinforced her beliefs that Nathanael's family's ways were not her ways. She was not even allowed to play cards in that strict Quaker home. She took pleasure in their fussing over her son and encouraged it, and then looked for excuses to shorten the visits.

The rumors of Kitty's reckless behavior at camp had reached Aunt Catharine's ears. One Sunday afternoon she invited Kitty to come by with her son. They sipped tea together in her elegant parlor, surrounded by the warmth of the blazing fire. Kitty felt nostalgic. For a few sweet moments, she felt ten years old again.

Catharine was anxious to learn the truth yet fumbled for the words. "Kitty, I simply cannot believe what the wagging tongues are saying. Is it possible that you behaved so wantonly at the generals' dinners in Nathanael's camp?"

"Wantonly, Auntie? By conversing and drinking wine with them?" Kitty felt the heat rising in her body and knew her face was blood red.

"Your Uncle Greene and I tried to teach you judgment and responsibility. I have been told that you danced with everyone *except* your own spouse at several of the socials. And that your gowns were extremely provocative, titillating the soldiers and even the young aides. Do you not consider that reckless behavior?" Aunt Catharine's voice shook and her eyes blazed. "It is certainly disrespectful to your husband." A log suddenly shifted and sent a scatter of sparks onto the stone floor.

Kitty answered slowly, staring into the fire and choosing her words carefully. There was stubbornness in her eyes that turned fragile. "I was exhibiting my joy and happiness after such a long miserable time away from Nathanael. I was also enjoying spending time in the company of the generals' wives, some of whom were envious of the attention I received. But wanton? No, I don't believe so."

Kitty's eyes now glowed with her own fire. "As far as not dancing with Nat, you know very well that he favors his bad leg and after a dance or two, he is finished. Yet he completely approves of my dancing with the other officers." Tears formed in her eyes and spilled down her cheeks. "I cannot believe I am hearing this from you, Auntie. You who encouraged my independence."

Aunt Catharine wasn't quite finished. "We taught you common sense, my girl. You, of all people, should honor my husband's position as deputy of Rhode Island and be aware that your behavior directly reflects upon us. Why, even your father is embarrassed by these rumors. Neither he nor I appreciate that your reputation as a self-serving, irresponsible woman is rubbing off on us."

"Do not bring my father into this!" countered Kitty. "I shall explain this to him myself, and I feel certain he will be more sympathetic to my situation than you have been." She closed her eyes, swallowing hard, and turned her face to the window. She put a hand against her mouth to still the trembling. When she thought her voice would be steady, she turned to face her aunt.

"Excuse me, Auntie," she said in a choked whisper. She had more to say but the words wouldn't come. Holding back tears, Kitty rose with care and left the parlor. She was shaking so badly that her legs wouldn't even carry her up the stairs. Several steps shy of the top, she sank down, her forehead pressed against the carved wooden rail. Catharine stared after her, indignation mingling with rising disbelief.

A deep melancholy overcame Kitty, a sadness she tried to detach from her body as she carried her son out the back door to her waiting carriage. Her eyes swept quickly over the beautiful home where she was raised. Sorrow, sweet and bitter, flooded through her as she left her home.

ക⊕⊙⊙⊃

Nathanael firmly upheld Kitty's honor. He liked the Greenes and appreciated all they had done for his wife when her mother died, but was incensed by her aunt's failure to stem the evil gossip by standing up for Kitty. He wrote them a letter asking them to support her, and even gave them permission to lovingly correct her. In his letters to Kitty he encouraged her to try to mend the situation, but told her not to go more than halfway in her efforts.

By late spring Kitty was weary of all attempts of reconciliation with her family. When she heard that some of the generals' wives were in New York, she made arrangements to leave baby George with Nat's family and boarded a schooner in Newport to sail to Manhattan. Upon landing, a carriage picked her up and drove her to the headquarters/residence of Henry and Lucy Knox, located at the foot of Broadway.

Kitty knew Lucy was embarrassed by her weight and compared her full-bodied figure with that of Kitty's own tiny body.

But she hoped that now that they both had babies to discuss, Lucy would return to her fun-loving nature. Lucy had just given birth to her first daughter.

She knew Lucy was suffering the loss of her family's presence in Boston. Nathanael explained to her that when the Americans entered the city after the British evacuation, Lucy learned her parents had fled with the enemy's fleet. Kitty tried to console her friend as best she could.

Nathanael's and Kitty's reunion was joyful, yet tempered with his apprehension that the British fleet would sail into New York at any moment. To defend New York, Nat was given only four thousand men in his brigade. They had become more disciplined after the siege of Boston.

The city was braced for an invasion, yet the buzz of the town continued. This city of twenty thousand people, lined by fine homes and lovely trees, churches, shops, coffee houses and markets, was savored by its inhabitants. Still tensions were high; Kitty and Lucy witnessed "Tory rides," where the victims, tarred and feathered, were carried through the streets on rails. Oddly, the place where General Greene set up his camp in Brooklyn was "Tory country," where the Loyalists outnumbered the Patriots five to one.

The Washingtons were quartered in Richmond Hill in a fine home overlooking the Hudson River and the Jersey shore. Lucy and Kitty often made the two-mile ride for the midday meals, where they renewed their friendships with the other wives who had joined their spouses.

Near the end of June Nat and Kitty received a message that little George was sick in Rhode Island. Kitty immediately boarded a ship to return home. The baby quickly recovered and Kitty prepared to return to New York, despite Nathanael's protests. She engaged a carriage and driver and surprised everyone by arriving at General Knox's headquarters at the dinner hour.

In order to surprise her husband, Kitty asked George Washington's personal servant to allow her to enter unannounced.

"Hello my love," she beamed as she approached Nathanael's chair from behind.

Eyes widening in genuine disbelief, mouth slightly open, Nathanael was speechless. So were the others at the table.

She let her gaze settle over the room. There were no women. Where was Lucy Knox?

"Ki-ki-kitty, why are you here? I wrote you not to come." Nat had found his voice. A look of genuine embarrassment crossed his face.

"But I knew Lucy was here and..."

General Knox interrupted her. The skin of his face had been stretched and rounded by his excess poundage. "She left yesterday at my behest when we learned British gunboats were on the Hudson. I saw them myself and sent my wife to Connecticut, where she is safe." Looking away from her face, he glowered at her impertinence.

Nathanael slowly rose to his feet and turned to General Washington. "May I have a word with my wife, sir?"

His Commander nodded, and then called out, "After you've spoken privately, kindly invite Lady Greene to join us for dinner."

Closing the door quietly, Nat faced his wife and gently placed his hands on her waist. "Have you any idea of the danger you have brought upon yourself by coming here?"

Kitty was flabbergasted. She had expected an elated smile and a warm embrace. She looked down and said nothing.

"Did I not make it clear that thee should not come?" he asked her. "Thou purposely defied my orders."

She closed her eyes and shuddered. Nathanael was angry; he had reverted back to the dialect of his Quaker speech. "I thought you would be happy to see me," she whimpered.

"Oh my angel, if it were safe, I should be overjoyed. And because I love you so much, I must consider your safety before our personal wishes." He sighed and took her hand. "Let us now enjoy our meal, and then we will make plans for your return."

The following morning General Putnam scolded Kitty gently and encouraged her to return to Rhode Island. She promised to consider his words. That afternoon, she met up with Alexander Hamilton, who also encouraged her to reassess her plans. Smiling sweetly, she agreed to discuss it with Nathanael.

Then came the historic event of July 9, 1776. Kitty and Nathanael were thrilled that they were able to share it.

Martha Washington was in Philadelphia when the Declaration of Independence was read on July 8th, 1776. Her husband George received a copy of the document on July 9, and called for an assembly at the large Broadway Common. A brigade of Continentals and civilians met on the green and listened to Commander-in-Chief Washington read this declaration, ratified by the Continental Congress in Philadelphia just five days earlier.

When, in the course of human events, it becomes necessary for one people to dissolve bands which have connected them with another and to assume among the powers of the earth, the separate and equal station to which the Laws of Nature and of Nature's God entitle them, a decent respect to the opinions of mankind requires that they should declare the causes which impel them to the separation.

After the last paragraph was read, the crowd delivered a powerful unbroken roar of approval. Some of the men threw a rope around the statue of King George III and pulled it to the ground, smashing it to pieces. Independence had been declared. Now it had to be won.

British warships sailed up and down the Hudson without an American navy to stop them. They were adding more forces on Staten Island. Nathanael urged Kitty to return home until the battle was over, and this time she obeyed, knowing that Martha Washington was leaving as well. She had another reason to return home to rest. She was feeling nauseous and had no appetite. Kitty Greene, twenty-one years old, was pregnant with her second child.

TEN

1776–1777

New York residents cheered the news that Generals Charles Lee and Moultrie had successfully defended Charleston, South Carolina against a British force led by Generals Clinton and Cornwallis. But their mood changed when ninety-six British ships sailed through the Narrows, carrying Hessian soldiers and British troops. With General Gates away, emergency defense measures were needed.

When General Washington asked Congress for more field officers, he was told to promote from his ranks. So Nathanael received a commission letter from General Washington to announce a promotion to major general. Nathanael's friend Henry Knox visited the bustling field quarter office with the letter and a purple sash, which he draped with a salute and a flourish across Major General Greene's chest.

Just after reconnoitering and fortifying Long Island, Nathanael was stricken with a raging fever. He first felt weak while inspecting trenches along the waterfront. Seeing his pallor, one junior officer insisted on calling the company's physician. Within the hour Nathanael was in a wagon with his horse trotting alongside, on the way to his headquarters on Broadway.

On August 24, confined to his bed, he could only listen helplessly to distant gunfire. John Sullivan struggled to replace General Greene, but was unfamiliar with Brooklyn's terrain and fortifications. Nat's brother Kitt, sent from Coventry to care for him, was at his side when word reached them that the Long Island defenses had been overrun and Nathanael's troops trapped near Brooklyn. Kitt would write to Kitty that her husband had broken into remorseful tears at the dreadful news.

> *His response to the bad tidings was made especially pitiful due to his weakened condition. Trying to jerk himself out of bed only got him trapped in his blanket, which as we tried to calm him, held him in thrall like the frustration he is likely to feel for the rest of his days.*

"My poor boys!" he cried out. "What have we done?"

Yet the trapped army was miraculously saved on August 29 by General Washington. He commandeered every available vessel to form a ragtag fleet, manned them with the Marblehead Brigade of Massachusetts and boatmen from Salem, and removed the trapped Americans to Manhattan. This brilliant tactical improvisation transported his battered troops and all their baggage, field guns, equipment and even horses from Long Island across the Delaware River, without a single casualty.

The British soldiers, unable to reposition their troops or armaments, watched as the odd maritime escape unfolded.

A junior officer arrived at the infirmary to report to Nathanael that Washington had not slept for forty-eight hours, spending most of those long hours on horseback looking after his grateful troops. Even the British generals had to admit that his retreat from Long Island had been "a masterly military transaction, well-timed and executed."

Kitty finally received a letter from Nathanael; but the news was not what she had anticipated. By September 5, having recovered enough to report for duty, he learned that the army's position in New York had become as tenuous as what the British had faced in Boston. The Royal Army, now in control of the rivers, could land troops at will to cut supply lines from the mainland. Nathanael's army was in complete disarray, with militiamen quitting in droves as soon as their enlistments ran out.

Medical facilities were poor and the leadership was weakened. This merely intensified factional jealousies among the officer corps. Finally the order to retreat from New York was received. As it turned out, the British would hold it until 1783.

Kitty, finally over morning sickness, now had waited nervously for weeks without word from Nathanael. She only knew his troops had left Manhattan Island, but knew not their destination. Lonely and frightened, she slept as much as possible for her baby's sake. She may have become even more distraught had she known that her husband was now in command of two American forts: Lee in New Jersey and Washington on Manhattan Island. No one told her how he agonized over what he believed was a failure to protect his loyal troops.

In October a letter from Nat told her he was living at Fort Lee on the Jersey side of the Hudson.

Fort Lee was a new fortification, named for General Charles Lee after General Washington and his troops had camped near Burdett's Landing in preparation for the defense of New York City. Thomas Paine had found time during the retreat in November 1776—down a road which would become Main Street in the future city of Fort Lee—to compose a treatise called "The American Crisis," which began: *These are the times that try men's souls.*

Kitty felt quite relieved that her cousin Sammy Ward was with her husband, after his return from an unsuccessful assault on Quebec. Nat wrote that Sammy had been captured, imprisoned and finally exchanged and released. To her surprise, Kitty also read that her younger brother Billy Littlefield had asked to join Thomas Paine and William Blodgett as an aide-de-camp. For the first time in months, Kitty felt that a burden had been lifted from her shoulders.

Now Kitty begged her husband to allow her to rejoin him. To her delight, his staff responded with messages encouraging her to go. Nat knew that her radiant personality would be a balm to both staff and troops, but he knew her safety was foremost. He blatantly denied her request, sending her into bouts of despair. Then she heard the bad news that followed her request and begrudgingly acknowledged his insight.

Fort Washington—the last American stronghold on Manhattan—fell to the enemy before the eyes of Nathanael and his staff, watching helplessly from across the river. General Washington had issued a discretionary order to Nathanael to abandon the fort and move its three thousand soldiers to New Jersey. Instead, Fort Commander Colonel Magaw decided to dig in. Howe's forces attacked the fort before Washington reached it to assess the situation. During General Howe's attack, fifty-nine Americans were killed and two thousand eight hundred and thirty-seven were taken as prisoners of war. General Greene quickly withdrew his remaining troops to Hackensack and joined General Washington's division.

During the last half of her pregnancy, Kitty was content living in Nathanael's family home in Potowomut. She was getting along with her in-laws and with Nathanael's siblings. She enjoyed playing with George in the pleasant fields surrounding the home and taking him down to the river below. She studied French and read books and practiced sewing and stitchery with her sisters-in-law.

Then a British fleet was spotted in Narragansett Bay. The citizens of East Greenwich watched in fear as the ships sailed up the western passage, landing in Middletown—close to Newport. They held their breath as the troops, under the command of General Henry Clinton, came ashore and pillaged wherever they went. Kitty was in a state of panic. She knew her home in Coventry, Nat's home in Potowomut and even her Uncle Greene's home were all high on the list for destruction. With nowhere to go, she felt terrified. And she had just read the words of Nathanael's aide, Thomas Paine: *These are the times that try men's souls.* Feeling powerless to protect her son and unborn child, she fought a hard battle against hopelessness. The next letter from Nathanael did nothing to boost her morale.

General Lee's troops are expected to join us today, without the General, who became prisoner last Friday. Fortune seems to frown upon the cause of freedom. I hope this is the dark part of night which generally comes before day...

I hear a fleet and army have made their landing in Rhode Island. God forbid that they should penetrate into the country with you as with us... We are fortifying the city of Philadelphia and doubt not that we shall be able to keep the enemy out this winter. The city is under martial law; the Quakers horridly frightened for fear the city should be burnt... I have no hope of coming to New England this winter.

Kitty felt a strong sense of desolation. She wondered what happened to the affectionate tones of Nathanael's letters. Now she felt fat, unloved, lonely and desperate. Then everything changed.

On Christmas night General Greene was given orders to counterattack by re-crossing the frigid river into New Jersey. George Washington was at his side. Arriving on the opposite shore, he collected his men who had been landing up and down the river. During a brutal blizzard the troops marched to Trenton and found a large Hessian force sleeping. Kitty read with wonder Nathanael's description of what followed.

We attacked the town by storm early in the morning. It rained, hailed and snowed... The action lasted about three quarters of an hour. We killed, wounded, and took prisoners of the enemy. Our troops behaved with great spirit.

Should we get possession of the Jerseys, perhaps I may get liberty to come and see you. I pity your situation exceedingly; your distress and anxiety must be very great. Put on a good stock of fortitude. By the blessing of God, I hope to meet you again in the pleasure of wedlock. Adieu, my love.

In January of 1777, Kitty learned that the Continentals attacked the enemy garrison at Princeton and won a complete victory, flushing out the last of the Redcoats from Nassau Hall. After two stunning victories, the Continentals settled down for the winter on the high ground of Morristown.

What wonderful news to begin her new year! Kitty felt certain that Nat would be coming home soon. She missed him; his strength; his warmth; his touch. She fell to her knees, praying for his return.

ELEVEN

1777

The last stage of Kitty's pregnancy was a difficult one, requiring the services of several medical doctors. She knew she would be delivering this child without Nathanael and gratefully accepted his family's assistance and care in their home in Potowomut. Kitty gave birth to a healthy baby girl in March and named her Martha Washington. Nat's brother Kitt wrote him the happy news and in early April, Kitty received a loving note from her husband.

> *My Angel,*   *April 8, 1777*
> *Thank God for your safe delivery. When I shall see the poor little one, God only knows. I am exceedingly happy at your being in Potowomut, and rejoice to find the brothers so kind and attentive to your wants. Mrs. Washington and Mrs. Bland from Virginia are at camp. Pray, my dear, are you determined to suckle your baby or not? On that depends your liberty...*

Kitty was resolute in taking both children and joining Nathanael in New Jersey. She knew from Nat's letters that his headquarters was near Basking Ridge, in the home of Lord Stirling—a showplace home surrounded by lawns, vineyards, fruit orchards, stables of fine horses and a park with deer. And Lord Stirling himself was an interesting man, one she was most anxious to meet. A general in the Continental service, this Native American, whose proper name was William Alexander, had lived in England and petitioned Parliament for the title of *Earl of Stirling*. He was turned down by the British, but assumed the title *Lord* upon his return to America. His wife and daughter Kitty lived with him at the headquarters/mansion, and Kitty Greene was determined to spend time with them in that setting.

Her travel preparations were firmed up and, as she packed to leave, she was hit with fatigue and stomach problems. Her fever shot up, and the doctor was summoned. He diagnosed pneumonia and forbade her to travel, ordering her to bed for a month. Alone in her debilitated state, she meekly obeyed. Nathanael was not told of her illness and became frantic when he received no news from his wife. She believed the family had written him about her illness and confinement, but this was not the case. His reply to the news of her illness assured her of his deep concern.

> *My sweet love,*   *May 20, 1777*
> *I pray almighty God may restore your heath and comfort again. Nothing would give me greater pleasure than to come and see you but…the general (Washington) will not permit me to go…I feel a blank in my heart, which nothing but your presence can fill up. There is not a day or night, nay not an hour, but that I wish to fold you to my heart.*

Knowing that Nathanael could not come home, she again made plans to join him in his New Jersey camp. He told her to bring everything necessary and urged her to write Lucy Knox if she needed anything. Unfortunately, he added the following words to his loving letter, which infuriated her and detracted from his message of love.

> *But remember when you write to Mrs. Knox that you are writing to a good scholar; therefore mind and spell well. You are defective in that matter, my love; a little attention will soon correct it…People are often laughed at for not spelling well…Nothing but the affection and regard I feel for you*

makes me wish to have you appear an accomplished lady in every point of view.

This reprimand, well-intended as it was, wounded Kitty. Nat's words seemed to imply that she was inferior to Lucy Knox and that he, her husband, was ashamed of her. She continued making her preparations to join him at his headquarters, now situated in Morristown, New Jersey. His hosts, Mr. and Mrs. Abraham Lott, were looking forward to meeting Kitty.

Kitty, in the face of Nathanael's criticism, went shopping for an updated wardrobe. Thin from her sickness and tired of her old clothes, she found outfits to complement her sleek physique. She thought about her competition. Both Lady Stirling and her daughter Kitty had become a source of irritation to her because of Nathanael's letters, where he mentioned their polished manners, elegance and fine education. Kitty worried that Nat had changed. She understood that his world had expanded, while hers had stayed the same.

She set out in a carriage for her journey overland, accompanied by her son, baby daughter, a female nanny and one of Nathanael's aides, Billy Blodget. The trip was rough and uncomfortable as they passed between Rhode Island and the New Jersey camps. The byways were dusty and interminable, the air hot and humid, and the roadside inns were often little more than hovels. The ferries operated only at the whim of the owners. The jarring of the coach contributed to Kitty's tremendous headaches and dizziness, and she knew she was becoming ill once more. Looking through feverish eyes at her smiling son George and sleeping daughter Martha, she felt grateful for her beautiful and uncomplicated children.

Pale and exhausted, Kitty regained a portion of her strength four days later. The carriage pulled up at the Lotts' home and headquarters—Beverwyck. The morning sunlight was so bright it hurt her eyes, blinding her more than the darkness of her sleep. She felt his lips touching her hair. His breath was warm against her skin. Kitty experienced that odd sense of slipping backwards, of falling into something. Reaching out to him, she let herself fall. Nathanael smiled, a sweet, delicate smile—beautiful enough to break her heart. She and Nathanael fell into each other's arms for the first time in twelve months.

The tears came in uncontrollable waves, great gut-wrenching sobs that seemed to shake her from head to toe. "My angel, you are home with me now," he said in a voice that was barely above a whisper. He watched the tears spill from her eyes, and he fought to blink back his own. Lifting her from the carriage seat, Nathanael carried her into the house.

⚜

Kitty slept for two days straight. When she awoke, she found herself in a small bedroom with Martha Washington at her side.

"Where am I?" she asked bleary-eyed and dazed. "Oh Patsy, you are here. And where are my babies?"

"Hush, Kitty. You are with me in my home." Her eyes smiled on her young friend. "Your children are here as well," she answered, stroking her hair. Kitty nodded, grateful for Martha's warm maternal touch.

"And Nat? Is he here?"

"Your husband is off attending to his many responsibilities. He spent all night at your bedside, but I am sending him back to the Lott house tonight so he can get some sleep."

"Oh mercy, I missed his reunion with his children. Did I faint? What happened to me?"

"You were exhausted, my dear. The doctor examined you and said you must keep to bed for three days. Fortunately, I have the time and the resources to care for you here in my quarters," explained Martha.

"Three days! But I must feed my baby. And speak with my husband." Kitty was beginning to panic. "And I've not yet met the Lotts, have I?"

"All in due time, my dear. You will move into their home when..." She paused, choosing her words carefully.

"When what? What were you about to say?" Kitty's eyes were large and expectant.

Martha reached for her thin hand and squeezed it gently. "The British are leaving and your husband is under orders to take his troops to the south."

She closed her eyes. The tears squeezed through her lashes as she began to weep. Words came between sobs. "When? How long has he known this?" Panic fluttered in her throat and curled all the way down to her toes.

"Kitty, you must calm yourself," Martha answered very gently. "He's just received orders this week. He will leave in two or three days."

"No, Lord, this cannot be! I've come so far to be with him. Will he send me back to Coventry after all I have done to get here?" Her voice rose in alarm. She pulled at the bed covers in an effort to get out of the bed.

"Kitty, listen to me. He wants you here, nearby at the Lotts' residence, so he can see you and the children. It will comfort him having you close by. You must be supportive. This is very difficult for him as well."

Kitty angrily brushed the tears from her cheeks. "Does General Greene really believe our marriage can endure by seeing each other only once a year? His children don't even know him, nor he them," she sobbed. Martha gathered her in her arms. Kitty let her hold her while she cried.

"Darling, we are at war. We must encourage our husbands and stay strong for them. It will not be easy, yet we must." Her face was calm, her manner relaxed.

"Patsy, please send for my husband as soon as he returns. And bring me my children, if you will."

Kitty turned her head to the wall, still trembling with anger and frustration.

TWELVE

1777

Just before General Greene departed for Philadelphia, he asked Martha Washington if she would watch his children so he could spend time alone with Kitty.

"Of course I will," she agreed with an affectionate smile. "Surely you know how fond of them I've become in just these few days."

Wrapping a warm shawl over her thin arms, Nat settled down beside his wife on the sofa. "I want to tell you something that I believe will help you understand this war and my place in it." He spoke quietly and put his arm around her shoulder, snuggling her close.

"Kitty, why are you angry at General Washington? Is it because he refused to allow me to go to Coventry for our daughter's birth?"

Kitty blinked, astonished at his discernment. Her anger had abated because she *did* like George Washington, but she now blamed him for sending her husband away again. Pulling on her curls and twisting them around her fingers, she looked down and said nothing.

"The day I begged him to let me go home he was quite ill. He summoned all his officers to his bedside and asked us to whom the command should fall if he were to die." Nat paused, carefully considering his next words.

"General Washington's throat was inflamed and he spoke with difficulty. Looking from man to man, his eyes finally locked on mine. The others noticed and were silent. After a moment, General Washington nodded in my direction."

"Oh my," Kitty gasped. A glint of wonder filled her eyes. "What did the others do?"

"Nothing. When the General spoke he was seldom interrupted. He told us, 'If my generals think you are my favorite, they are correct. But my decision to pass the command to you upon my death was determined because you are the most able of my men.'" She felt his hand on her chin as he tilted her face toward his. "Imagine, Kitty. Those were his very words." He straightened his shoulders as he told her.

Kitty searched his eyes and saw a strong man without pride. She saw humility.

"Then he said that I was his strategist and tactician. He said my men respected and obeyed me, and that my loyalty and honesty were valued by him. Once again he surprised us by saying that he had approached Congress and asked that I be commissioned lieutenant-general."

"And they accepted his request?" she asked incredulously.

Nat laughed softly. "Of course not. They told him his rank as our leader was major-general and they could not give me a higher rank."

"So that is why he could not spare you. He needed to know you would be able and ready to take his place if he died." She brooded over this. Gradually her face softened. "And that is why General Spencer is in command in Rhode Island and you are here." Kitty sighed passively. "And now he will send you to Philadelphia. Am I correct about this, Nat?"

He grinned. "You are as clever as you are beautiful, my angel. General Washington believes I am the only one he confides in to present our position before Congress." Holding her face between his gentle fingers, he kissed her tenderly. "Please forgive him, my love. Please allow me to leave for my next post in peace."

Kitty nodded. She faced him with an encouraging smile. The combination of fragility and stubbornness in her face made his heart ache. Looking into her eyes, Nathanael saw the inquisitiveness and the unmistakable intelligence that enlightened her every expression.

He stood up stiffly and limped from the room. Kitty heard him ask to see the children. He was determined to spend the last few hours in Morristown with his beloved family.

⸎⊙⊙⸏

Only one month after eleven thousand strong American forces proudly marched through the streets of Philadelphia, they were forced to leave the city behind to the British troops. Nathanael had stationed his brigade between Philadelphia and the advancing British troops, led by Generals Howe and Cornwallis. As the enemy proceeded forward, the citizens fled from their homes on foot, carrying clothing and furniture and prodding their cattle before them. Nathanael described this in a May 20, 1777 letter to Kitty, and chided her for not writing.

> *My dear, it is now a month and upwards since I received a line from one of the family. I think it exceeding unkind; if you are unwell and incapable of writing surely some of the brothers might do me that friendly office. I returned last night from Peeks Kill after a long, tedious and hard journey. To crown all I fell from my horse upon the top of an exceeding high mountain, cut my lip through and otherwise bruised myself. Never did I undergo more fatigue in less time.*

He ended the letter with words about the citizens. *The country all resounds with the cries of the people.*

General Greene fought throughout the entire invasion, sitting astride his horse for over thirty hours and forgoing sleep for more than forty. He only collapsed on a bed after he was overcome with a severe attack of asthma. His skillful strategy helped to avert a complete disaster at the Battle of Brandywine that could have wiped out his army. Pushing them forward with prolonged speed for four miles over broken country to join up with Sullivan's troops, they fell into position and permitted Sullivan's exhausted men to fall back through his ranks. That action prevented a total defeat and allowed a planned retreat by Washington and his generals to Chester. Both Generals Washington and Greene were miraculously unscathed after exposing themselves recklessly to enemy fire in a battle with high casualties on both sides.

The young French volunteer, the Marquis de Lafayette, was shot in the leg in the Battle of Brandywine. An aide to General Washington, he had been commissioned as general in the Continental army at the age of nineteen. This very wealthy Frenchman was serving at his own expense as a volunteer on George Washington's staff. He had left behind a young wife and small child in France, as well as a brilliant social life.

"Why would he do that?" Henry Knox asked his friend shortly after Brandywine.

Nathanael smiled. "He told me it was for the cause of liberty. He's a Frenchman, but liberty is a universal goal. He appreciates and admires our commander-in-chief as well."

"And General Washington thinks highly enough of him to have put him on his personal staff. I think he made a lasting impression when he asked for no salary and told the General that he'd come to learn and not to teach.'" Henry chuckled. "I have never asked you. Do you like the Marquis?"

"I am indebted to him," answered Nathanael with a slow smile. Opening his jacket he exposed a small jewel. "He's a Masonic brother of mine. The night I suffered so badly with my asthma attack, Lafayette stayed beside me and helped as much as he could. Just before he left, he gave me this jewel of our brotherhood." He smiled at the memory. "I still remember his comforting words, and as he walked away, he asked me to wear this throughout the war."

Henry nodded respectfully. "And I'm sure you shall oblige him, my friend," he grinned.

eꙮꙮ

It took Kitty some time to recover. With her children safe and Nathanael away, she decided to make the most of her time as a guest of the Lott family. Mr. and Mrs. Abraham Lott were an older couple and one of the finest families she knew. Their daughter Cornelia was full of life and a grand companion for Kitty. Everyone doted on her children, and soon the games, concerts, sewing circles and frugal dinner parties were in full swing. Kitty was studying French and taking some music lessons as well. Dancing parties were arranged at the Lott's home. Handsome Colonel Cary was Kitty's frequent partner.

Once again Kitty's *inappropriate* behavior became the theme of conversation in the camp, set in motion in Boston by her "good" friend Lucy Knox. When the rumors reached Nathanael in Philadelphia, he went looking for Henry and found him reading in the large sitting area. Nathanael paused and watched him for a few moments, completely absorbed in a volume of poetry.

This particular room was colder and emptier than the parlors in the other headquarter homes; woodwork and mantelpiece were painted white, the chandelier was brass and crystal and hung over a round mahogany center table, bare except for a candelabra. Tall mahogany bookcases stood against the back wall and in the corner beyond the mantel.

Nat dropped slowly onto a chair across from his friend. "Pardon me, Henry. May I interrupt you for a moment?" he asked awkwardly. Henry looked up as Nathanael continued. "What do you hear from your Lucy about Kitty and Colonel Cary?"

Henry Knox abruptly averted his eyes and closed the heavy tome. "Not a thing; why do you ask?" Knowing the answer, he hoped to avoid Nat's next question.

"The man himself came into Headquarters talking about what a pleasant dance partner she is, how charming and lovely." His expression darkened and his eyes ignited. "I do not want to hear from other bloody men about my wife's charms, especially when I've not seen her for nearly nine months."

Nathanael's candor threw him off. "Nat, why hasn't she come to camp? She always came before. Have you invited her?"

Nat snapped as his eyes narrowed in suspicion. "I know not why. I've asked her to join me several times. She gives me excuses in every letter, but I believe she simply doesn't want to come here." Raw hurt gleamed in his eyes. "And I have no inclination why."

"Write her again this evening, Nat. Tell her you need her at your side, and how much you miss her. She'll be pleased to know how strongly you care."

Nathanael stood up, saddened by a despair that turned the room dark and the air thick. Henry watched him limping slowly out the door through the broken shadows.

Hunched over his desk, Nathanael felt a heaviness building inside him as he reached for the pen. Life wasn't that simple, that straightforward. It was tangled and twisted, and he couldn't erase the last nine months. What had he done wrong with his wife?

No matter how hard he tried, he could not escape the truth. Kitty must not feel his love. He had not been able to be a proper husband. His mouth curved into a sad smile, and his heart twisted inside him as he began writing.

Dearest Kitty   *November 2, 1777*

I am happy to hear you are so agreeably employed. I wish the campaign was over that I might come and partake of your diversions. But we must first give Mr. Howe a stinging, and then look forward to a joyous winter of pleasant tales... In the neighborhood of my quarters there are several sweet pretty Quaker girls. If the spirit should move and love invite who can be accountable for the consequences? I know this won't alarm you because you have such a high opinion of my virtue. It is very well you have. You remember the prayer of that saint—tempt me not above what I am able to bear. But I promise you to be as honest as ever I can.

Yours,
Nathanael

He had not conveyed his true feelings because he was unable to write them. His jealousy infuriated him, yet he recognized it sneaking silently through the words he wrote. No one could offer him yesterday for today, yet he needed to clear his head and move forward. His instincts shouted at him to burn the letter, but instead, he handed it to the messenger who would ride out in the morning.

THIRTEEN

1778

Kitty read and re-read Nathanael's letter, which stirred up so many memories of her husband: walking hand in hand on the beach, watching his eyes sparkle in merriment, reliving the comfort and warmth of his body next to hers. Missing him was painful. She had discovered that blocking him from her mind was possible and had finally reached the point of enjoying life without him at her side. His written words confused her and the suggestion of other women's interest in him made her angry. She was startled to realize she was flattered by his jealousy. With so many thoughts spinning around her, she carried the letter to Cornelia Lott and asked her to read it.

"His words torture me, Cornelia. I know I love him dearly, yet I admit I have enjoyed my freedom here with your family and my children. I confess there are days I scarcely think of him at all. Is that wicked?"

Cornelia studied her friend's eyes. "Kitty, do you not see the love he has for you between the words? He wants you at his side, and questions why you are kicking up your heels while he is fighting for the country."

Kitty wrinkled her nose in annoyance. "Are you also going to berate me? I wonder which hurtful rumors have reached him now, for surely that is the reason for his bizarre message."

Cornelia appreciated her high-strung girlfriend. Life with the Lott family had given Kitty the attention she craved and allowed her the freedom to enjoy her self-centered world. But

Cornelia knew that Kitty loved her husband in her incomparable style.

"If you are asking my opinion, I would suggest that you go to him as soon as you can," smiled Cornelia. "I only hope one day to find a man as strong and principled as yours."

The next morning Kitty made plans for the ride back to Rhode Island. Leaving her children once again, she set out to join Nathanael at his camp in Pennsylvania. It was an unusually cold February. Accompanied by only an aide, she bundled herself up and suffered through the long carriage trip to the west bank of the Schuylkill River, twenty miles from Philadelphia. As she descended into the Pennsylvania valley, she was awarded a breathtaking view of the high ridges and the Schuylkill River. But it was the sight of human suffering that seared her memory forever.

The Continental army was in tatters; the men had no protective clothing. The fortunate ones were covered by ragged blankets or dressing gowns to keep from freezing. The others huddled in their tents or huts, stripped of most of their clothing, and what they wore hung loosely from their wasted bodies. These soldiers had eaten no meat for days, and subsisted on hand-to-mouth provisions brought back from forages into a countryside depleted by the raids of the enemy. The men had to build their own shelters—little log huts, chinked with mud, a door at one end and a clay fireplace at the other. Each hut measured fourteen by sixteen feet and housed twelve men. Even the officers occupied the tiny log cabins. Noticing them on her arrival, she was sickened with the realization that one of these huts would be her next home.

To Kitty's great relief, by the time she got there Nathanael had taken residence in a spartan farmhouse. As the carriage approached the home, her cousin Sammy Ward charged through the door, grinning from ear to ear.

"Welcome to Valley Forge," he beamed, helping her down from the carriage. She threw her arms around his neck in relief, holding back her tears.

"Oh Sammy, it's so good to see your smile. And look at you: such a smart uniform!"

He laughed gleefully. "I'm an aide-de-camp in your husband's brigade, sweet Kitty." Looking into the carriage, he frowned. "But I do not see the babies. Where are they?"

"I took them back to Rhode Island and left them with Nat's family. And I am relieved I left them there. From what I've seen, these circumstances are deplorable. The poor soldiers look like they've not eaten or bathed in weeks." She shook her head in pity, watching his eyes stealing uneasy glances at her.

"You should have seen where we were living until Nathanael heard you were coming." Pointing down the road to the village of small huts, he added, "Even General Washington stayed there until Lady Washington arrived. He's since moved to a nicer home not far from here." He hugged her tightly. "Oh, Kitty, Nathanael will be so happy to see you. The poor chap has been ever so lonely."

Nodding slowly, her expression full of concern, Kitty responded. "I have missed him also. But what about the troops, Sammy? Can nothing be done for them?" Tears popped into her eyes.

Sammy led her inside to a chair by the fire. "Warm yourself now, Kitty. Nat will be here shortly." Seeing her glazed expression, he answered her question. "We are doing what we can for the soldiers. You do know that even Congress had to flee from Philadelphia, and yet the enemy rests there comfortably. So now we must make do on our own. Lady Washington, Lady Knox and the other women have already begun sewing and knitting clothing for the men. I am certain they will welcome more hands." He grinned at her shamelessly distressed expression.

Kitty exhaled noisily. Turning away from Sammy, she began unpacking her trunk of elegant gowns, purchased shortly before the trip. Sammy's brow was knitted in concern as he watched her search for a place to hang the gowns.

"I do not like sewing, and I prefer knitting even less. But I will join them if that is what is needed."

After a short time he spoke up. "I do hope you've brought warmer and more practical frocks with you. There is no partying in this camp and there hasn't been since we've arrived. Not even card playing."

"I should have stayed in Morristown," she mumbled under her breath, her lips twisting at the corners. Yet she kept her true thoughts to herself. *If it weren't for Nat's letter, I would still be there. And now I must worry about returning to Rhode Island in the spring, most likely pregnant again.*

Sammy sensed her unhappy reflections and regretted being the messenger of bad tidings. "Here now, I'll help you unpack so you will be ready for your reunion with your husband," he replied.

∽∽⦿∾∾

Nathanael rode slowly, apprehension and uncertainty about seeing Kitty clouding his thoughts. This had never happened before. His memories of their past reunions were joyous and filled with laughter and love. She had always come to him excited and buoyant, eager to enjoy their marital bliss. Was she suffering the same insecurity and nerves as he?

He heard them conversing as he drew near the house. Stepping inside, he heard the conversation stop abruptly. Kitty's wide, apprehensive eyes locked with his for a long moment.

Nathanael felt embarrassed by his awkward greeting. "Thou looks lovely, Kitty."

Her sensually molded lips smiled shyly. "I can't believe my blessed eyes are finally filled with you."

Sammy took several steps toward the door. "Pardon me, but you two have a great deal to catch up on. I'll see you later." Neither noticed him leave.

Kitty held open her arms, and Nat walked across the room into them. "Oh Kitty," he breathed. "You have finally come." She searched his weary hazel eyes and saw a stray tear ease out of one corner. Lifting her fingers gently to his cheeks, she brushed her hands across them, feeling his skin.

"Nat, my love, I need to be with you," she said simply, pulling his head down to hers. He kissed her softly and saw that her eyes were still and calm. The fire burned low. The warmth was comforting.

He cleared his throat. "Kitty, the children?" he murmured.

"Later," she answered, standing on tiptoes to reach up and slide her arms around his neck. She caressed the back of his head, looking into his eyes. She wanted to comfort him, but even more, she wanted to kiss him. His gaze held hers for a long, tense moment before dropping to her mouth. He lifted a hand to brush a rebellious curl out of her eyes.

Kitty stroked his chest beneath his cloak, loving the feel of his coarse, dark hair under her fingertips. Nathanael skimmed his hand along her throat to the curve of her neck and let it rest there while his thumb gently massaged the tight muscles. It felt so good she wanted to purr.

"Kiss me," she rasped, clutching at air until she gained a handful of his hair.

His mouth was hot, and she melted into him. Her soft breasts pressed against his chest. His mouth took absolute possession of hers. His hands were everywhere, caressing, stroking, teasing, as his mouth covered hers again and again. With each breath, she drew in his unique scent.

They were both panting for breath when he ended the kiss and stepped back. His face was taut with passion. The way he was looking at her made her feel bold. She moved restlessly against him, her hands slowly easing down his sides. His body was as hot as his gaze. He could barely breathe because of the ecstasy she evoked. Beads of perspiration covered his brow.

Heat seared the inside of her skin and skittered along her nerve endings. She clutched his shirt, twisting the cotton. Kitty couldn't breathe. She made a sound in her throat, a guttural plea that had him lifting his head to stare at her. His mouth was vulnerable, his eyes glazed with a hunger that matched her own. She noticed his pupils were dilated and nearly filled the irises, and she could see herself mirrored in them.

Nathanael hid his relief behind his grin. Lifting her fingers to his lips he whispered, "Come with me, my angel. Welcome to your new home."

FOURTEEN

1778

Nathanael couldn't hear enough about his children. When Kitty told him the Lotts were calling his daughter *Patty* instead of *Martha*, his smile blossomed into a joyful grin. Learning that little George was speaking sentences and playing soldier completely astounded him. After countless questions, he suddenly turned to her with a dejected look.

"Oh Kitty, they don't remember me anymore, do they?"

She reached out and squeezed his hand. "Of course they do, dear. I speak to them every day about their father. I tell them how much you love them."

He shook his head. "It's the war. We've become victims, each one of us. Dear Lord, even my children are victims." He turned away to hide the unshed tears standing in his eyes. "And do you know what pierces my very soul, Kitty? That I am forced to take food from the poor farmers to keep my army from starving."

Kitty's head jerked upward, her eyes wide with apprehension. "Surely you pay them?"

His eyes were cloaked in sadness. "Yes, we give them useless Continental notes, which are worth almost nothing." With a sharp intake of breath, he continued, "Oh Kitty, they even hide their livestock. Or they try desperately to transport them to Philadelphia, where the British pay gold for them. The Quaker farmers are convinced that God's favor is with the British over us, since they have plenty, and we have naught."

Kitty hurried to him, wrapping her arms around his waist. He lifted her face to his, searching her troubled eyes for a long moment. "There's more, my angel. And it involves a shift in my position," he added solemnly. Her gaze loosened and color flooded her face.

"The Quaker Mifflin deserted his post as quartermaster general. His Excellency wants me to take it as my own." He held up a hand to cut off the question forming on her lips. "There will be no need for a major general if there are not provisions to feed the army. They are counting on me to provide those resources, foraging for food and supplies. General Washington believes I can do that. At the moment, he has had to add that position to his many other responsibilities." He bowed his head, awaiting her reaction and murmured, "How can I say no?"

She surprised him. "Dear Nat, you must do what you feel is right." She reached up and kissed him on the lips. "And I know you will."

The following day Nathanael was called to a meeting by His Excellency. Also in attendance were John Sullivan, Henry Knox, Lord Stirling, and Alexander Hamilton. George Washington passed a letter around the circle. "Here are the slanderous words written against each of you. The author is Dr. Benjamin Rush, signer of the Declaration of Independence and Surgeon-General of the Armies of the Middle Department. Along with Horatio Gates, Tom Conway, and Thomas Mifflin, his intent is to remove me from my command. And because you are my friends and confidants, you are being vilified as well."

The men said little after reviewing their character denigration in the written word. Nat smiled to himself as he read that he was "*a subordinate parasite who was timid, speculative, without enterprise and a flatterer of His Excellency for his own self-interest.*"

George Washington retrieved the letter and brought the gathering to an end. "No one is to even consider defending my honor with a duel. Let us strive to forget the attacks and lead our army to a praise-worthy victory over the true enemy."

⁗⊙⊙⌇⌇

In late winter the Nathanael Greenes moved three miles down the Pottstown Road into the comfortable quarters of Moore Hall, the home of William Moore. This gentle family had been constantly tormented by their Tory neighbors and was happy to have the general, his wife and their military guards as guests. Here in Moore Hall, Kitty, the expert in living in the moment, flaunted her knowledge of French and communicated with the foreign officers in camp—Lafayette, dePortail, Pulaski, Steuben and Kosciusko. Her vivaciousness and verve were a blessing to the morale of the officers, as well as the troops. Moore Hall was frequently filled with visitors, and one of her favorite officers was the young and handsome Marquis de Lafayette. The two of them spent hours sharing stories of their distant families, singing French songs as she accompanied them on the piano, and enjoying their mutual interest in French literature.

Another of Kitty's favorite officers was the dashing Brigadier General Anthony Wayne, who helped save the army from starvation by rounding up cattle on foraging expeditions and bringing them to camp. This debonair, handsome general was only eight years older than Kitty. Married to Polly Penrose, daughter of one of Philadelphia's most prestigious families, he once took his young bride to Nova Scotia, where she suffered hardships she never thought possible. When they returned to Waynesborough, she vowed never to leave home again. She never did, even when her husband camped only a short distance away. Anthony Wayne became an incurable ladies' man and was wildly besotted with the lovely Kitty Greene, who in turn found him charming and a remarkable conversationalist.

These two men, and several others, competed for Kitty's attention during the long winter at Valley Forge. They brought her gifts, tendered her endless compliments and placed themselves at her service.

Martha Washington watched and wondered. One evening, after she and George retired for the evening, she mentioned her concern.

"George, is it my imagination or were all the men here this evening captivated by Kitty Greene?"

George Washington grinned. "She certainly brings the laughter and fun to the party, does she not?" He and his wife were very fond of Kitty and her children and considered them family. They both admired her strength and pluck.

"For example, take a look at General Wayne. Why, he's practically falling all over her, and she allows it."

"Patsy, do you think Nathanael is concerned about this attention?" George knew Kitty was a beautiful woman, but he also understood that his wife felt no jealousy of his admiration. Martha was aware that some of the other officers' wives felt threatened by Kitty, but she felt secure in her husband's love.

Martha smiled. "No, I believe he is the most trusting man I have ever met. He thinks she is oblivious to the havoc she causes."

Nathanael detested the drudgery of providing the army with clothing and provisions, but accepted the post as quartermaster general for one year because of his love for the weary commander-in-chief. General Greene gave Congress his conditions: he would appoint his own subordinates—Cox of Philadelphia and Pettit of New Jersey—and retain his major general's rank and pay. He also wanted Jeremiah Wadsworth, whose monetary credit was excellent all over America and was helping finance the war, as his commissary general. Congress was desperate enough to accept.

General Greene went into private partnerships with his assistants Cox, Pettit, and Wadsworth, overlapping official duties with those of private enterprise. They bought interests in several ships under the name of Nat's brother Jacob. These vessels engaged in privateering, which was a legal and popular type of speculation. Even George Washington, the most respected gentleman of his day, wanted an interest in a privateer. But members of Congress condemned this venture because they had not been consulted or included. The intransigence on their part brought anguish and eventually monetary losses to Nat and Kitty. Yet during the war, when the stores had no supplies, Nat, as quartermaster general, was able to fill his warehouses from his own private resources, maintaining the army and keeping it from ruin.

Within a very short time Nat had formed a chain of supply depots from Delaware, Pennsylvania and Jersey to the Hudson. Cloth, cattle, canvas, grain and forage began trickling in from regions not swept bare by both armies. The soldiers regained some weight and minimal clothing was provided to all.

As spring arrived, General Washington ordered a thorough housecleaning of the entire encampment. Windows were added to the small huts, fresh boughs and clean straw were brought in, and the men cleansed themselves in the icy streams. Because of General Greene's competent quartermastering, they now had soap, vinegar, shoes and new shirts and pants. Tossing out nets to capture fish and planting garden plots enabled them to eat fresh food.

When the army congregated in May to celebrate the completion of the French alliance, the officers and ladies crowded together under a marquee of tent cloth and a throng of excited civilians watched nearby as the American army performed the drill they had learned from General Steuben. These clean, mended and self-respecting soldiers stepped out with their heads held high and executed their moves with precision and confidence. Kitty and Martha Washington wiped away tears of pride and then rode back from the parade to the banquet tables, where they enjoyed wine and a sumptuous meal prepared for this momentous occasion.

France had promised to come to America's aid against the British fleet, but it would take time for reinforcements to arrive. The generals decided their army would remain at the Valley Forge encampment and await the next British move. The time had come for the wives to return home, and for once Kitty left earlier than the others. She had received word that their daughter Patty suffered from the rickets, caused by a lack of calcium or vitamin D. Preparing quickly for her return to Rhode Island and distressed to leave Nathanael again, she was looking forward to reuniting with her small children. Nathanael was able to accompany her as far as the Hudson. As he held her to kiss her farewell, he tenderly stroked her belly. Once again, Kitty was with child.

After his arrival back at camp, Nathanael penned a letter to his wife.

I have only time to tell you now that I am here in the usual style, writing, scolding, eating and drinking. But there is no Mrs. Greene to spend an agreeable hour with. I hope you got home safely. Pray write me a full history of family matters; there is nothing that will be so agreeable. Kiss the sweet little children for their absent papa. You must make yourself as comfortable and as happy as possible. Write me if you are in want of anything to render you so.

FIFTEEN

1778

Kitty was happy to be far away from the eyes of her friends during the miserable months of her pregnancy. Returning to Rhode Island, she found her family in a state of fright because of the British forces roving around Newport. British soldiers were entering homes and stealing provisions and then burning the houses to the ground. Her friend Martha Varnum, staying in nearby Warren, witnessed raiders shooting rifles to frighten the residents while stealing their belongings. Terrified for the safety of her children, Kitty wrote to Nathanael and pleaded to live elsewhere.

Nathanael urged her to go to a place he owned in Westerly, a small coastal village near the Connecticut border. Soon she and the children relocated to the comfortable farmhouse they called *Liberty Hall,* where they were entertained by watching the countless vessels sailing through the bay. Kitty took her small children to the rivers behind the farmhouse, and let them dip their toes in the rushing waters and play with the minnows. They ate an abundance of fresh fish, milked cows for rich creamy milk, and tended their large vegetable garden together. Kitty felt content and safe there.

Through Nathanael's letters Kitty learned of the British evacuation of Philadelphia and their advance into New York City. She implored him to return to Rhode Island and help drive the enemy from Newport. When he explained that his army must remain near New York City to keep the British bottled up on Manhattan Island, she resorted to manipulation: *You've not been home in three years and I've ridden all over the country to be near you. I'm carrying your third child and you've scarcely even seen the second.*

In one of Nathanael's letters, dated July 17, 1778, he revealed his own sentiments.

This news I am sure has done violence to your feelings, but I trust that I shall meet with no difficulty in obtaining your forgiveness hereafter. At the close of the war I flatter myself I shall be able to return to your arms with the same unspotted love and affection as when I took the field. Although I have been absent from you, I have not been inconstant in love, unfaithful to my vows, or unjust to your bed. And I feel equally secure in your affection and fidelity.

General Washington, after reviewing General Greene's and several other officers' written advice, came to the conclusion that Newport did indeed need an expeditionary force to expel the enemy. He called Nathanael into his headquarters office.

"Please sit down, Nathanael. I have your letter here, and I wish to verbally respond to it." His Excellency studied him with insight. "Yes, I do expect more from you because that is what you've always given me. And I know of your devotion to the army, the citizens and especially to me." He smiled, watching General Greene with certain shrewdness evident in his eyes.

"Because of your respect for me, you accepted the position of quartermaster general. We were victorious at Valley Forge, and General Steuben received the glory. But without your selfless attitude and tireless effort, he would not have had an army. I know that to be a fact."

Nathanael flushed and remained silent as he listened to every word, letting a slow smile unfold.

"Now I realize that I often fail to show my appreciation to those closest to me. I should have told Congress that you deserved the glory for Brandywine, but I feared they would accuse me of showing favoritism toward you." Letting out a long weary sigh, he flashed a grin at Nat. "However, I've found a small way to make amends. I will send you back to Rhode Island to face the enemy at Newport, as commander of one of the divisions."

The instantaneous expression of gratitude in Nathanael's smile profoundly touched General Washington.

"Your Excellency, how can I possibly thank you for this honor?" asked Nathanael, noticeably shaken. The firelight illuminated the plane of his face and cast the hollows into deep shadow.

"You need not, son. I owe you this."

Sending General Greene back to Rhode Island was a timely move since the newly-arrived French fleet had just attacked the British garrison at Newport Harbor. Shortly after the attack, the area was hit by a severe storm, disabling and scattering the French fleet. The British wreaked mayhem on Newport Harbor, plundering and pillaging whatever they wanted.

In spite of the excitement all around him, Nathanael returned directly to his home in Coventry, where Kitty and his children had arrived the day before from Westerly. He set aside the rest of the day to spend in peace with his family.

The following day Nathanael gathered his troops around him, setting up division headquarters in his own home. The barren yard was filled with tents and soldiers huddled in silent, gloomy groups. Their nightly campfires startled Kitty—their grotesque shadows and flickering lights reflected on the bedroom's walls and ceilings.

The children were shy but fascinated by this tall soldier who was their father. He approached them slowly and gently, and soon two-year-old George willingly followed him around the house on his sturdy chubby legs. Little Patty, as they now called her, was more timid, yet in a short time let him pick her up and hold her on his lap.

"Can you show me the river, George?" Nathanael asked, tucking his son's small hand in his. "I want to see the fish you and Mama catch."

George beamed up at his father, leading him through the back yard and down to the river. Kitty followed, carrying Patty, giving them some private time alone. The ground, carpeted with soft moss, gave her a magical sense of isolation. She listened to the singing of the gentle wind in the tree tops and inhaled the sweet and heavy air—damp with secret, growing things.

"Look! Cows!" shouted George, pointing a plump finger at the distant field. "Mama milk them. Me help her," he grinned happily, scampering to keep up with Nat's deliberate walk.

Kitty followed leisurely, heavy and graceless with her distended stomach. She felt relieved knowing Nathanael would be with her at the birth. She needed his strength and his encouragement. Feeling abundantly blessed, she watched him play with their son from a short distance.

Patty squirmed and tapped Kitty's arm. Just in front of them were butterflies, each sporting the most amazing colors—reds, yellows, greens. They stopped to watch as one glided beside them, wide-winged—the brightest blues imaginable—with wings rimmed with solid black.

"Oh Patty, you shall finally know your father. He is such a good man. And your mama will be so much happier now." She hugged her daughter close, tenderly setting her down to rest on the late summer grass, and then eased herself awkwardly to the ground beside her. Breathing deeply, Kitty soaked up the sliver of sunlight on her face and absorbed the aroma of the deep forest—a hint of flowers, of water-drenched moss, of trees and light, pure air.

A sudden sweet gust of wisteria washed over her—the very scent of childhood and home. Kitty closed her eyes, sorely missing her family, especially her Aunt Catharine and Uncle Greene. She smiled thinking about his newly elected post: Governor of Rhode Island, and looked forward to visiting them after the baby's birth.

eↄ◌ↄↄ

"But you promised, Nat! You said you would request a leave of absence to be here for the birth of our baby!" Tears formed a bright line of silver along her lower lids.

"Angel, how could I have promised? You are still weeks off and I must return to my camp. I will try to persuade General Wash..."

"You've neglected me for too long," she interrupted with a shriek. "And it's so wrong of you. Henry Knox stayed with Lucy when she had her last baby. But you gave Colonel Cox and Biddle leave to attend their wives. What about us?" Kitty's pretty face had hardened into a sullen glare.

Nathanael knew that reasoning with Kitty while in this state would be fruitless. He needed to let her calm down first. As he approached her quivering body, her face went sharp and she pulled away, bitter tears stinging her eyes. Kitty refused to give her husband an opportunity to comfort her.

Kitty stared callously at him, her voice ringing with finality. "I hate your army! I hate this place and I hate your position as quartermaster. Everything comes before your wife and your children." She paused, trembling. "I even hate you at this moment," she wailed, lurching from the room.

Nathanael sank into a chair, head in his hands as silent tears fell to the floor. *Lord, you know I've tried to be a good husband, and a good officer. Is it so difficult to do both? Why can I not reach my wife and convince her of my love? Help me, God. Please help me.*

Moments later his brothers Kitt and Jacob entered silently, their faces heavy with concern, and placed hands on his shoulders in a comforting gesture. He looked up at them through red-rimmed eyes.

"Thou is suffering greatly, brother. We are here to offer thee comfort, if we can," murmured Kitt, noticing how the weariness showed in the drooping slope of Nat's shoulders.

"What is wrong with me? Why is my marriage so filled with anguish? Help me understand my Kitty, as you have spent more time with her than I." His face had drawn inward, a pale knot of apprehension.

"Nathanael, our Kitty is but a frightened child. She fears she will die birthing this baby. Does thee understand she nearly died after Patty's birth? She needs you with her." Kitt spoke softly.

"Nay, she shall not die! I will not allow it!" His gravelly voice quaked in fear.

Jacob's compassionate voice was low. "Then tell your General thou must stay here with her. I believe he will understand."

Nat nodded slowly. He looked up, offering them a fragile smile. "I must go to Boston forthwith, and from there will request a leave of absence. I have Pettit and Cox at the camp, who are more than capable. Perhaps His Excellency will appreciate my plight."

His brothers smiled. Kitt answered for them both. "We will pray for that resolution."

In his request for leave Nathanael wrote to his commander-in-chief:

My wife is very desirous of my staying until the event of our child's birth. Since she has her heart set upon it, I wish to gratify her, for fear of some disagreeable consequences, as women sometimes under such circumstances receive great injury from being disappointed.

The leave was granted. Nathanael was able to travel to Boston with the promise to return well before the baby's birth. Kitty, comforted and relieved now that the soldiers had left her home, made an effort to participate with Nat's family.

"Kitt, would you allow the children and me to visit you in the forge?"

"Does thee wish to work there, sister Kitty?" he answered bewildered.

She laughed easily. "No, but I should like you to show my son what you and his uncles do, so he will understand how and where his papa grew up."

General Greene spent the amount of time necessary to converse with John Hancock and his assistants about the upcoming economic situation of the army. Nathanael suggested levying federal taxes to keep the army afloat, explaining to the Congress that the colonies were still fighting for freedom. Justifying that his wife needed him at her side, he left after several days.

On their ride back to Rhode Island, his aides Rob Burnet and Billy Blodget kept Nathanael's mind off his problems, sharing humorous stories and telling lighthearted tales.

"Kitty should be so pleased to have me home a month before her delivery time, right boys?"

"Aye, you are a noble man and a considerate husband. She will be well-pleased," smiled Rob. "We must make haste for it is beginning to rain."

Cantering to a nearby tavern, they were intercepted by a boy who worked in Nathanael's forge. "I carry a message from Jacob, sir. He told me to find you with great haste."

Nat read the missive with a somber countenance. "We must go now, boys. My wife is in labor, and it will take us three hours of fast riding to reach her." He spurred his horse into action.

Three drenched men rushed through the door of Coventry after an exhausting ride. "Is she okay?" gasped Nathanael as Jacob hurried toward him.

"She is suffering pain and…"

"I must go to her bedside this moment." Nathanael cut short his brother's words.

"Thou is soaked and shivering. Change thy clothing and drink something warm before you go to her. The doctor is with her as well as Mother Greene and Peggy."

Nathanael nodded and obeyed. Before entering the room, Jacob pulled him to the side. "Nathanael, the doctor fears the baby may not live. The birth is too early, and…I'm so sorry."

Pushing gently past his brother, Nathanael reached the bedside. The relief in Kitty's eyes was overwhelming. He cupped her chin, covering her dry lips with kisses as his hand stroked her hair.

"Nat, the baby is coming too soon, but I cannot stop it," she sobbed, her voice panic-stricken.

"Kitty, take deep breaths and listen to Mother Greene and the doctor. God will do the rest, and I will be at your side," he smiled tenderly, attempting to mask his own fear.

For the next hour Nat dabbed Kitty's pale cheeks and forehead with cool water as they prayed together. She bore down hard, finally delivering a tiny infant who entered the world with a feeble whimper. Kitty fell back as Nat's stepmother wrapped the fragile child in warm coverlets.

The doctor smiled warmly at them. "You have a baby daughter. She's tiny, but with your help she will pull through. God bless you."

Nat and Kitty exchanged exhausted looks. A glint of wonder filled her eyes and he felt smarting tears stinging his own. Together, they would will this baby to live.

"Nat, may we call her Cornelia Lott Greene, after my friend?" she asked hesitantly.

Taking both her hands in his, he gave her his lopsided grin. "Of course we will, my love. Rest now. Sleep. I will watch over baby Cornelia."

Kitty slept for nearly a week. Sleep was her refuge. Her recovery was slow and arduous. During that time little Cornelia Lott fought for her life. With the assistance of a wet nurse and the constant care of Nathanael's family, she gradually began to gain strength and weight. After eight days, mother and daughter spent the daylight hours together in her bed. When Nathanael joined Kitty at night, he lovingly tucked Cornelia into the cradle beside them.

"My little girl, you are a brave one," Nat whispered to his child as he arranged her in the tiny bed. "But you will now grow strong and become a vital woman, just like your mother."

Climbing into bed, he cuddled Kitty. "My angel, I love you

more each day. I'll love you when you're rocking our grand-children." She shook in the circle of his embrace, but it wasn't from the cold.

Kitty felt her strength returning and knew that Nathanael would leave soon. She felt the warmth of his breath and savored the thrill of being close to his hard body and inhaling his presence.

"Nat? When must you leave?" she murmured between sleep, burying her face in his chest.

He rumbled pleasantly from somewhere way down in that big chest. "Soon, Kitty. But I will suggest to His Excellency that I set up camp in Middlebrook, New Jersey again. We'll be close to the Lotts. Won't they be thrilled to meet our little Cornelia Lott?"

In spite of her drowsiness, Kitty's eyes flew open with glim-mering anticipation. "Oh yes, Nat. I would love that. When will the children and I join you?" Her bright smile touched his heart.

"In three or four weeks, I believe. I shall find us a nice home near the Lotts and then send for you." Leaning over, he ten-derly kissed her mouth—a sweet kiss that traveled through her body.

"But you must fully recover before you make the trip. Mother Greene must assure me."

She giggled. "Let not your heart be troubled, my husband. Not only will I be strong and well, but I'll come with a new wardrobe. And one for each child."

"Yes you will. And I shall give you my blessing to do so."

When he kissed her good-bye, he could not have known it would be his last night in their Coventry home.

SIXTEEN

FEBRUARY 1779

"How trim her figure looks so soon after the birth of baby Cornelia," smiled Martha Washington, gazing fondly as Kitty whirled gracefully across the floor to the strains of lively fiddle music. "She's so lovely in her fashionable French gown! I am fond of the shorter skirts that accentuate the shoes and the ankles." Her eyes sought Nathanael's. "You must be so proud of your beautiful Kitty, General Greene."

Nathanael was conscious of the guests' eyes on his spirited wife as she swirled with the music. Her rose-colored silk dress had been carefully selected for the affair: an off-the-shoulders frock with tight-fitting sleeves and a square neck filled in with rare old lace. The skirt, complete with lace-edged flounces, swayed gracefully as she danced. Her mass of dark hair was coiled high upon her well-poised head, with dainty ringlets bouncing along with her movements. Nestled in the hollow of her throat she wore her golden locket, a treasured gift from Nathanael's aides containing Nathanael's picture.

As if on cue, Kitty's gaze drew him out and she blew him a gentle kiss, cooling her face with her silk and ivory fan. Her smile touched him like a warm breeze. Laughing softly, he turned his attention back to General Washington's wife.

"She is delighted to host this small party in our parlor," he grinned. "After all, the last time we were joined by our wives at headquarters you women were made to suffer the horrid circumstances of the encampment at Valley Forge. And, if my mind serves me well, there was no dancing. It appears that Kitty is determined to make up for lost time."

Even the women present admired Kitty's sweet smile and poise. As she approached a small group of ladies, she overheard her friend Jane Stickle Crosier speaking to an officer's wife.

"Isn't Lady Greene lovely? Why the grace she exudes! Twenty-five summers have left no mark of care upon her joyous nature."

Her friend nodded. "She seems permanently surrounded by a bevy of bright faces. With her brilliant conversation and quick perception, she delights all within the magic of her presence."

Middlebrook Valley was a paradise compared to Valley Forge, and General Greene's headquarters at the Van Veghten House were comfortable and clean. The handsome dwelling was constructed of Holland brick and situated along the banks of the Raritan River, under the cover of a New Jersey mountain range. In contrast to the miserable conditions of the soldiers in Valley Forge, Kitty now found them well-fed and well-clothed. The generals and their wives welcomed her warmly, and Nathanael's aides were enchanted by her enthusiastic outlook. The enemy was far away, her husband was close and Kitty was content.

Commander-in-Chief George Washington strode purposefully across the room to Kitty's side. She laughed breezily as she countered her dancing partner Alexander Hamilton's light banter with clever, witty comebacks, all the time keeping in step with the music.

"Lady Greene, may I accompany you back to our spouses for a bit of refreshment?" he offered, nodding to Alexander Hamilton. "You must be in need of a beverage and some rest," he added with a bemused look in his eyes.

Kitty's brow furrowed slightly and her snapping large eyes widened as she linked her arm lightly through his. "Did you suggest rest, General Washington? Why, I can dance forever without pause. Per chance you have forgotten the ball at the Knox's Academy, celebrating the first anniversary of the

French alliance?" she added saucily, chin held high, eyes alive with mischief.

"Indeed I had not forgotten that ball. Why I believe you danced all evening, attended by every gentleman in the room." They had reached the table where their spouses were seated. Nathanael rose to offer Kitty his chair, inwardly groaning at his stiff knee joint. He relaxed back into his chair with every appearance of ease. Lady Washington placed a cool glass of wine in Kitty's hands; her gentle eyes settled on Kitty's flushed cheeks.

"My dear, please rest a spell. You've just given birth to your precious Cornelia Lott. Your body cannot endure such strenuous movement." She gave the younger woman a quick, assessing glance.

Kitty's eyes smiled as she sipped the chilled wine. Reaching over to stroke her husband's hand, she stared boldly at George Washington. "Would you like to make a wager that I can outlast you on the dance floor, General Washington?"

Now she had their attention. George Washington met her gaze and shook his head slightly. A wide smile spread across his face as he looked over at Nathanael. "Shall I take her up on it, Quaker preacher? What say thou?"

Nathanael and Martha laughed easily. The impetuous charming Kitty Greene would have her way. Martha knew her husband loved a challenge, and at least this one was harmless.

"Darling, make your wager. Lady Washington and I will be the judges." Nathanael set his pocket watch on the table. As the dancing began, he felt some of the tightness around his mouth ease up.

Martha sighed, closing her eyes. She didn't dance, except the first dance of the evening with her husband, yet suddenly she was overcome with weariness. Peering over at Nathanael, she caught his slow proud smile as he watched his wife dance with his commander-in-chief.

"General Greene, I am curious. May I ask you how you injured your leg?"

Nathanael shot her a startled look, and then shrugged. "It was an act of disobedience, I fear. I was but twenty, still living under my father's rules. He forbade his sons to visit the dance socials, but I often sneaked out my second-story chamber window by jumping to the ground. It worked well many times, until the night I slipped on the roof and crashed to the ground, twisting my knee."

"Oh my—how painful. Did you get medical assistance?"

Nathanael laughed. "No, I was foolish and rebellious. I danced on the leg all evening and suffered permanent impairment."

She nodded with understanding, finding him to be even more endearing than ever.

Several days later, Nathanael recalled the evening in a letter to a Rhode Island friend.

We had a little dance at my quarters a few evenings past. His Excellency and Mrs. Greene danced upwards of three hours without once sitting down. Upon the whole, we had a pretty little frisk.

⁓∽⊙∾⁓

These were possibly the happiest days of Kitty's marriage. Living with her children and her husband together in a comfortable home, she felt secure and loved. She attended tea frolics and dinners with Cornelia Lott and other female friends. Nathanael's aides, especially Cox, Pettit and Wadsworth, could not do enough for her.

Living in bachelors' quarters nearby were other army friends from Valley Forge. General Wayne, wifeless as usual, General Steuben, and Major Henry Lee were among her favorites. She greatly missed practicing her French with the Marquis, who had returned to France for a lengthy stay with his own family. She smiled thinking about his newest child who shared a name with her own son: George Washington Lafayette. Her latest distinguished friend, enigmatic Henry Lee, "Light-Horse Harry," entertained her, playing the part of the proper and elegant soldier, exuding an air of vigor and verve.

In the midst of all this activity she slowly realized her husband's usual smiles of admiration became less frequent, especially during their evenings at the headquarters soirees. One evening she noticed him staring at her in blank silence before scowling, and she questioned him about it.

"Please sit beside me, Kitty. I think the time has come to talk about this," he answered in a soft and calm voice. "I have noticed that you have become overly fond of wine, and although I want you to enjoy yourself, too much wine can damage both your health and your personality."

Kitty's eyes widened in genuine disbelief. "Are you saying that I behave improperly when I drink wine?" The words were clipped and cold.

"I fear that your soft qualities of a polished lady become diminished after several goblets of wine. And I know you desire my officers and their ladies to continue to hold you in high esteem."

"Like the pedestal on which you place Lady Stirling and her daughter Kitty?" Her eyes blazed in indignation, boring into Nat's with such force that his quiet words seemed to ring like a bell.

He sighed. "Your jealousy of the Stirlings is unfounded and foolish. I have never judged you against them, and if I should, you would not be lacking."

"Oh, then it must be your high standing in the army, second only to His Excellency, and I cannot possibly measure up to the image of a high-ranking general's wife!" He watched helplessly as tears spilled from her eyes.

"Kitty, you are worthy of the best. It is I who often does not measure up." Nathanael had damaged her pride and shamed her, and felt her humiliation as if it were he who had been rebuffed.

Kitty continued to enjoy the merriment in Middlebrook, as charming and fun-loving as ever. Nathanael tried to bring up the subject of her drinking on several other occasions and was met with an intractable silence and an unspoken refusal to change her ways. Hiding behind this unique veil, Kitty successfully shut her husband out, triggering a chasm in their blissful marriage. He could feel her heart and spirit fleeing to the outer banks of their covenant.

Nathanael was transferred to a camp on the Hudson in May and Kitty hoped to follow him. She did not want to return to Coventry. Nevertheless, she received his letter in June outlining the arrangements he had made for her trip home to Rhode Island.

Kitty paid a tearful farewell visit to Martha Washington.

"Oh Patsy," she sobbed, throwing herself into Martha's arms. "I fear I am pregnant again. And if I am, I shall not be able to join you at camp the following winter."

"Dear child, please get control of yourself," the older woman reproached her tenderly, pulling her close to her bosom. "You know a child is a gift from God, conceived in love. This little one is a part of your husband. Be courageous for your baby." Her soft gray eyes blinked back tears of longing; she had never been able to bear a child for George.

Capturing the sides of Kitty's face with her hands she added, "And I know that you will find a way to return to us when the time is right." A weak smile formed on her lips.

"But now I must go back to live with Nat's Quaker family again, who will try to raise our children like them, and make me feel useless and..." Kitty was crying so fiercely she was shaking in Martha's arms.

"Hush now, Kitty. You will become ill if you keep this up. The Greene family has been so good to you, and by loving them, you make your husband proud. Please consider your words." Her kind tired face revealed her unspoken pain.

Martha Washington knew how to comfort and console Kitty, and Kitty believed her motherly advice was heartfelt. Wiping away her tears, she went home to pack, thinking of all the good things she and her children would find in Coventry. She looked forward to the lush summer smells of the land and upcoming visits with her family.

SEVENTEEN

1779–1780

General Washington had a huge problem. Having lost Savannah to British forces in December 1778, and with Charleston begging him for more detachments, how could he prevent the British from overrunning the Carolinas while he was pinned down on the Hudson-Delaware line?

The collective hope of the Continental army was that this year the British would admit that their American colonies were lost for good and sail away. Yet the fall of 1779 was extremely bloody as Loyalists and Patriots attacked one another at various locations. An American attempt to retake Savannah was a disaster. The two small bright spots were the success of American privateers against British merchantmen and John Paul Jones' capture of a British frigate.

General Washington and his soldiers settled into winter camp at Morristown for the second time. He rented an eight-room house for many of the officers. Nathanael Greene, along with General Knox, Colonel Biddle and Colonel Wadsworth, resided in the best house available in the town of New Windsor, New York. The dwelling was dubbed General Knox's Headquarters, and Kitty's brother Billy Littlefield, who had distinguished himself at the Battle of Red Bank and was everyone's favorite, was also lodged there.

As Kitty predicted, she experienced difficulties and roadblocks readjusting to her life in Coventry. She tried to revive her relationship with Aunt Catharine and Uncle Greene. Her aunt fussed over the children but treated Kitty in a brusque cool manner, and Uncle Greene was away.

"I look forward to Uncle Greene's return and introducing him to my little family," Kitty offered, as a way to open the possibility of a return visit.

Aunt Catharine's eyes avoided hers. "As you wish, Kitty. We will contact you." Her lack of enthusiasm sent daggers through Kitty's heart.

Nathanael's brothers held a lengthy heated dispute over family financial affairs, during which Kitty was an unwilling spectator. No one asked her opinion or advice, and she felt shunned and lonely.

Kitty suffered her customary pregnancy bouts of nausea, but now she felt upper abdominal pains, accompanied by the vomiting of blood. Miserable and yearning for an invitation to join Nathanael, she looked to her children to keep her going during the day. Every night she withdrew to her bedroom, sipping wine to relax and reach the oblivion of sleep.

Nathanael's letters in response to her situation were consoling and admonishing at the same time. In one of them he counseled her on how to deal with a snub from General Horatio Gates.

Don't be mortified at the neglect he shows you. It is a greater reproach to his politeness and want of breeding than to your want of merit... you should rather pity him than resent his pitiful behavior, marking him as a little dirty genius who enjoys a malicious triumph over a female—who never did him injury—because he doesn't like her husband.

He also commented on her wine drinking, a subject that she had imprudently shared with him in a letter. His next letter admonished her actions and her quick response told him that his continual criticism demoralized her and weakened her self-respect. In reply, he penned the following words.

I did not mean to humble you in your own opinion... You must be sensible how capable the most finished characters are of improvement, and how subject human nature is to err. My love for you, the respect with which I wish you to be treated, make me anxious to have you appear to advantage in all circumstances. It is from this principle that I hold out a clue to direct your steps, not from a want of being sensible how happy I am in the real jewel I possess.

Unfortunately for Kitty, he included a book of English grammar with that letter, requesting she study it carefully. Two days later, she received another letter from her husband.

My resolution failed me. I have queried with myself frequently in this way: If I do bar her from the pleasures she so much admires, will she not think it unkind? Verily. Will she not think me more the tyrant than the husband? Undoubtedly. Will it not lessen her affection? Most certainly. Will it not mortify me to have her affection diminished? Indeed it will. Don't I love her most dearly? Inexpressibly so. I know the value of health and am exceedingly hurt to see it bartered away for a few moments of fleeting pleasures. I have spoken to you so many times to so little purpose, and I was ashamed to repeat the subject. Yet I knew your health was in danger; indeed I foresaw its downfall and consequently my own misfortune and your distress... I am going to Washington's headquarters this afternoon to consult Dr. Shippen on your case.

Dr. Shippen advised dipping into salt water every day to control the nausea, a recipe she promptly rejected. Kitty gave up hopes of rejoining her husband in the near future. In October, forty-two British transports arrived and the troops prepared to embark. They committed their final acts of destruction and then headed away from Newport as American soldiers arrived from the mainland. The enemy had departed.

Nathanael's sense of worth was dealt a mammoth setback as well. His year of quartermaster general was over and he expected to be given a field command at His Excellency's discretion, as was discussed at the time he accepted the quartermaster position: a post he never wanted to begin with. An updated list of new field commanders was sent to headquarters. All the other generals' names were recorded on the roster, everyone's name but his own. When he read the letter from his commander-in-chief directing him to focus on the immediate needs of the quartermaster's division, he felt betrayed.

General Greene held out the letter to Henry Knox, who read it with disbelief. A cold silence fell.

"I don't know what to say, Nathanael. Surely this has come as a total surprise," he muttered, placing his hand on top of Nathanael's forearm.

"I never imagined General Washington would surrender my field command. Had I known, I would not have accepted this position. Henry, you know I believe in the cause of our fight, and I would defend with my life our God-given rights." He paused, his words coming slowly and carefully. "I feel more enslaved by my own countrymen than I did by the British."

"Nat, General Washington had his hands tied. This is a decision of Congress, I feel certain. How will you proceed?"

"I can serve at their disposition or I can resign." It was hard to focus on the task at hand and even harder to see the finish.

"Think carefully before making any decision, my friend," he said, sounding relieved. "You will find the solution."

Before he could reach General Washington, his brother Kitt arrived at camp, angered by rumors circulating around East Greenwich. Reaching Nathanael, he sank into a chair, dropping his gaze.

"Look me in the eyes, Kitt. What is wrong? Is it my family?" His shaggy brows lifted in silent query.

"Nay, brother Nathanael. They are well. I'm ashamed to tell thee and express the family's doubts, but I must," he answered, his face crumbling.

"Go on now. Whatever it is, I know you are only the messenger." He smiled affectionately at his older brother.

"Rumor has it that you've taken your commission and quietly put it into companies, selling to the army at inflated prices to make money for you." His eyes pleaded with Nat that his words be false; his expression was as raw as his voice.

"Oh Kitt, is that it? That rumor has been around for some time. I believe someone in the Congress or a jealous fellow officer may have started it because of my foraging activities." Digesting Kitt's accusation, Nat felt something shake loose inside, like pebbles skittering downhill before an avalanche.

A furrow formed between his brows. "Kitt, the truth is I've made no such investment. However, I have heard that some members of Congress are questioning my ethics about giving positions to family members. You know I gave Jacob and Griffin positions as my buying agents, but they have proven to be reliable, honest partners for years. I never saw it as a problem. People are gunning for me now and scrutinizing my every move."

"I believe thee, Nathanael. Please forgive me for my doubts."

"I forgive thee; thou art my brother and I love thee. Now, let us share food and warmth. And please tell me all you know about my Rhode Island family." Nathanael hid his relief behind his smile.

☙✿❧

The winter of 1779-1780 would be considered the worst weather for years to come. Ice formed on the ocean as far as the eye could see, and Newport Bay was frozen solid. Yet Kitty was determined to join Nathanael in New Jersey. Naturally, her friends and family were horrified at her absurd and selfish plans to leave home at this time.

"Pray consider this carefully, child," pleaded Mother Greene. "Thou art putting thyself at risk."

"I must go to Nathanael, Mother Greene. I need your blessing. Please."

"Then thou shalt have it," she smiled. "I shall cover thee in prayer."

Traveling to Morristown in a howling snowstorm, taking only her son George with her and leaving the others with Nat's family, they arrived at the comfortable headquarters at last. Less than a month later, attended by the camp doctors, little Natty—Nathanael Ray Greene—was born. The camp buzzed with excitement: "A son is born to General Greene and Lady Kitty!" was heard throughout, and the soldiers outdid each other in crafting novel and heartfelt gifts for the baby.

Nathanael invited his wife to join him on a business trip to Philadelphia, leaving their sons with a camp nurse. Kitty was delighted to walk around the city for the first time. Although divided in political views, it remained as gay and brilliant as before. Nat showed her Carpenters' Hall, where Sammy Ward's father met with the First Continental Congress, and then took her to the State House, where the Declaration of Independence had been signed four years prior. He indulged her whim to shop for the new fashions, and even accompanied her to many of the shops.

They visited the home of General Benedict Arnold, commandant of the American forces in Philadelphia, and his young bride, Peggy Shippen. Peggy, the beautiful daughter of a Loyalist judge, married Ben Arnold shortly after meeting him. She had socialized with the British officers during their time in the city and met Ben shortly after the British evacuation of Philadelphia. Kitty found Ben and Peggy to be hospitable and stimulating conversationalists.

General Greene's meetings with Congressional committees did not fare so well. Debts in the quartermaster department were exorbitant, and when the Congress tried to hold Nathanael personally responsible for them, he offered them his resignation. The Congress would not accept it until the accounts had been settled. Nat gave final notice of his refusal to serve the department, and several incensed members resolved to dismiss him from the service, especially when they knew he had private speculations along with some army subordinates.

George Washington was shocked and angry. He sent a letter

to Congress explaining it was impossible for officers to support themselves and their families on their salary, and even more difficult now that Congress would not assist in food and clothing expenses. As to Nathanael Greene's dismissal, General Washington wrote: *Never let such a tragic event take place if it is within your abilities to prevent it.* That letter probably saved the army from the loss of one of its most competent generals. To Kitty and Nat's joy, Congress dropped the resolution against him and accepted his resignation as quartermaster general, freeing him to be a soldier in the field.

Jacob wrote that Kitty's older brother, Simon Littlefield, passed away at twenty-nine years of age. He said little Patty was on Block Island with her grandfather. Cornelia was at Potowomut with Nat's family, who adored the girls and considered them charming.

Kitty returned to Rhode Island with her sons so she could live with all four children. Visiting Block Island for the first time since the war began, she spent days reconnecting with family and friends, and visited her brother's grave. She found the islanders indifferent to the war and oblivious to the change in government, simply passing their days farming and fishing.

Time stands still here, she thought, *but my world has been changed beyond understanding. Nineteen years since Mama died, and I'm standing here looking down on the same rocks as before I left Block Island for the first time.*

She returned to Newport with Patty and was met at the dock by the Marquis de Lafayette, who took them to the French headquarters. Over five hundred homes had been torn down for firewood; gardens were ruined, stores emptied and commerce was non-existent. She was appreciative and impressed to see how the French were fearlessly attempting to set things in order in this ravaged port.

Nathanael wrote to his wife that he thought he would be sent to the South, but nothing had been determined for the upcoming campaign. Naturally she wanted to join him again in New York. In September he wrote that he had been given temporary command of the entire army while General Washington was in Hartford, and could not possibly attend to his family for the present.

Furious at his words, she refused to write him for weeks at a time. When she finally wrote, she lashed out, motivated by her raging envy.

> *If you are too busy for your family, how can you find time to visit Lady Stirling and her daughter, Kitty Duer? Is there a particular attraction possessed by them that you find lacking in me? If so, I deserve the courtesy to be told.*

Her husband wrote immediately and had the letter hand-delivered by a French officer returning to Newport.

> *Let me ask you soberly whether you estimate yourself below either of these ladies? You will answer me No, if you speak as you think. I declare upon my sacred honor, independent of the partiality I ought to feel, I think they possess far less accomplishments than you, and as much as I respect them as friends, I should never be happy with them in a more intimate connection. Though our felicity is not perfect, we have a great foundation for solid and lasting happiness. I can assure you that I never enjoyed a moment's rational and refined happiness until I had the good fortune of being united to you.*

It was only a few days later that Nathanael wrote her about Ben Arnold's treacherous attempt to deliver the West Point fortress to the British. Arnold had offered his services to the commander-in-chief of the British forces in any way that would restore the former government. Major Andre, aide to the British commander, saw a great opportunity to receive information from one of Washington's most trusted generals. This information would be coded in letters from Peggy Arnold to Andre. Everyone would be well-paid for their betrayal.

Ben Arnold's plan was to take command of West Point and hand it to the British, for a sum of twenty thousand pounds sterling. The letters from Benedict to his wife, which she obediently passed on to the enemy, sent the news that General Washington was on his way to West Point. Major Andre, in disguise, made his way through the American lines to West Point and left with sensitive documents for his commander. Waylaid by the Americans, Andre was arrested and the papers, which clearly implicated Ben Arnold, were confiscated. It was indeed the blackest treason.

After telling Peggy what happened and leaving her in a "feigned" state of despair, Arnold escaped to a British man-of-war docked in the Hudson. General Washington arrived and found Peggy completely out of control: ranting distractedly and tearing her hair. She seemed hysterical with her blouse open and her breasts exposed. Even Alexander Hamilton believed she was entirely unacquainted with the plan.

Only later did they realize it was all a show to delay the pursuit of her husband. General Washington cried when he learned that Benedict Arnold had betrayed his trust so flagrantly.

Subsequently, Nathanael was given Arnold's position as commander and was on his way to the post on the east bank of the Hudson. During the eleven days that he held Ben Arnold's position, he convicted Major John Andre to death by hanging.

Kitty was saddened by the saga of the Arnolds, but content she and her family were moving to a comfortable winter home on the Hudson River. She began preparations for the trip, starting with a shopping trip to Providence. Upon her return, she received devastating news from Nathanael.

My dear Kitty,   *October 14, 1780*
*   What I have been dreading has come to pass. His Excellency General Washington, by order of Congress, has appointed me to the command of the Southern Arm. General Gates was recalled to undergo an examination into his con-*

duct, after he fled from the enemy at Camden, leaving his own men behind. I have been given his post. This is so foreign from my wishes that I am distressed exceedingly... The moment I was appointed to the command I sent off Mr. Hubbard to bring you to camp. But alas, before we even have the happiness of meeting I am ordered away to another quarter. How unhappy is war to domestic happiness.

I wish it were possible for me to stay until your arrival, but by the pressing manner in which the general urges my setting out, I am afraid you will come too late to see me. God bless you, my love. With the truest love and sincerest affection, I am Yours.

N. Greene

She was shattered. There was not even time to kiss him good-bye. This misfortune was more than she could bear. With the letter he forwarded a few stock certificates which were not negotiable at the moment and could be worthless. He told her that the stocks, the farm in Westerly and one in New Jersey were his entire fortune. Nathanael urged her to make her own decisions, suggesting she move to Westerly if her discontent at Coventry became unbearable.

Kitty doubted the love they shared would survive this final separation. *It is already a near-casualty of the war. There are days during our infrequent reunions where we feel like strangers, and when we recapture the joy of being together, the army rips us apart again.* She knew Nat was suffering as well. In a state of despair she wrote that she would not be held responsible for the consequences of a long separation. But the moment he sent for her, no matter what the difficulties, she would go to him.

Nathanael spent his final days in the North in Philadelphia, assembling and equipping a "flying camp" of eight hundred light-horse soldiers and one thousand infantry. Henry Knox promised artillery, and requested the promotion of Major Henry Lee to colonel to lead a mounted legion of light-horse. He was hopelessly short of arms, clothing, hospital supplies and blankets, yet before the end of his stay, Knox received word that Congress would send funding for the journey. A group of mountain riflemen who had fought against the British in the Carolinas, inflicting terrible casualties, was now available to come to Greene's support. On November 1, 1780, General Nathanael Greene, with a last backward glance for Kitty, departed Philadelphia and traveled southward into history.

EIGHTEEN

1780–1781

Nathanael's final stop before heading south was to George Washington's camp headquarters.

"Welcome, General Greene. Shall we retire to my board room?" George's greeting was formal but warm as he clasped his friend's hand in his own.

Nathanael turned to his aides to dismiss them for the afternoon and followed his commander upstairs. His Excellency had requested time alone with him and Nathanael joined him in a large high-ceilinged room, flanked by a pair of vast sunlit windows. Four broad tables were spaced about its length, each one surrounded by books and tomes and papers.

"I am so sorry Nathanael. I know you applied for leave to say goodbye to your family. I simply could not spare you at this time." The words were out of his mouth before he even closed the door.

"I understand, sir. Please do not worry yourself."

"Oh, but I do. I am certain Kitty was terribly upset that you could not go to her. Was she also devastated that you had to move to the South to lead the southern command?"

Nathanael slowly nodded and smiled at his friend. "I had never mentioned the possibility that I might be chosen as commander, so as not to worry her. I think the actuality of the event utterly stunned her."

George was quiet for a moment, his expression turning thoughtful. "I have sent word to Rhode Island to see to your family's comfort. If they wish to come to camp this winter, she will be well cared for, as will your children. I know she enjoys being among her women friends," he said, with a trace of a smile, "and we all enjoy her cheerful spirit."

There was a sense of humility in his behavior, and a dismal reflection in his eyes. "I wish I could have granted you the leave you requested, but …"

"Please, sir. It is I who should apologize to you for the momentary anger I felt at being denied the request. You have not been home in five years. I know how much Mount Vernon means to you and Martha, so there is nothing more to say on the subject of my disappointment."

General Washington lifted his gaze and inspected the man sitting across from him. From the beginning George had recognized a quiet intensity in him, making him aware of an underlying strength that separated Nathanael from other men. This was the reason he wanted to keep General Greene close, even though he needed him in the South. Nat had the confident strength of a born leader and kept his men's ready allegiance with deceptive ease. He also possessed an enormous strength of character and integrity.

"You will hold the command from Delaware to Georgia. There is not a man in this army I trust more to accomplish what I need done. You will weaken them and break the hold they possess over the South." He paused, leaning toward Nathanael across the desk, raising one expressive eyebrow as he sought his eyes.

The enormous responsibility and faith of his commander completely humbled Nathanael.

General Washington's voice jarred him from his reflections. "There is not a general officer in this army whose military ability and knowledge I respect more. Now, go and rest before dinner. I've invited a few of our friends to join us tonight."

⌒⊙⊙⌒

Kitty enjoyed visiting the French command at Newport. She took pleasure in the French custom of men and women sharing drinks and conversations together after dinner. As a married woman without her husband, she knew she would be criticized by the proper English ladies. Nevertheless, she enchanted the French commanders with her lively conversations in their native tongue.

During her stay in Newport, she attended dinners at Count Rochambeau's headquarters and later accepted an invitation to a dance in the home of Baron de Viomenil, where she was the belle of the ball. Kitty invited her new friends, Claude Blanchard and Captain Haake, to visit her in Coventry, and was shocked a month later when they arrived, unannounced. Nevertheless, she entertained them graciously, with charm and dignity.

Because of her love of fashion and color, Kitty found the pageantry of French parades captivating. The artillerymen dressed in iron gray coats with red velvet lapels. The infantry had long waistcoats trimmed in their regiments' colors, and wore white feathers: some with red plumes, and others with white and green. She dreaded returning to the dull, unexciting life in Coventry, but looked forward to being with her children and reading Nathanael's letters. General Washington offered to make his headquarters a relay station to dispatch letters between the Greenes, and often sent personal notes along with the letters. On December 17, 1780 His Excellency sent these words to Kitty.

If you will entrust your letters to my care, they shall have the same attention paid to them as my own, and forwarded with equal dispatch to the General. Mrs. Washington, who is just arrived at my headquarters, joins me in most cordial wishes for your every felicity; and regrets the want of your company. Remember us to my namesake, who I suppose can now handle a musket.

Nathanael's letters strongly discouraged Kitty from joining him in the South. He wrote about the dismal conditions of the roads and the people, explaining that the bitterness between Patriot and Loyalist was beyond anything he'd seen elsewhere.

In a letter dated January 17, 1781 he penned: *The difference between Whig and Tory is little more than a division of sentiment at home, but here they persecute each other with little less than savage fury... The sufferings and distress of the inhabitants beggars all description, and requires the liveliest imagination to conceive the cruelties and devastations which prevail.*

Kitty learned that Nathanael's entire force now numbered less than three thousand men, but that only half of them were actually with him at any given time. She grieved knowing that he could not crush the British or even drive them from the land. He explained to her that he employed tactics of guerilla warfare: keeping the enemy on the run and neutralizing British influence in the Carolinas and Georgia. He confided to her that he had never before felt so inadequate to face his task.

Feeling that her place was at his side even under such duress, Kitty requested, through a letter to Martha, that General Washington allow her to visit Nathanael. His Excellency sent a message to Coventry inviting Kitty to visit him in Providence, but she was detained because little Natty was ill. It wasn't until the end of March that Kitty heard back from General Washington regarding her request.

I can neither advise you to nor dissuade you from the measure, because the true footing upon which the journey should depend is, in my opinion, the encouragement given to it by General Greene, who having a view of all circumstances before him, can alone determine the propriety of it.

She chose to remain in Coventry. Spring had arrived, flowers were blooming and Kitty was anxious to share outings with her children in the forest and meadows behind Spell Hall.

Kitty was tending to Natty when Patty burst through the door. "Mama, where are you? George is high in the tree! Come see," squealed Patty, cheeks flushed with excitement.

"Here I am, Patty. I'm changing your brother's nappy. I'll be there shortly."

"Come now, Mama! He's hanging from the tree!"

Kitty scooped the half-dressed baby under her arm and raced out the door, chased by a whirlwind of fear. Patty followed after her, dragging Cornelia Lott as they tried to keep up.

"Over here, Mama. Look at me," he laughed, hanging by his legs from one of the lower limbs of a tall hickory and waving vigorously with both hands.

Kitty heaved a sigh of relief, willing herself to relax. Placing Natty on the ground next to her girls, she dragged a rock over to stand on, hooked her arms around his small waist and pulled him to her chest. Stepping down from the rock, she gently lowered George to the ground.

"You wanna do it, Mama? It is so much fun. I will show you!" Eyes sparkling with mischief, he smiled his slightly goofy smile—the one that reminded her of his father.

"I think I'm too big to do that, son. And you frightened your sister and me too." Smiling warmly as she hugged him again, she added, "Why don't we go back home and make some lemon water. I'm certain you must be thirsty."

Kitty was surprised by the sense of pride that welled up in her as she watched her children skipping through the meadow. The morning was glorious: the azaleas seemed borderline arrogant in their display of fuchsia and white, while merry heads of daffodils danced with elegant tulips in their joyfully elaborate sweeps. Spring's ripe scent filled her senses and was heightened by the sleepiness of the field. *This is such a lovely spot down by the river,* reflected Kitty. *I must remember to be thankful more often: for my children and for my loving husband.* Birdsong rose from the trees alongside the path leading to the house, and to Kitty's ears it sounded like Heaven's chimes.

ॐ

En route to the Carolinas, General Greene had been forced to leave General Steuben in Richmond, Virginia to train the new recruits and forward the supplies to the Southern Headquarters. He arrived at Charlotte with his aides Captain Pierre

Duponceau, Colonel Lewis Morris and Major Rob Burnet, and was greeted by General Horatio Gates, the man who was required to transfer his command to Greene. Nathanael would later write to both Kitty and His Excellency that Gates had received his successor with dignity and composure—and perhaps with some relief.

The day before General Gates was scheduled to leave camp, he approached General Greene.

"Will you be conducting the investigation of my conduct, sir?" asked Gates.

"No sir. General Steuben will preside over the court about your conduct inquiry, and he is in Virginia. Why do you ask?"

"I am anxious to have my name cleared before I leave," answered Gates, smiling bravely. After a moment he searched General Greene's eyes. "What is your opinion of my rumored conduct?"

Nathanael paused a long moment before responding. "I have inquired into the battle and I believe the flight following it was general, officers and soldiers alike taking care of themselves. I am convinced that reports of your actions were misrepresented." The slight gruffness in his voice was at odds with the slow smile that spread across his face.

Gates returned a weary smile. "Thank you for your confidence, sir. That will not, however, clear my name with General Washington or with the Congress."

"Perhaps it won't, but I intend to share my research into the matter with both of them."

Gates bowed his head. "Greatly appreciated, General. I will ask no more of you. May I take my leave?"

"Go in peace, General." As Horatio Gates stood to leave, he took a long final look at his successor, who had risen to his feet to return his salute. He finally understood why His Excellency found this man to be so worthy. Gratitude radiated from his eyes as he soundlessly exited the room.

Shortly thereafter, Nathanael appointed Colonel Otho Holland Williams, who had served under his command previously, to adjutant general. Cavalry Officer William Washington, a kin to George, was chosen as Nathanael's "right arm," since the infantry followed his orders fearlessly.

The moniker of "General Greene's right eye" was given to Light-Horse Harry Lee. He loved danger, and asked to be sent out to reconnoiter the enemy, becoming the right eye of Nat's command. He dressed his three hundred men, half of them mounted cavalry and half light-infantry, in tight-fitted green jackets, white leather breeches and plumed steel helmets. Only twenty-four years old, Light-Horse Harry set out to convince General Greene of his worthiness.

NINETEEN

1781–1782

I n early spring, Kitty received another devoted letter from
her husband.

My dearest,

*I am delighted to hear that you and the children are in
good health. I am quite sensible to the fact that your happiness will not be complete until I return, as you must understand the void in my heart as well.*

*I am grateful you and my children are not at headquarters
this winter. The situation there is far worse than even last
year. His Excellency has informed me of the mutiny of the
Pennsylvania Line. A general carnage was prevented when
Anthony Wayne came upon the scene, and after a warning
volley was fired over his head, Mad Anthony tore open his
clothing, exposing his chest, and yelled, "If you mean to kill
me, shoot me at once." No shot was fired; the troops calmed
down and set out for Philadelphia, along with General
Wayne, hoping for an opportunity to negotiate.*

*His Excellency fears New England may follow suit, and
if general mutiny occurs, we are all in danger, for the British
will swoop down on the camp and do infinite damage. You
are safe in Rhode Island, and that is where I want you to
stay. You asked if you could come southward: my answer is
nay. Nay, because of my great love for you! The trip is long
and hazardous and there would be little safety for you as you
traveled.*

Beyond that, our conditions are quite deplorable. My

orders are to weaken Cornwallis and I must do battle whenever the opportunity presents itself. I cannot risk you being here under these circumstances—and shall not waver in my decision no matter how agonizing the separation is at present.

Benedict Arnold has proven himself as committed to the enemy as he once appeared to be to us. His wickedness is beyond comprehension. He now holds the British commission of brigadier general, and is in Virginia causing havoc along the James River trying to cut off supplies and troops headed my way. Your friend, General Lafayette, has been ordered to Virginia with three regiments to aid General Steuben and squash Arnold's attempts.

I am awaiting news of General Morgan. Reports tell us that one thousand enemy troops are approaching his position. It is 2 a.m. and sleep does not come. My restless mind finds solace in writing to you as to none other. My love to my dear children. Kiss each one for me.

With my sincere love and affection,
Nathanael

He did not discuss his battle strategies with her, nor boast of how he had lifted the morale of his army by his self-sacrificing spirit. It was months before Kitty learned of his motto: "We fight, get beat, rise, and fight again."

Rather than confront directly the much larger and better-equipped British army under General Lord Cornwallis, Nathanael attempted to wear down his opponents by engaging them in a series of small battles. Cornwallis began to press Greene but he, through careful planning, eluded him. General Greene's force included a number of prisoners, baggage and supplies, which weighed him down, yet his strategy of keeping rivers and streams between his army and the enemy turned out to be advantageous.

In March, General Greene lured General Cornwallis to the Guilford Court House in North Carolina, on the ground of his own choosing. In this area, amid forest and hills and little clearing, Greene made his stand to fight. The British were compelled to accept the ground or retreat. Cornwallis resolved to fight. Greene arranged his forces in three lines: untrained militia up front, militia under the command of seasoned officers next, and the Continental soldiers in the third line. The second and third rendered good service and the British forces were stopped, crippled and ultimately incurred many more losses than the Americans. Cornwallis retreated to Wilmington and General Greene freed the colony of North Carolina from the major forces of the British army.

On March 21, 1781, just before the battle was fought, his friend General Washington sent support in a letter written from New Windsor, New York.

Your last letter has relieved me from much anxiety, by informing me you had saved all your baggage, artillery and stores, notwithstanding the hot pursuit of the enemy. I hope your reinforcement may be such as will enable you to prevent them taking a part in the upper country. You may be assured that your retreat before Cornwallis is highly applauded by all ranks, and reflects much honor on your military abilities.

After freeing North Carolina, and doing so with an inefficient and poorly-equipped army, Nathanael Greene received another missive from General Washington on April 18, 1781.

Your private letter of the 18th arrived safe to hand. Although the honors of the field did not fall to your lot, I am convinced you deserved them. The motives which induced you to seek an action with Lord Cornwallis are supported upon the best military principles; and the consequences, if you can prevent the dissipation of your troops, will no doubt be fortunate. Every support that is in my power to give shall cheerfully be afforded to you.

By May Nathanael wrote Kitty that Cornwallis had withdrawn from the state and that the British troops remaining in the Carolinas were retreating toward Charlestown. He told her to be patient: before long, he would write her to join him. At least that was his fervent wish.

Nathanael strategized his next move to drive the British out of South Carolina. These forces were under the command of General Lord Francis Rawdon. They met in the Battle of Hobkirk's Hill, where the British won an empty victory as Greene withdrew his forces and formed a well-fortified camp that Rawdon chose not to attack. The fact that Greene's army had not been destroyed encouraged the Patriots of South Carolina, resulting in many of them joining General Francis Marion's forces against the Tories.

Now General Greene began a siege of Fort Ninety-Six, which he gave up once General Rawdon's force approached. But Greene's troops had become veterans as a result of the past battles, and now resolved to fight on to victory. At this point, General Rawdon refused to battle and withdrew. General Greene's army had grown in great numbers and needed reorganization and new equipment. Nathanael ordered Generals Marion, Lee and others to take their band of men and press the British from every quarter. This movement was successful and morale was restored among the military and the civilian populations.

Finally, General Greene attacked the British at Eutaw Springs on September 8, 1781. His forces numbered two thousand and the British two thousand three hundred. Nathanael had prepared a surprise attack but two deserters of his own army informed the British of their approach. The British were driven back but not destroyed. Nathanael recalled his forces, and the British were forced to retreat. This struggle caused the breakdown of the Tories' morale and nearly ended their control in South Carolina. Their only stronghold left was Charlestown. General Greene kept his army in position ready to strike at the British in Charlestown, but the surrender of

Cornwallis at Yorktown initiated the evacuation of the British from Charlestown.

General Greene's troops had received no payment for over two years and were in desperate need of essentials, including clothing and medicine. After touring the hospitals, Nathanael wrote the Congress a concerned, compassionate letter, begging them to help.

Our sick and wounded have suffered greatly. The extent of our hospitals, the malignity of the disorders, and increasing sick troops since the battle of Eutaw, the little means we have to provide for them and the great number of our physicians who fell sick in service have left our sick and wounded in a most deplorable condition. Hospital stores and medicines are exceedingly scarce. To afford the sick and wounded all the relief in my power, I visited the hospitals from this camp to Charlotte. We are in great need of your assistance.

During all of this, Kitty and her children stayed at Nathanael's farm at Westerly. In Nathanael's absence, and because he was no longer involved in the ironworks, the Greene brothers were forced to divide the family properties. His beloved Spell Hall was given to Jacob and the farmhouse at Westerly became Nat and Kitty's home.

Their friend Colonel Wadsworth was a frequent visitor to Westerly and brought them provisions from the warehouses of his and Nat's private company. These visits were made at Nathanael's request; nevertheless, they provided fodder for local gossiping tongues: *In General Greene's absence, Kitty Greene is using his home for trysts with an attractive general.* Several of her acquaintances went so far as to place a charge of adultery against her name. She was distraught that no one cared enough to defend her, and became overwhelmed with gloom.

Kitty vented her aggravation and pain through letters to Martha Washington and her husband, narrating the devastation and helplessness she suffered because of this vicious dishonesty. *My heart is broken; my tears are abundant. I fear for my sanity at times. My children do not deserve this, nor do I,* she detailed in her theatrical writing style. Both of them encouraged her to remain as mentally and emotionally strong as possible and to hold her head up high in public.

In October, before receiving Nathanael's confirmation, Kitty read in the *Providence Gazette* that General Lord Cornwallis had surrendered his entire army to the Americans and the French at Yorktown, Virginia. Even though the garrisons of Charlestown, New York and Savannah were still intact and protected by powerful fleets, this piece of news brought hope to the Patriots and to their families. With her husband's permission and encouragement, Kitty enthusiastically prepared for her next reunion with him, and in December of 1781 she was on her way to Nathanael's camp in South Carolina, accompanied by six-year-old George and William Blodgett, one of Nathanael's favorite aides.

❧❧❧

Kitty stopped over in Philadelphia, primarily to seek comfort with the Washingtons, but more importantly to grieve with them over the loss of Jack Custis, Martha's son by a previous marriage and her only surviving child. He had signed up and gone to Yorktown as his stepfather's aide-de-camp, where he contracted typhus fever. Just two weeks after the celebration of the British surrender, the Washington family was forced to deal with the grief of Jacky's death. Only twenty-seven years old, he left behind a widow with four children under the age of five.

"Oh dear Patsy, my heart is breaking for you. He was so young. Poor Nelly, with those small children. How can you bear this?" Suddenly it hit her: sorrow. Only this time it was for someone else, not for herself. Almost gratefully she bent under it as the tears thickened in her throat.

Martha smiled through her tears. Her face opened in kindness as she held her young friend. "God will give me the strength, my child. As He does for you in your trials."

"I shall be here for you, in every way," responded Kitty. Her own emotions poured out in sobs that nearly choked her. Her concerns seemed weak and meaningless when confronted with the death of Martha's son. Knowing that this strong woman had outlived her four children genuinely grieved Kitty's heart. She made up her mind to change her manner and do her best to cheer both Martha and George, resolving to encourage them. Surely her son George, a darling child who charmed a smile out of everyone he met, could work his magic in their lives and entertain them with his presence.

General Washington later praised her efforts in a letter to Nathanael, ending his missive with: *Your Kitty thinks no difficulties are too great to be surmounted.*

A heavy snowstorm kept Kitty and George in Philadelphia longer than she expected. This gave General Washington an opportunity to share his ideas about George, of whom he was very fond.

"Kitty, my namesake George needs a good education, for he is bright and will certainly be a leader like his father," he began, joining her and Martha, seated before a blazing fire. The light of the fire blurred the lines that time and pain had etched into his face.

"And he shall, once we get settled," smiled Kitty, her eyes shimmering at his interest in her son.

George cleared his throat as his gaze lingered on Kitty's face. "What better time to start than now? We have tutors here in Philadelphia, and while you are at winter camp with Nathanael, we could take advantage of that. He will be reading and writing in no time at all." His voice became gentler then, along with his expression.

Kitty had already left behind three children, and was looking forward to spending time sharing George with his father. She knew better than to expect an opportunity of tutoring him at camp, but felt strongly against leaving him behind. He had been her companion through some of her bleakest times.

There was a knock on the door. General Washington

absently asked who was there, and suddenly her son appeared: bounding toward them with his lopsided grin. Kitty bent down and scooped him into her arms, feeling his legs circle her waist while his short arms twined around her neck. Someone had just bathed him and he smelled of an unfamiliar soap. Kitty rained kisses on his face, and wondered how she could bear leaving him—so small and yet so endearing.

"Hello, son," greeted General Washington, extending his large hand. George grinned and went to him.

"Good afternoon, sir." He turned to his mother, as if seeking instructions. Then he climbed on General Washington's lap. Kitty giggled and the general's face brightened into a huge smile.

"General Washington, please allow me to mull over this generous offer. I only wish I could discuss it with my husband, but you and Lady Washington are as close to family as I have here, besides my son. And I do understand you are concerned for our welfare. Pray give me a few days."

"Of course, my dear. With this storm you will not be going anywhere. We have time to look into the possibilities," grinned General Washington, lifting the boy down as he rose slowly to leave. What she saw in his eyes brought tears to hers as it became achingly, wonderfully clear. This great man had made a decision to watch over her and her family, protecting and nurturing them in a way Nathanael could not.

In the end, Kitty did leave George with the Washington family. Martha and George eventually adopted Jacky and Nelly's youngest children, Nelly and Washington Custis, and for a brief time, little George studied and played with them while he lived in the home of Charles Pettit. Martha and Charles made the necessary arrangements for his schooling, hiring an excellent tutor for the child—Dr. Witherspoon, president of Princeton.

TWENTY

1782

With growing pride and delight, Kitty realized that her husband was considered a war hero for his victories in the South. What a difference from her last visit to Philadelphia, when Nathanael had been under fire by the Congress and she had felt like an outcast. Once the word was out that she was in Philadelphia, she was invited—frequently as the guest-of-honor—to one fete after another. Kitty basked in her new stardom.

Verbal and written messages were exchanged between Nat and Kitty, through friends coming from and traveling to Nathanael's headquarters. She sent word by John Mathews, governor-elect of South Carolina, that she would resume her journey in late January and arrive at camp shortly after that.

Tell General Greene that I claim the privilege of being met by him personally at least five miles from headquarters.

Having no idea when she would see her son again, she wept at their parting. Her tender words spilled out between sobs when she kissed George goodbye.

"Mama, why am I staying here without you?" he asked, rubbing his eyes as the tears leaked through his lashes. He didn't understand time or distance, but understood his mother was sad because she wasn't going with her.

"My sweet son, it's only for a short time. You will be happy with General Pettit and his children. And I shall see you in my dreams every single night." Sorrow ripped at her voice. A sound was torn from deep in her chest, a sob of utter despair. She would later remember that moment as nearly suffocating her.

He went to her and reached for her face, holding it between his small hands. "I will see you soon, Mama. Papa too."

Kitty and Major Rob Burnett set out on the long trip, and when they arrived at Mount Vernon, they gratefully accepted Lucy Knox's invitation to linger for a few days. Already overwhelmed with the sorrow of leaving her son, Kitty needed the laughter and levity that her friend Lucy always provided. Lucy was presiding at Mount Vernon in Martha Washington's absence, and the two ladies spent joyful days in pleasant pursuits, discovering they still had a great deal in common. Each morning, over a leisurely breakfast on the terrace, they soaked up the spectacular view of the Potomac River while discussing their daily plans.

Kitty decided she would stay in this happy environment as long as possible, basking in the splendors of renewed friendship as well as a comfortable environment. She expressed regret at having left her children behind, but knew she could not have enjoyed this undisturbed freedom with them.

The time came to join Nathanael. Under military escort, with Major Rob Burnett at her side, the carriage approached General Greene's camp on the Santee River above Charlestown. Kitty spotted several men on horseback in the distance, waiting on the knoll.

Abruptly, a lone rider broke away from the others and advanced toward them at full gallop. Dismounting his horse, he pushed his long legs into the carriage and scooped Kitty up into his arms. They had not seen each other in almost two years.

"Oh Nat, I cannot believe this. You are with me, and that..." Her breath caught on a sob.

His heart beat strong and steady against her body. His skin felt warm and amazingly soft molded next to hers. His breath, where it feathered across her shoulder, was life-sustaining and vital. Kitty knew Nathanael was fundamental to her very foundation in everything that mattered.

He lifted a hand and gently brushed the back of his knuckles over her cheek. Hooking an arm around her shoulders, he pulled her close. "This time I will not let you go. From here forward we're staying together." He felt tears clogging his throat, but held them back.

Kitty snuggled against his chest on the ride into camp. Her eyes were soft and sleepy when they met his. She dozed, and he let her. A gentle purr puffed her lips where her cheek rested against his shoulder. He beamed when he looked above her breast and saw the gold locket glinting in the sun, carrying his picture. There was no wind, and he clearly heard the birds' morning calls in the surrounding trees. Nathanael could not remember when he felt such deep peacefulness.

✿◉✿

Nathanael had aged. He was much thinner than she remembered, his skin drawn tightly over his cheekbones. His face was darker, bronzed by the unrelenting southern sun. His beautiful hazel eyes had lost their twinkle, replaced by clouds of worry and concern. Kitty thought he looked as old as George Washington, who was at least ten years his senior. She thanked God that he had escaped serious illness and injury, yet she knew he had given the better part of his life to the American cause.

Kitty's maturity, hastened and sculpted through long months of hardship and loneliness, was pleasing to Nat and he celebrated it. She had come a long way from her tempestuous youth. Her unfailing good humor and charm were still a strong part of her character, and the headquarters staff and soldiers seemed delighted with her presence. Even the ladies enjoyed her cheerfulness and inspiring conversation.

"My Kitty, I believe you are rejuvenating this old husband of yours," he grinned. "The officers have told me I look at least five years younger since you've arrived."

"And I have become quite fond of the wisps of gray in your hair." She laughed easily. "Do you know how proud I am of you, dear Nat? Your generals have told me that only you could have accomplished what you did under such deplorable conditions."

Nathanael shrugged. "They are simply being kind. I only did what was asked of me."

Her eyes snapped. "Listen to me, Nathanael. You had not a day of leave during the year of bitter fighting! You planned a brilliant strategy and handled the supply problems as well. Who else would have endured such hardships? You..."

Interrupting her discourse with a soft kiss, he shook his head. "I did no more than any other Patriot would have done." Kitty looked up and noticed that the vanished sparkle in his eyes had been restored. Perhaps her arrival had revived him after all.

He threw Kitty a tired smile. "Speaking of duties, I have invested my commission in a sizable tract of land off the coast of Georgia on a small island called Cumberland. My hope is that the timber grown there will be marketable."

Kitty was startled at his words. "Then we own more than the farm in Westerly?" she asked.

"Yes Kitty. And in addition to that, the governors of the Carolinas and Georgia, in gratitude for my service in the South, have bestowed on me some land holdings: property abandoned by Loyalists who fled to England. They also gave me a piece of frontier land."

"Dear Lord," she gasped. "I cannot believe what I'm hearing. Can you explain yourself, Nat?"

"They are rather sizable. About twenty five thousand acres in North Carolina on the frontier. Not usable now, but we can give them to the children one day."

Kitty was speechless. She thought they were virtually homeless, and now her husband casually informed her of their vast land holdings. "And in Georgia? You also mentioned Georgia," she murmured.

"Yes. Both Georgia and South Carolina have graciously given us abandoned plantations, each comprising about two thousand acres."

Kitty shook her head and appeared genuinely mystified. This seemed too good to be true. "But you've not seen them, have you, Nat? Are they even habitable?"

"I know not. We will find out after the war. If I had my preference, I should go back to Rhode Island and forge iron. But my brothers have the business now, and so we must find another life."

His quiet words shivered through her. She watched the sadness cloud his features. Then she giggled. "Cheer up Nat. Now you can be a gentleman farmer like our dear friend General Washington!"

Tea frolics and dinner parties were back, and Kitty was winning the affection of everyone at camp. Even Nathanael was amazed at her popularity, and took pleasure observing her in her element. He was relieved that he could make time to converse with his generals and soldiers while his wife enjoyed organizing social activities and making new friends.

She quickly befriended John and Edward Rutledge, political refugees from Charlestown who had been wealthy but now camped near the army. Their families remained prisoners in British-held Charlestown, where John had been elected the state's first governor in 1776. He escaped in 1780 during the British siege, and turned to the army for protection.

Edward, ten years younger than John, was the youngest signer of the Declaration of Independence. Seized by the British after the fall of Charlestown, he was sent to St. Augustine as a political prisoner, and caught a horrible case of arthritis. He could barely walk, and was forbidden to return to his home. He camped with his brother in the vicinity of the army, and soon both of them became Kitty's good friends.

Among her other latest friends were Colonel William Washington and his beautiful new bride, Jane Elliot. Jane had nursed him as a prisoner after his wound at the Battle of Eutaw Springs, and he became a visitor at her plantation home outside Charlestown during the intervals of campaigning against Clinton.

Captain Nathanael Pendleton, Jr., a member of one of

Virginia's wealthy families and a fine musician, was also a new favorite of Kitty. After joining the command of General Washington, Captain Pendleton was taken prisoner and spent four years of captivity in New York City. He was then transported to the home of a physician and fell in love with the doctor's daughter. After his release, George Washington excused him from further service. But Nathanael Pendleton chose to fight again and was assigned to General Greene, distinguishing himself in the Battle at Eutaw Springs. He received a special citation from Congress for his bravery.

Nathanael Greene explained to Kitty that he was commanded to guarantee thousands of dollars in his name to buy clothes for his soldiers. Hungry and unpaid, they were on the verge of open revolt. He bought them uniforms on credit from Charlestown merchants through a speculator named John Banks. Nat's signature was on the promissory notes.

"There is really no great concern, Kitty. I feel certain that eventually this will be backed up by the government; now they say they are on the verge of bankruptcy, but this too shall pass."

"And with all the land we now own, we can sell some off if necessary," she added, looking hopeful.

The Greenes attended a dinner party given in their honor. The home overlooked the Ashley River and was situated between headquarters and the city. Before dinner, the guests' conversations were interrupted by a loud knock on the door.

"I am here to warn you that you are in great danger this evening," exclaimed a breathless young woman, wild-eyed and disheveled, as she hurried over to the officers. "I am the sweetheart of one of your soldiers here at camp. Just today I overheard a discussion between some of the soldiers and British officers in Charlestown." She paused slightly as the women approached. Kitty looked up at Nathanael with startled eyes.

"Would you like something to drink? Water, perhaps?" offered Nathanael.

"There is no time. Please, you must know that they plan to

capture General and Mrs. Greene this evening, here at the dinner. You are not safe here, sir. You must depart quickly."

Kitty let out an audible gasp as her hand flew over her mouth. She reached up and gripped Nathanael's forearm with her small fingers.

"We thank you deeply, miss," he said, unable to hide his gratitude. "Go in peace. I will not betray your trust, and we will leave immediately."

Within ten minutes the Greenes and the other officers were gone from the residence. Forty-five minutes later, the house was surrounded by British dragoons, shouting for the American officers to surrender. All had reached their camp safely.

An investigation took place and several soldiers were found with incriminating documents in their possession, revealing that the British army in Charlestown was recruiting some of Nathanael's soldiers. Sergeant Gornell, the ringleader of the mutineers, was brought to the parade ground and executed in front of the entire camp.

As he walked composedly to his execution, he turned to the threadbare soldiers and handed them his coat, hat, and sleeve-buttons. Then he made a public statement that his trial had been fair, advising them to discard any thoughts of mutiny. Calmly, he gave the hand signal to the firing squad to end his life.

This put a stop to the threatened insurrection of troops, but it deeply troubled Nathanael and Kitty. Fearful for her mental state and knowing how much she missed her children, he prepared for her to travel with several of his aides, ailing in health, to Kiawah Island for recuperation. Fever was spreading through the camp and Nathanael was worried about Kitty's health. With the arrival of hot weather, Nat knew it would lift her spirits to be near the water.

"But I do not want to leave you again, my love. Now I shall be without my husband and my children," she sighed, looping her arms around his neck.

She tipped her head back and Nathanael touched a hand to her face. "This will be merely a brief separation," he promised. "Soon we'll be a united family, and none of us will be deprived."

Dr. Johnson, a camp surgeon, Colonel Washington and his wife, and four aides, including Nat Pendleton, all accompanied Kitty. Cooks had been sent to prepare the kitchen, and they were welcomed by a delightful dinner. The menu included duck, chicken, crab, beef, fish, prawns and potatoes, washed down with an expensive wine.

Over the next two weeks everyone recovered, renewed by the ocean, healthy sea breezes, horseback riding, and rest. In a letter to General Greene, Nat Pendleton commented: *Mrs. Greene, who is the very picture of health, observes and laughs at everything about her. Her cheerfulness is greatly appreciated.*

General Greene wrote to Pettit that his wife was enjoying the fresh air, fruit and vegetables which were abundant there.

> *The people are very friendly, and strive to render this country agreeable to her, but the fevers fill her with apprehensions. She is a very great favorite, even with the ladies, and has almost rivaled me where I least expected it; her flowing tongue and cheerful countenance quite triumph over my grave face. I bear it with great philosophy, as I gain on one hand what I lose on the other.*

In September, Nathanael was stricken with a severe bout of fever. Kitty rushed back from the island holiday to nurse him, but by the time she arrived he was at his desk writing once again, making his endless appeals for clothing, food and a bare subsistence for his suffering men. He received only one reply, from the man named John Banks.

Banks convinced General Greene that he had connections in Charlestown and could feed and clothe the army through these channels if Greene would provide him with $1,500 cash.

He offered to bill the Superintendent of Finance in Philadelphia for the balance as it fell due. Greene's commissary department was in such a low state that he had two choices: providing for his men through Banks or turning them loose to forage for themselves. He accepted the proposal.

TWENTY ONE

1782–1783

rs. Greene has so much the spirit of the military about her that she is determined to be in uniform with her husband, and therefore prefers deep blue with yellow buttons and buff facings. She begs that you will be so obliging as to procure a very small pair of gold epaulets for her. You should not be surprised if she should mount her Bucephalus and enter the town at the head of the army.

Captain Morris described the anticipation of the departure of the British garrison in a letter to his fiancée. The British authorities had reached an agreement with Nathanael's command to allow the withdrawal to be carried out without harassment to the British troops, but no time limit had been set. Kitty began planning activities in anticipation of this glorious day. To her great delight, her friend Anthony Wayne's arrival for the event brought her renewed vitality.

Nathanael had put General Anthony Wayne in charge of the Georgia campaign, and after its successful conclusion, he joined Nat's staff near Charlestown. General Wayne was extremely rank-conscious and already had uniforms tailored to his specifications to present himself as a spectacular figure. He and Kitty designed marching uniforms for some of the officers in the parade, working together while engaging in lighthearted conversations.

"I take pleasure in your eccentricities, Anthony." She threw him a bright smile. "And my husband tells me you are a fearless soldier as well as an innovative leader."

General Wayne grinned, eyes twinkling at the praise. "Did he not mention 'a fine strategist'?"

Kitty shook her head in feigned disapproval. "So they no longer call you by your moniker *Mad Anthony?*"

He laughed, head tipped back, the sound big and flowing. "Of course they do, my dear. I'm still mad; I'm just no longer unstable."

On December 14, 1782, the British morning gun boomed for the last time over Charlestown. They completed their final stage of evacuation—ten thousand inhabitants and slaves, led by General Alexander Leslie—departed the area and slowly boarded the ships at the wharf. Bound for St. Augustine, the West Indies or England, many citizens wept openly, leaving their homes and possessions to follow the British drums. Nathanael asked General Wayne's light infantry to follow behind them, leading the vanguard of American troops into Charlestown. With colors flying, drums beating, and heads held high, they herded the red-coated enemy down King's Street to Gadsden's Wharf. General Wayne's ragged infantry was light-hearted as the Patriots shouted out their welcomes.

At 3:00 p.m. General Greene and Governor John Mathews rode their horses side by side into town, followed by a long procession of officers and other notables. Kitty was dressed in blue and gold and accompanied by the prominent ladies of the state, riding in their phaetons. Following behind them were the citizens of the surrounding areas. The cheering flag-waving crowds were comprised of Patriots, who had been forced for so long to repress their loyalties. Now they deliriously celebrated the triumphal soldier, who after hardships and war fatigue was now in possession of his city and country again, owed, in great part, to the leadership of General Nathanael Greene. They recognized that he had accomplished what most people thought to be unattainable.

Some of the balconies were lined with well-wishers waving quietly, but most of the owners of the finer homes had left town or were unwilling to participate in the festivities. These people were associated for so long with Great Britain in customs and commerce and were not pleased when General Greene and his ragged army marched in. Just five years ago Charlestown was a thriving city: most of the homes had a garden and a court-yard. Now, the town was largely in ruins and presented a dismal scene. Kitty hoped the bells of St. Michael's Church would wel-come the victorious army during their celebratory march, but sadly, the enemy had taken them down and carried them off.

The Greenes moved into the stately stone residence of John Rutledge on Broad Street, a wedding gift from John to his nineteen-year-old bride, Elizabeth Grimke, and now the new army headquarters. They opened it to Charlestown society on Christmas 1783.

After two years of separation, the Rutledge family was happy to be reunited and eager to share their home with the Greenes and their staff. The Edward Rutledges lived across the street, and soon Kitty became an official hostess with the socially well-established Rutledge women. Lady Greene, as she was now known, was esteemed by both the army and the town people. Yet she was saddened by the separation from her children. Nathanael wrote to Sammy Ward that *a divided fam-ily leaves a blank in the heart that often causes a flowing tear, and yet my Kitty cannot think of returning without me.*

South Carolinian families moved into Charlestown to set up homes in the residences of the departed Tories. Kitty, part of the higher echelon, grieved over the shattered city, seeing little resemblance to the pre-Revolutionary days. The leaders decided to change the name to *Charleston,* giving it less of a British ring. It was Kitty's idea to give a ball to honor the vic-torious army. Nathanael was not in agreement with the plan.

"Oh Nathanael, the citizens need to gladden their hearts after so much loss. You, as the most prominent general here, should host a gala for them. It will be a lovely time."

"Angel, we are so short of currency as it is. How can we justify spending it so frivolously?"

In the end, Kitty had her way. She enlisted Mad Anthony

Wayne, Colonel Thadeus Kosciusko and their staffs to help her decorate the long assembly room of the mansion with garlands of magnolia leaves, vibrant buntings and festoons of multi-colored hanging paper flowers. She called it the Victory Ball and invited all the elite couples in Charleston. The army minstrels, dressed in elegant new uniforms, played minuets, country reels and other dances for the guests.

Nathanael opened the evening by dancing with his lady, and then asked Mad Anthony to take his place, citing his knee injury as an excuse. Anthony Wayne still carried a musket ball in his thigh from Yorktown, but did not let that stop his entertainment.

Kitty was in her glory as she twirled around the dance floor. Nathanael watched her with pleasure. Her blue and gold gown, adorned with small, delicate epaulets similar to her husband's, clung to her dainty body as she dipped and swayed with supple steps. After a while her eyes found her husband's across the room. Fluttering her lashes, she sent him a wide happy smile. Nathanael went to her, politely dismissing her dancing partner.

"Oh darling, I am honored. Two dances in one evening," she teased, eyes large and expectant.

Leaning down, he gathered her in his arms, so close he could smell the scent of lilacs on her skin. His lips brushed her ear, and when he spoke, his breath stirred the dark tendrils of hair at her cheek.

"You are too beautiful to be left in the arms of so many others," he confessed. "I wanted to hold you again and tell you something that will bring you happiness."

Her brilliant eyes flickered. "Really?" She let out a delightful laugh. Her body gravitated toward his with a mind of its own, and he held her there so that where he swayed, she swayed; where he dipped, she dipped. His touch felt good, so good; the wrap of his arms seemed like the warmth of the sun after a long, long winter's night.

"Lady Greene, you were correct. Thank you for insisting on this gala affair," he whispered, his eyes pouring out tenderness.

"Thank you, my darling. This is your finest hour and your men are victorious. This ball is an honor to you and your soldiers." Her eyes sparkled brilliantly, giving off shades of gray-blue-green. Their colors made him think of the great blue heron. Abruptly, they turned supple and calm.

"And I love you more with each new day," he said softly, so no one would hear. "Finally, for the first time in so long, I feel a sense of ease and gratification, so I needed to hold you in my arms when I told you this."

Kitty beamed. Contentment seemed suspended in the air surrounding them. She believed this dance was the highest moment of the Revolution.

⊷⊙⊶

After the initial excitement, the residents of Charleston started feeling less hospitable to the army's continued presence in their city. The soldiers were seen as another group of occupiers rather than their liberators. Mad Anthony had taken the bulk of the army across the Ashley River to James Island, and from there they acted as police while civilian government was being restored. General Greene tried to force the state legislature to financially support the troops, but without a word of a peace agreement, he could not disband the army.

Nathanael and Kitty traveled to Savannah the second week of January and were welcomed enthusiastically by Georgia's state officials, who promptly escorted them to Mulberry Grove—a rice plantation fifteen miles up the Savannah River. This vast estate had been awarded to General Greene for his services in the South, and although suffering from neglect, it held a great deal of promise.

"The view of the Savannah River is exquisite," beamed Kitty, "and this plantation house could be fixed up properly and provide us a lovely home, if we choose to live in the South."

"The time may come when we live half a year here and the other half in Rhode Island," proposed Nat, glancing at his wife to gauge her reaction. "It is only a two week journey by water."

They found problems pending on their return to Charleston. Formal peace with Great Britain had not been declared. There was no guarantee that the enemy would not return to claim the land. Although his troops were weary and wanted to go home, General Greene had no choice but to keep them together. Some left camp without orders and never returned, and the numbers were dwindling.

Kitty observed a continuous change in the people's attitude toward them, feeling a growing resentment on the part of the South Carolinians over the power of Nathanael's position. Because he insisted that the state maintain the Continental Army until the war was over, they called him a military dictator. Some discredited him, whispering he was in partnership, for his own gain, with the dishonest agent Banks, who had invested other people's money in ill-conceived speculations that went bad. Drained by the heavy burden of his financial problems, Nathanael attempted to explain the situation to his wife.

"Our land holdings can't be converted into money, so to produce income we must cultivate or sell land. This is a bad time to do so in our impoverished economy." His lips forced a sad weak smile.

"But Nat, must we begin pinching pennies again? We've been doing that throughout the war, and now..."

"Vicious rumors are circulating in Philadelphia that I entered into a secret business partnership with John Banks to make a profit on the sales to the Southern Department." He sighed loudly, and all the strength seemed to drain from his body.

"Let not your heart be troubled, Nat. Those who know you will never believe them, and the others don't matter."

"Sadly for us, a letter from John Banks was discovered that says that Rob Burnet has entered into partnership with him, and that I am his secret partner."

The knot in her belly twisted. "*Your* Rob Burnet?"

"The same. I cannot believe Rob would knowingly take part in a scheme to profit off the army." He hung his head, unable to look at her. "That is betrayal."

"What can you do, Nat?"

"Congress has ordered me to make a deposition of my conduct. General Wayne and Colonel Carrington are also under orders to do so." Searching her face with stricken eyes, he continued. "Congress will not honor the debt until I've proven myself innocent, so I have asked that all monies from Philadelphia be sent directly to me. How can I trust John Banks to pay the merchants?"

An emotional storm was rolling within Kitty: frustration, sorrow, and exasperation formed a whirlpool of contending winds. "How much are you responsible for?"

"More than $200,000.00," he answered quietly.

She slipped an arm around his waist, drawing his lower body close. "I believe in you, and so will Congress. Simply hold your head high, as you have so often told me," she added with a gentle smile.

Charleston merchants pressed General Greene for the payment of clothing given to Banks. He was compelled to satisfy them after judgments against him were handed down in the South Carolina courts. Forced to borrow heavily from three wealthy friends—Robert Morris, the Marquis de Lafayette, and his own business partner, Jeremiah Wadsworth—he was able to pay them.

Almost eight years to the day that the Battles of Lexington and Concord were fought, word was received that the preliminary Articles of Peace had been signed by Great Britain and the United States in Paris, France. On April 16, 1783, the War for American Independence was over.

In Charleston soldiers and civilians rejoiced with a display of fireworks and dancing, but General Greene's troops went hungry that night, for there was almost no food in the commissary.

At long last Nathanael could disband his army, with a fraction of their overdue pay sent out with their orders. The North Carolina and Virginia regiments were the first to leave. The soldiers from Pennsylvania and Maryland had to wait for the transport ships, which finally arrived in July. As they pulled into port, Nathanael handed Kitty her ticket to Philadelphia.

"Oh please Nat, do not send me back without you." She clamped her teeth together to keep the desperation from her voice. "You promised we would be together when we reunited with the children," she whimpered, her eyes building up tears.

"Kitty, I must resolve the Banks scandal. Knowing how much you miss the children, I want you to be home with them so you can hold them again. In just three months I'll be there with you, in our home again," he smiled, glancing outdoors through the bay window. The moon was in the third quarter, far from the hovering rain cloud. The air was cool. He felt a sense of space without end.

"But I dread sea travel. And what if you never make it home?" She shuddered at the thought of having to share the news this way. "And, I am carrying your child, and I am already experiencing the familiar symptoms of early pregnancy: nausea, head..."

He cut into Kitty's words. "What? You are pregnant?" he asked incredulously, thinking of his enormous financial burden.

Crushing sadness filled her eyes and he instantly regretted his words. Moving closely behind her, he hooked his forearm across her chest just above her breasts, drawing her back against him, his chin resting on the top of her head. He wrapped his other arm around her waist, experiencing her sobs.

"Oh Kitty, please forgive my heartless question. I so desperately want to go home with you and help you through this pregnancy. You have my word I will return to Rhode Island as soon as I can. You realize I must be the last man out of Charleston, and need to tend to our land holdings in an attempt to get some money for our future." He lifted a finger and carefully wiped away the stream of tears on her cheeks. "Believe me when I tell you that I am truly happy we shall be welcoming another little Greene to our family. Please forgive my selfishness in thinking only of our financial troubles."

Kitty mopped her eyes on her sleeve. She slowly turned around to kiss his mouth. The kiss was slow, deliberate and devastating.

"I am happy to know I'll see our children soon, and I will pray daily for your safe journeys, Nat. The Lord will unite us once more, and then it will truly be 'until death do us part.'"

TWENTY TWO

1783

A disheartened and queasy Kitty left her husband standing desolately on the dock as she sailed away to Philadelphia, accompanied by Colonel William Pearce and Colonel Kosciusko. Keeping to her room for most of the trip, she read, wrote and slept. When she reached Philadelphia, she had an overwhelming impulse to kiss the ground when she disembarked.

There was a mutiny of soldiers the previous month, sending the Congress fleeing to Princeton. Nevertheless, the victory celebrations and parties continued, and Kitty soon found the energy to attend them. Her old friend Anthony Wayne, recognized as Pennsylvania's foremost war hero, was front and center. Since his wife Polly was absent, he and Kitty attended many of the functions together. Eyebrows lifted and tongues wagged once again.

Naturally Kitty needed new gowns and accessories for the social events. She purchased a striking wardrobe of Philadelphia's latest fashions, reflecting the bold colors and styles from the postwar era. The new gowns had hoops, arranged to bounce as the ladies walked, and shortened petticoats to expose silk garters and tassels. Kitty and Wayne created a fashionable couple; her dark beauty and lovely dresses complimented the elegance of his impeccable self-designed uniforms.

Many young ladies vied for a place in Mad Anthony's life. The belles of the city considered him dashing and challenging and competed for his attention, buying him gifts and baking him sweets. Kitty was amused and happy to share his attentions, until she met Mary Vining, the sister of a Pennsylvania congressman. Young, dark-eyed Mary Vining enchanted every man she met, but she chose to give her heart to Anthony Wayne. Kitty watched her closely, surprised to discover that even the Marquis de Lafayette fell under Mary's charms. What annoyed Kitty the most was that Mary conversed freely in fluent French while she sometimes struggled to find the right words.

"Anthony, is Miss Mary informed that you have a wife?" she asked nonchalantly, running her finger slowly around the rim of the wine goblet.

"Naturally," he grinned. "Everyone knows my wife Polly refuses to come to camp."

"Is your wife aware that you still wear the inlaid sword Mary sent you some time ago?"

Mad Anthony regarded her with amusement. "You know a great deal about me, do you not?"

Laughing lightly, she shrugged and said matter-of-factly, "Of course I do. And since we're the talk of the town, I must stay informed of my competition."

Changing the subject, Kitty mentioned her new purchase. "I do hope Nat isn't angry with me. I've just acquired a phaeton and a pair of horses," she smiled, observing him under thick lashes.

"Will you be riding the horses?" he asked vaguely.

"They are for the carriage I've recently ordered," she answered in a coy manner.

"Good Lord Kitty! What did all this cost?" He looked genuinely startled.

"I've charged the total, $1,400, to the company Nat owns with Charles Pettit. Do you find this too pricey?" She raised her eyebrows at him, tucking a strand of hair behind one ear.

Anthony slowly shook his head. He knew the company was on the brink of insolvency. And he knew Nathanael well enough to know that, although he would pay the bill somehow, he would be upset by Kitty's irresponsible behavior.

Nathanael was furious. Alone, ill with fever and despairing over his financial matters, he sent his wife a sharp reprimand expressing disapproval of her foolish actions. Kitty, who had just returned from a gala house party on the bank of the Schuylkill River, was angered by his criticism and refused to answer the letter, tearing it into tiny shreds.

Three days later, she received another dispatch from Nathanael, dated August 1, 1783.

Notwithstanding all I wrote you the other day, I do love you most affectionately. I have not been pleased with myself since I wrote that letter and you know self-reproach is a painful companion. I am merely thinking of the future of our family, and wish you to be as economical as possible. But at the same time, I have no desire to deprive you of one rational amusement. My letter, I am afraid, was both indelicate and severe, as you have naturally a generous disposition and perhaps a little vanity at being thought so, which renders you a prey to the artful and designing.

This did not entirely mollify Kitty and she did not answer it. His next letter reached her three days later, explaining how disappointed he was to not hear from her, especially since he had received the bill for her expenditures. Agonizing over how to pay it, he added that he already owed Pettit for taking care of little George and arranging his education in Princeton. At the mention of her son's name, Kitty wept. Longing to see him and the others, she quickly made plans to withdraw George from his school and drive back to Rhode Island. She picked him up from Witherspoon's household at Princeton.

"Mama! Mama! You are here!" shouted the joyful, tall and slender child, racing toward her.

Scooping him into her arms, she held him tightly. "Darling, I told you I'd be back for you." She bent down beside him. "Let me look at you. Oh my," she whispered, tears welling in her eyes, "you are nearly a young man now. Wait until your papa sees you."

They drove in the new phaeton to Rhode Island, stopping briefly in New York City. Kitty showed her son where she had her first view of Manhattan Island in 1776. From there she and George drove the familiar roads to Coventry, where they would be reunited with the other children. Kitty's mind was filled with memories. It was difficult for her to accept that Coventry no longer belonged to her and Nathanael. Peggy was the mistress of the farm now. *My poor Nat will suffer greatly,* she thought. *He built this home with love...for his family. And now I must find us another place and try to close that door behind us.*

After picking up her little girls and baby Natty from their Uncle Jacob's home, Kitty gained a belated sense of purpose. Her children were seven, six, five and three and she would soon have another baby to nurture. Feeling contented and focused, she found them a renovated house on Mill Street in Newport, owned by the Crary family, and rented it with Nathanael's credit. Kitty commenced turning the dwelling into a cheerful home, optimistically anticipating her husband's return by the year's end.

❧

The weather was bitterly cold for riding, but Nathanael was looking forward to his reunion with John Cox, his former assistant quartermaster. John and Nathanael stayed in contact through frequent correspondence and were anxious to finally see each other. The sun wasn't quite down yet, but the light was gray. The days were marked by this protracted twilight, darker shadows gathering among the trees while the sky remained the color of tarnished silver. He and his aides could just make out the house in the distance, and gratefully directed their horses toward it after almost two months of traveling.

Nathanael limped toward the door, stepping back when it flew open. John hurried across the porch to welcome him with a strong embrace. Each man wore a huge grin as they walked over the threshold together. There was another man standing behind in the shadows. Nat thought he recognized his stance and walked in his direction.

"Your Excellency?" Stopping dead in his tracks, he regarded the man with a dazed expression.

There was no answer. The three men stared at each other for a long moment. General Washington tried to speak but his voice would not respond. Nathanael fell into his arms, unshed tears standing in his eyes.

They talked about their shared grief at Lord Stirling's passing, commented on their triumphs and losses during their three-year separation, and reminisced about times they spent together. Memories rushed out and filled the room. The hours flew by as the men enjoyed warm food, drink and conversation. Finally John retired for the night, but the two generals had too much to convey and talked into the early morning.

"Do you know that Mad Anthony and I will be neighbors in Savannah?" grinned Nathanael. "The Georgia Legislature gave him a plantation called Richmond. Naturally, he grumbles that it is not as handsome as Mulberry Grove, but the land is fertile and he looks forward to being a planter."

"Do you? Will that be your goal in Georgia?"

Nathanael shook his head slowly. "I'm not as convinced as General Wayne that a fortune is to be made out of growing rice." Frowning, he added softly, "And as a Quaker, I'm opposed to slavery, even though I realize no plantation can be worked without them. If I do farm, I will find a way whereby my slaves will become free workers on the land."

General Washington sighed. He knew how much Nathanael yearned to return to the iron forge, yet his dreams had been forcefully altered. Kneeling down to the grate, he arranged the firewood and kindling stored on the hearth.

"I agree with you on the subject of slavery. I desire that we not possess them as slaves, but rather work with them as paid servants."

Nathanael told him about the ride to Philadelphia. "There was so much gratitude expressed by the countrymen as we rode through the towns," clarified Nathanael. "I even heard shouts of 'Long life to Greene!' from some of them. There were times I could regrettably spend only moments with them since I had a travel schedule to follow."

George smiled at his dear friend. "If only Lady Kitty were with you, your social schedule would have been overflowing." Then he turned somber eyes on Nathanael. "How is she? Is she finally reunited with the children?"

General Greene nodded. "She's found us a home in Newport, and from all accounts, is happily preparing it for our rather large family." He offered a tired but cagey grin. "Has Lady Washington learned that we shall welcome a new baby shortly?"

They leaned toward each other across the table. His Excellency smiled, watching Nathanael with fondness illuminating his eyes. "Congratulations, Nat. You have such a fine family. Speaking of which, I do hope Lady Kitty was pleased with my namesake's brief education at Princeton." He closed his eyes and touched his right temple lightly. "We must get some sleep. Tomorrow we will ride together to Princeton to meet with the Congress. We can continue our recollections during our ride."

Nathanael grimaced at the mention of Congress, and George gently patted his shoulder. "I believe the Congress will support your dealing with the Banks affair."

"From your mouth to God's ears." Nat unfolded his long legs and rose up in sections.

The following morning the victorious commanders rode into Princeton side by side, followed by a long line of staff officers. The townspeople removed their hats, cheered noisily and waved madly out of deep esteem for these two generals—the only two commanders to continuously serve from the beginning of the war to its finish.

The Congress anticipated General Greene's arrival, but no formal reception was offered him. Nat had expected nothing more, but General Washington was deeply insulted at this lack of respect. His friend had done more than anyone in the field to attain the country's independence. A Congressional committee, with member James Madison, voted Greene the gift of two pieces of field artillery taken from the British. Commander-in-Chief Washington was honored to present this to his friend.

General Greene's thoughts, standing before them and searching out the few friendly faces he knew, were enveloped in deep sadness at having his character questioned. All he had wanted was a warm welcome as a persecuted brother who had suffered hard for their common cause.

"My fellow gentlemen, I left my home in Rhode Island more than eight years ago, and have visited my family and friends but once in that span of time. I have successfully completed my task assigned to me in the South, and with the consent and approval of General George Washington, I now humbly ask your permission to resign my commission as major general in the Continental Army of the United States of America."

The main army had not yet disbanded because the British evacuation of New York was not completed. As Nathanael awaited the response from Congress, he finalized all military business. He wrote the Congress requesting payment for the debts incurred on behalf of the army.

Free to come and go while awaiting Congress's response, he visited his old friends: Lafayette, Von Steuben, Charles Pettit, Thomas Paine, Anthony Wayne, John Cox and his closest companions, George Washington and Henry Knox.

"Nathanael, do stay to ride with us into New York next week. The last of the British will leave, and it should be the crowning glory of our conquest." Henry and Nathanael were sharing a drink before the warm hearth in Henry's parlor.

"Thank you, my friend, but I am anxious to return to my family. Congress has just now granted me permission to return home."

"Splendid news! But could you not wait just one more week?"

"I promised Kitty I would be there by November's end, and I shall," he grinned shyly.

"Old man, let me ask you a personal question." Henry dropped his gaze to his hands. "Are you shamed by the rumors of Anthony Wayne's constant attention to your wife?" The fire kindled, snapped and crackled. Little flames leaped.

Nathanael grinned at his friend. "I trust them both, and by now I've become accustomed to Kitty's conquests," he answered warmly. "In fact, I asked Mad Anthony to attend her at the social functions when I was not around. And I would have asked the same of you, Henry."

Having settled this topic, Nat changed the subject. "Will you be returning to Boston before becoming Minister of War?"

"Yes, Lucy wants to spend time there. And if you come by, my brother now runs the bookstore. He will be happy to supply your children those books I promised you at the war's beginning."

"Just one more thing, Henry. Have you heard that Banks received money from the Financial Security, money designated to pay those who supplied my troops? I just learned the merchants were never paid. He used the money to pay off his own business debts."

Henry straightened up with a jolt, his eyes meeting Nathanael's directly. "And you are left with the debt," he alleged.

"Yes, but I'm told he has property. I shall try to force the sale of enough of his land to cover his debts to me."

Henry shook his head sadly. "Nat, did Major Burnet betray you, as rumored?"

Sorrow rose up and sucked the air from Nathanael's lungs. "He is my friend and was my aide for six years. He claims he was not involved."

"There is proof of his signature on the army contracts."

Nathanael stared hard at his friend, his expression as tender as his face. "If he is proven guilty, I must forgive him. He was facing the same situation we all faced—no means of support at the end of the war. If he fell with the promise of a lucrative position, I can forgive him."

Henry smiled. He remembered a conversation with General

Washington about Nathanael's qualities. The commander-in-chief spoke of his lack of deceit, of his integrity and loyalty, and how he was a forgiving counselor.

The night before Nathanael's departure to Rhode Island, he and General Washington shared dinner. George gave him his blessing and they agreed to visit each other, in Georgia and at Mount Vernon. Still, George felt a gripping foreboding at their farewell.

"Is this farewell, or simply *adieu,* meaning we'll see each other soon?" General Washington asked lightheartedly.

General Greene, dressed in full uniform, rose to salute his commander one last time, respectfully and affectionately. "If I know our women, we shall be reunited shortly," he grinned.

"God bless you. Go in peace and return quickly," added Nat's commander-in-chief, wrapping a firm arm around Nathanael as he met his eyes. The disquietude he felt at that moment was spreading, becoming heavier by the minute. He silently prayed that his eyes did not reveal his crushing premonition that this would be the last time he would ever stand before his beloved friend.

TWENTY THREE

1783-1784

Nathanael Greene's homeward journey took place by sea. Drained and fatigued, his entertainment onboard consisted of reading nautical tales of adventure, conversing with the crew and captain, and sleeping. On November 27, 1783, as the ship approached Newport, he climbed to the top deck. His eager eyes scanned the docks in nervous anticipation of his reunion with the family.

The captain handed him a spyglass. "Good Lord, General Greene. It would appear that all of Rhode Island has come to welcome home their honored son," he grinned broadly. "I hope you have a speech prepared for them."

Stunned into silence, General Greene shakily stepped down to the cheering and whistling crowd. He was searching for Kitty when the governor, the commander of the Kentish guards and the state congressmen pushed forward to greet him. Smiling shyly, his eyes continued to seek out his wife and children. Stepping up to the platform, he finally heard her delightful voice.

Madly waving her handkerchief, she called out to him. "Welcome home, my General. We are over here."

His eyes filled as he caught sight of a tall lad, dressed in a continental blue jacket and buff breeches, stepping forward to award him a crisp, military salute. Beside him stood his little brother, dressed identically, who also attempted the salutation. Two beautiful little girls in white bonnets held tightly to Kitty's hands, and with her encouragement, curtsied and smiled up at him. He hesitated only seconds before he reached out his long arms to gather them into a vast embrace. The tears fell freely as Nathanael gave up this moment of gratitude to God.

"Kitty, we are making a spectacle, are we not?" he chuckled, wiping tears and leaning over to kiss her soundly. "What will my Quaker family think of us?"

"They are enjoying this reunion, my love. Why look, they are just over there, beaming with happiness at your return."

Nat looked over her shoulder to see his entire family, in addition to his former aides, Sammy Ward and Billy Blodget, all lined up for their personal moments with Rhode Island's war hero.

The governor spoke first, followed by several other dignitaries, and finally General Greene was asked to say something. He gave a short talk about appreciation and duty and then humbly accepted the gratitude of his peers and the Kentish Guards.

When the muskets were discharged in a thirteen-gun salute, Nathanael could no longer contain his emotions. Again he drew Kitty into his arms and held her as she wept. He stroked her cheek, felt her tears on his fingertips, then buried his face in her shoulder and went quietly and completely to pieces. He was finally home with his family. They would never again be separated by war.

The festivities continued in Freeport for more than a week, leaving Kitty and Nat exhausted. At long last, they were allowed to quietly resume their family life. Kitty was run-down and constantly tired, expecting another child. Nathanael finally had ample time to become reacquainted with his children.

"George, you do remember me, do you not?" he solemnly asked his older son.

The eight-year-old child's head nodded in assent as he dropped his eyes. Nat realized he must go slowly with them all, and was grateful he had the time to do so.

Three-year-old Natty stayed close to his big brother and mimicked his actions. But the girls, now five and six, barely remembered their father and were timid and reserved for the first few days.

"Let me read travel adventures to you," he suggested, opening his old copy of *Gulliver's Travels*. "Tomorrow we shall act out the parts, and each of you can choose which character you want to play."

They entertained themselves primarily indoors since Christmas was approaching and the air was frigid. They visited family in Potowomut and Coventry, and traveled together to see the Knoxes. Kitty and Lucy relaxed in the joy of seeing their children reunited with their fathers.

Nat loved watching Kitty, admiring her poise and dignity. She possessed a confidence in the way she talked and carried herself, but still managed to retain the soft hazy edges he loved.

Their friends also came to visit them in Newport: Colonel Kosciusko, Jeremiah Wadsworth, the Baron Von Steuben, and Kitty's favorite, the Marquis de Lafayette. The Marquis swiftly won the children over, dramatically begging them to call him "my dear marquis." After repeated attempts, they learned to pronounce it correctly. He entertained them with his enchanting stories, told in the soft tones of his French heritage.

Taking Nathanael and Kitty aside one evening, he surprised them. "Kitty and Nathanael, I ask you to seriously consider sending George to France for his higher education, under my guardianship, of course." They said they appreciated the offer, but George was much too young to go now.

Nat was determined to stay out of the public eye, turning down the many offers presented to him. Congress asked him to partake in peace negotiations with the Indians. General Washington and Henry Knox tried coaxing him into donning his uniform and joining them in Philadelphia at a meeting of the American Revolution officers. He politely rejected them all, even the paid ones, to stay home with his family. Kitty was nearing her delivery date and he was determined to be home for this birth.

He continued to support the proposal of a temporary state tax to pay the war debt. Nathanael believed each state should cover the expenses of their soldiers. He felt he should also be given his back pay for the past six years, thus providing for his family's living expenses until they could settle in Georgia. If he could get the state taxes to cover the expenses of feeding and clothing the Continental Army, he could recuperate the enormous sum he had put down to supply his Southern troops.

❧◉❧

"Oh Nat, I am finally at peace. The war is over, the tension of our endless separations is gone, and we are a family once again," she smiled, watching the children playing games by the cozy hearth.

"A family about to grow larger," he grinned. "Do you think we should farm the children out to family when your time comes? I know your brother Billy would love to take the boys to Block Island."

"I think that's a brilliant idea, my dear. Perhaps the girls can stay close by, with your brothers. You know how excited Patty is to meet the new baby. She'll want to help out, and Cornelia will not be separated from her for one minute."

As if on cue, the little girls stood up and went over to their parents sitting on the sofa.

"Papa, can we dress up like poor girls and go ask for bread?" Cornelia's large hazel eyes beseeched her father's permission. Patty covered her mouth as the giggles escaped.

Kitty laughed gleefully, tossing her head back and holding her stomach. She knew they were referring to her beggar disguise, first worn to fool her family and then to prove a point about kindness.

Several weeks before, she instructed them about generosity and being charitable. She cloaked herself as a poor woman, concealing her face with a shawl, and visited the houses of her friends to beg for food. Most of them ordered her off, not recognizing her behind the disguise. Finally, at the last house she visited, the master of the house was so touched by her pathetic story of poverty that he gave her the loaf of dinner bread he was cutting for his family. Thanking him tearfully, she returned it the following day, without her costume. The story became the subject of conversation throughout Newport, mortifying the friends who had turned her away.

"What I think, young ladies, is that it is time for bed," answered Nathanael, offering them his asymmetrical grin. "Now, whose turn is it to read the bedtime story?" He scratched his head as if he were concentrating.

"'Tis Mama's turn," they cried in unison. Patty ran into the library to bring the book to Kitty, who scooted over on the couch to make room for four more.

In March a healthy baby girl was born, and they named her Louisa. Kitty took the time to rest properly and soon recovered her strength. Once again she and Nathanael joined in the social activities of fashionable Newport, where Kitty was in her glory. Her daughters were thrilled to sit in her dressing-room, utterly captivated as their mother primped and applied make-up to her lovely oval face.

"A fairy princess," gushed Natty, watching his mother glide across the room, dressed for a dinner dance. "My mama is the most pretty princess in the world."

"And I, Natty? Am I the most handsome king?" asked his father.

"No, Papa. You are the bestest general in the world."

Kitty swooped him up and covered his face with kisses. "That he is, Natty. The very best general in the world."

A few months after Louisa's birth, Kitty and Nathanael agreed he would accompany Anthony Wayne on a trip to Savannah, Georgia to look over the possibilities of fixing up their plantation home and moving down there. They knew there was no likelihood of recuperating his fortune or paying his debts as long as they lived in Rhode Island. During his absence, Kitty took all five children for an extended stay on Block Island. When she returned home, she read Nat's letter from September, 1784.

I have attempted without success to get in touch with John Banks, but to no avail. I verily believe if I were to meet him, I should put him to death. He is the most finished villain that this age has produced. There is no crime but murder that he has not committed.

He promised Kitty that when he came back home they would go over the family's financial status and make a decision together. He mentioned that he would have to purchase Negroes, something he found repugnant, but necessary, if they were to live in Georgia. He ended the letter with these words: *I am not anxious to be rich. To have a decent income is much to be wished; but to be free from debt more so. I never owned so much property as now, yet never felt so poor.*

Nat returned three months later and sat down with Kitty to discuss their bleak economic position. Explaining that a recent storm had damaged Mulberry Grove, their Savannah plantation, he added that the rice crop was nearly destroyed. Repairs to the house were underway and new crops would be planted. Squatters had moved onto their property on Cumberland Island, selling their timber. Before leaving Cumberland Nat removed the squatters and sold a portion of the property. He told Kitty that he knew John Banks was hiding out in Virginia, and that he would find him and force his hand.

After all the facts were laid out, they concluded they would move to Mulberry Grove Plantation in Georgia. But first, Nathanael would make another trip down south to resolve the problems, and make one final effort to recover a substantial portion of the fortune lost in the John Banks debacle.

TWENTY FOUR

1784–1785

Nathanael did not find John Banks when he traveled through Virginia en route to South Carolina. He and Anthony Wayne rode to Savannah, where each had been awarded Savannah River plantations by a grateful legislature. Mad Anthony's plantations, Richmond and Kew, were adjacent to the Greene's acreage and their Mulberry Grove plantation. The two generals, propelled into the vocation of novice rice-planters, helped each other prepare the land for crops in fields neglected too long. They had purchased Negroes and good overseers on their previous trip, and felt optimistic about the future.

The generals visited Cumberland Island, accompanied by Colonel Hawkins. Nat wrote a brief description of the land in a letter to Kitty.

> *I find it a valuable property, and had I the funds to improve it to advantage it might be one of the first commercial objects on the Continent. The island is twenty miles long and a large part of it excellent for indigo. The situation is favorable for trade, the place healthy and the prospects delightful. On the seaside there is a beach eighteen miles long, as level as a floor. It is the pleasantest ride I ever saw.*

Nathanael wrote letters to Mr. Dennis De Bert in London, complaining about lumber stolen from his property on Cumberland by British naval vessels, and asking him to trace the whereabouts of the vessels. He asked De Bert to find the vessel owners and get them to make amends. He also requested that De Bert act as his agent in London to seek outlets for the sale of his live oak.

In a letter to the Marquis de Marbois, Nathanael described and extolled Cumberland Island.

The island forms one part of the harbor of St. Marys, into which there is an easy entrance and twenty-four feet of water on the bar. Shipping is perfectly secure from all weather stresses. The island is upwards of twenty miles long and three miles wide. There were a few settlements here, but they were broken up when the war came. The soil is excellent for indigo. The island is covered with live oak and red bay timber: both of the best quality for ship building. In the north there is good quality pine timber. The island is healthy, abounds with good water and shell fish. The quantity of acorns growing on the live oak affords food for hogs which net a prodigious profit. Horses thrive admirably on the island, but horn cattle not so well. At present there are over 200 hundred horses and some mules.

Little Cumberland Island lies north of here, and is parted from it by a narrow creek. It is full of timber but the soil is not good. It is surrounded by marshes and contains more than 2,000 acres. Half of great Cumberland and one half of little Cumberland belong to my purchase. I am going to lay out a town towards the south end of Great Cumberland, and many people have spoken for lots. There are 20 families settled on the island since the war. There are multitudes of deer and wild fowl to be got on the island, and green turtle in great numbers during season.

In the same letter Nathanael described their trip to the city of St. Augustine, in Spanish East Florida. Nat and Colonel Hawkins traveled down the inland waterways by canoe to visit the Spanish governor, Vicente Emanuel de Zespedes, and his family, hoping to recruit settlers to colonize and develop Cumberland Island. Although they did not succeed in their endeavor to interest Spaniards to settle on Cumberland, he did enjoy the time spent with the Royal family and their friends.

Wadsworth, working from Connecticut on behalf of Greene's interests, believed that Marbois might get a sizeable order for timber from the French government but Nat told him in May of 1785 that he would not sell more than a fourth interest in Cumberland Island, as he had good offers down there.

While Greene was attempting to make his investment in Cumberland Island profitable, his earlier debts still hung precariously over him. He wrote to the Marquis de Lafayette to interest the French navy in a timber contract with him, and asked Tom Jefferson in Paris to help expedite matters. Lafayette was agreeable, but through a misunderstanding, Greene's attempt ended in failure. Even his hopes of interesting friends like Wadsworth and Seagrove to invest in the islands were growing dim.

In the meantime, Kitty was once again "husbandless." During her time without him, she was forced to accept the truth that they were poor, shattering her dreams of wealth and leisure. They now lived on credit while the debts mounted daily. Their southern property needed money to develop it, money that seemed to be unavailable at this time.

As if this were not enough to weep over, she thought, *I'm pregnant again. And I cannot even run off to winter camp with Nat to escape all these problems. Where is our financial relief? From where shall it come?* Yet she managed the family and the house until Nathanael's return in late spring.

Just before his return to Newport, Nathanael stopped in Virginia to search for John Banks and learned the speculator had fallen victim to fever only a few days before. He left no assets behind and Nathanael would never collect the funds owed him. There was no hope of getting out from under his Charleston debts. The Greenes had no choice but to move to Mulberry Grove, cultivate rice, and sell other properties when the market was favorable. Kitty saw no good options for their immediate future.

After Nathanael returned, Kitty, under a dark cloud of depression, took to her bed with uncertainty and fear. Her strength seemed to ebb away as her tears flowed freely. Even her children, who had always brought her laughter and gaiety, could not raise her spirits. After a difficult final month of pregnancy, she gave birth to a little girl and named her Catharine, after the aunt she no longer saw. Kitty slept with this baby during her confinement, and the children believed baby Catharine was a special gift to the family.

When the older girls came down with a cough, Nat and Kitty kept the baby away from them. It turned into whooping cough, and to Kitty's despair, little Catharine was seized with fits of coughing. After the older girls recovered, Nat and Kitty helplessly watched the tiny baby grow sicker and weaker. Nat spent the nights awake caring for his daughter, and Kitty did what she could during the day. Late one afternoon Catharine's little throat simply closed up, impeding her ability to breath. She died in her mother's arms. When Nat carried her from the room, Kitty collapsed in grief.

For several weeks she lay in bed, falling in and out of sleep, her arms empty, her heart aching. She felt a deep hole inside, sucking her entire being down into a black pit. She could not eat. Nat pleaded with her to help herself. One afternoon she opened her eyes and saw him, looming large beside her. When she reached up to him, he pulled her to his chest, aware of her painfully thin shoulders.

"You're trembling," he whispered. Burying her face in his chest, she felt herself shaking in the circle of his embrace.

"The children?" she moaned. Her eyes had gone glassy with wetness. "Are they well?"

"Yes, my angel." Sorrow ripped at his voice. "They are all below, waiting for you to wake up. Would you like to see them?"

She shook her head slowly. "Not now, Nat. In a bit." Tears thickened in her throat. "When did you bury our baby?"

"Oh Kitty, you've been sleeping and with fever for several weeks now. We could not wait." Compassion flooded his heart.

She nodded and reached out to him, brushing his hand with her fingertips. "Fear not, Nat. It is better that I was not there. How are the children dealing with it?"

"We read, we talk about Heaven, we play with the new kittens, we…"

A fragile smile, tinged with sadness, broke over her face. "Ah Nat, you've always been so strong. And such a devoted father. I need you so, and I will forever be grateful. Please help me rise, and help me wash up."

Reaching out for his hands, Kitty inhaled sharply, pointing to the window. "The sun, Nat. Look at the sun. It will be a mango sunset." Nat watched in wonder as the sun, hanging low in the sky and still holding onto its burning white color, dropped slowly into the horizon, transforming itself into a red-orange orb.

"I see it, Kitty. Look how the streams of light burning through the clouds are dividing the horizon into triangles of opalescent colors."

She smiled a poignant smile. "There are no words to describe its beauty, but you've come close." Blinking back her tears, she added, "Perhaps it is our symbol that peace and harmony await us."

ꞓⱺꙊⱷ

As autumn approached and Kitty gradually regained her strength, she and Nathanael made preparations for their permanent move to Georgia. They shipped their furniture, the many books in Nathanael's library, and their personal belongings. Nat spoke with his brothers and cousin Griffin about new business opportunities: the sale of timber and rice from Georgia from aboard their merchant ships. Taking on more debt, he purchased several thousand more acres on Cumberland Island, because they were covered with live oak and pine. He made out his will and secured a ship to take him and his family to Savannah. Finally, he rented out the old farmhouse in Westerly.

Nathanael reluctantly signed new notes to keep John Bank's creditors at bay as he entered a new claim in Congress for his debts incurred on behalf of the army. He heard from former aide Nat Pendleton, now living in Savannah with a growing law practice, that another hurricane had ruined his second rice crop at Mulberry Grove. Old friends from Rhode Island, learning he was leaving the state, came to him with their pleas for reimbursement or sympathy for their wartime wrongs and injustices. Nat was tireless in his efforts on their behalf.

In the middle of this hectic preparation to relocate, Kitty sought him out, tears streaming down her cheeks.

"Are you ill, my dear? What is wrong?" he asked, apprehensively.

"Oh Nat, I thought my illness made me miss my 'complaint' but now I don't know," she sobbed. "It's been three months and I fear I'm with child again."

"Hush now, Kitty. It will be alright. I will get you a nurse to help you with the children," he assured her. "Please calm down. We will sort everything out," he murmured, holding her tightly.

Kitty's nervous system completely surrendered under this added stress. Nathanael placed her under the care of a doctor and a full-time nurse. With Kitty unable to assist him with the children, Nathanael hired the tutor who had been recommended by Yale's president, Dr. Ezra Stiles: Phineas Miller, a twenty-one-year-old Yale graduate and resident of New Haven, Connecticut. This cultured young man with kind manners and high intelligence turned down a more lucrative offer to accept Nat's terms of thirty-five guineas a year plus room and board. He would begin tutoring the Greene children in Rhode Island and then accompany them to Georgia when Kitty was well enough to travel.

Kitty was drawn to Phineas the moment she met him. The kindness and concern he exhibited toward her and the children was obvious. She quickly learned he was well-versed in the classics, and an inspiring conversationalist. Although reserved,

Phineas was responsive when addressed. She appreciated the quiet way he reached through her despair and offered her companionship. In later years she told friends that he did the most to bring her out of her depression.

Phineas Miller was not particularly tall, yet held his slender frame so erect that he seemed to tower over men half a head higher than himself. He wore his raven hair long and full, usually tied back. The Greenes learned to appreciate his quiet, confident strength and his unusual respect for both adults and children. The older children took to him instantly, forming a strong bond with their young tutor.

In October the Greenes embarked on their new journey. The vessel took seventeen days to reach Savannah, and the passage was difficult. One crew member was lost overboard. The ship faced dangerous weather conditions more than once. Kitty stayed below under the care of her nurse with one-year-old Louisa, while Nat assumed charge of the other children. The ship's creaking and pitching made Kitty violently ill, and her extreme fear worried Nathanael.

Fortunately, the children were far less trouble than Nat could have hoped for. The most pleasurable moment of the trip was the sighting of a large whale that passed close to the ship.

"What is that, Papa?" shouted George over the noise of the ship. He grabbed his father's coat sleeve and pointed excitedly at a large gray form not far from the ship.

"I believe it's a whale, my son! I've never seen one come this close to the ship. Stay here with the mate while I bring the others to the quarterdeck." What a wonderful thrill for his children, he thought as he went down to find them.

When the vessel reached the safety of the docks of Savannah, Nathanael assisted his cheerful children and pale, badly-shaken wife down the gangplank. The family eagerly stepped onto the soil of their new state of Georgia.

TWENTY FIVE

1785

Stepping off the vessel in Savannah, Kitty's eyes scanned the dock and caught sight of Nat and Susan Pendleton, standing next to Anthony Wayne. She managed a delicate wave and a warm smile, as she whispered a thankful prayer for their safe arrival. Mulberry Grove Plantation was located fourteen miles up the river and Kitty had arrived malnourished and worn out. Nathanael knew she could not make the trip, and gratefully accepted the Pendleton's kind invitation to stay in their Savannah home for a fortnight.

Nathanael sent the servants to Mulberry Grove to prepare the plantation house for their arrival. Phineas Miller stayed with the Greene family, tutoring the children and exploring the bustling seaport of Savannah. The Pendleton's lovely home stood on the corner of Bay and Barnard Streets, overlooking the Savannah River harbor's docks and warehouses. This forced break in their travels allowed Kitty to renew the brief connection she'd had with Susan Bard Pendleton.

"Kitty, I think about the stories my husband Nat tells of how you nursed him back to health when on that beach near Charleston. He will never forget your vitality and kindness to him."

"Yes, I was ill as well and Nathanael wanted me to breathe fresh sea air, so he sent us to Kiawah Island. But your story of meeting your husband is much more interesting!" Her eyes twinkled. "Wasn't Nat a paroled prisoner of war on Manhattan Island when you two met?"

"Indeed he was, and I fell for his intelligent conversations. Oh, and he wasn't too hard on the eyes either," grinned Susan.

The women enjoyed each other's company. Kitty was in awe of Susan's New York polish and hoped to learn from her. After a week's time, she felt she had made a close female friend in the South.

Every day Kitty grew a little stronger. The women were soon shopping at the fashionable shops on Broughton Street. Their favorite shop was run by Ann Taylor, who imported European petticoats, the British Anderson's pills, Irish linen, French nappies, men's silk hose, and many other foreign delights. The town theatre was nearby, and they attended two different presentations, enjoying the performances of *The Fair Penitent* and *The Tragedy of the Orphan*. As her vitality returned, Kitty found additional gratification in the dinner parties the Pendletons offered, allowing her to converse wittily in her flirtatious style with Mad Anthony and the other guests. The Pendletons seemed to be charmed by her, and even after her health returned they encouraged the Greenes to remain with them longer than the original two weeks.

In November, accompanied by Nat Pendleton, they left the city for their plantation home, traveling by two carriages sent from Rhode Island. Their first sight of the property was at the bend turning onto Augusta Road. Passing through the gate and meandering down a lane surrounded by a lovely forest of unfolding live oak trees, the children were enchanted by the beauty of their new home.

Spellbound, swiveling her head back and forth like a puppet, Patty asked, "Is this real?"

"What are those, Papa?" Cornelia pulled on Nat's arm and pointed worriedly to the moss draping the trees. "Are they ghosts?"

Nathanael laughed and explained that the Spanish moss did not hurt the trees and was not a ghost. Kitty was fascinated with the wild vines and masses of yellow jasmine, making the forest almost impenetrable through the narrow lane. The network of live oaks formed a shadowy arch above the carriage trail and forced them to look up and search for squirrels and birds. As the forest ended and the Savannah River approached, tall shrubs took the place of the oak trees.

They could see a wilderness of marshlands on one side and levees of rice fields on the other. Green meadows bracketed by vast forests of pine yielded to thick wild bush.

"This is ours, as far as the eye can see." Nat spoke with reverence. "In the whole, we have more than two thousand acres of oak and hickory and well-timbered pine land."

The carriages traveled slowly, eventually pulling up to a two-story brick mansion, encircled by a grove of mulberry trees. The mansion house, with its porches across the first and second stories, lay a hundred yards from the river's edge on the western bank of the river. Vines of sleeping honeysuckle ran up one wall of the porch and climbing rose vines twisted up the columns.

Nathanael gave the restless children permission to run through the fields, and asked Phineas to accompany them.

"But Phineas, please don't allow them to go down to the river. 'Tis better for all of us to be there together to watch them," added Kitty. She wanted to gauge the danger herself before allowing the children to explore it. Nat Pendleton stood by, quietly observing Kitty's reaction, sensitive to the fact she was seeing the house now as her permanent home.

"This truly is amazing, Nat," she said softly. "I am in awe of the trees and the flora. I wonder why there are so many mulberry trees. Do you know?"

"I was told they were planted with the intention of promoting a silkworm farm. Unfortunately, that was not successful but the trees have grown and enhance the beauty of our dwelling."

"Who built this plantation?" Kitty continued to admire the symmetry of the lovely trees lining the pathway.

Nathanael reached for her hand. "A man named John Graham—a wealthy Scotsman and outspoken Tory—built it before the war. After 1776, he could no longer maintain his property because of the Patriot raids. When Savannah was evacuated in 1782, Graham, who was lieutenant governor of the British administration in Georgia, fled with the fleet, leaving a huge fortune behind. The state confiscated it and gave this plantation to me in appreciation of my service."

Kitty smiled. "But surely the mulberry trees were planted before that."

He chuckled at her curiosity. "Yes, my love. The original owner of the plantation was John Cuthbert, who sold it to Dr. Patrick Graham. He is the one who planted the mulberry nursery around 1740. That would make them about forty-five years old now."

She laughed lightly, glancing over her shoulder as Nat Pendleton walked down to the river bank.

Nathanael led her through the front door and into the parlor. As they entered the huge vestibule, Kitty paused, breathing in the incredible smell of the house. It smelled like standing in the middle of a deep forest with a sliver of sunlight on your face—a hint of flowers, of water-drenched moss, of trees and light, pure air. Wide glass panels flanked the double door, offering a lovely view of the Savannah River and its tree-covered bluff. Just below, at the water's edge, stood an old rice mill.

"Look in the distance, my love. You can see the midstream islands and the South Carolina shore." Nathanael, pleased with her feelings about this large, abandoned house, knew it would take a lot of work to make it livable. They wandered hand-in-hand through the large rooms until they reached the kitchen, set apart from the main house. Two massive chimneys were built at each end of the mansion to service the many smaller fireplaces throughout the house.

"This will certainly dry out the rooms in the rain, and warm us in the winter," said Kitty. "But Nat, I don't think our Spell Hall furniture will fill these large rooms properly, do you?"

"Oh, I've failed to mention there are many fine pieces of furniture left by the owners and stored in the outbuildings. We can look them over and you can choose whatever you want to bring back here. Of course, we'll purchase new pieces when we can, and..."

Kitty abruptly threw her arms around his neck. "Oh Nat, this is beautiful. It has so much potential. It will be perfect for our children, and I'll have you right here with me to put it back in proper condition." She snuggled against his chest.

Nat grinned. "So you don't find it impossible to repair?"

"Good Heavens, no! It is more than I ever expected, and when we plant our flower gardens, and our fruits and vegetables, we'll be living like the King and his Queen." She dashed back to the large parlor. "I can just see General Washington dancing here with me! Won't he simply love it?" she giggled.

At that moment the children, tired and muddy yet full of laughter, charged into the room.

"Have you been to the river?" Kitty fixed her eyes on Phineas with a questioning look.

"No, Miss Kitty. They've been all over the property, and got muddy at the water machine used to clean the rice," replied Phineas.

"Mama, Papa, there are so many buildings!" shouted George. "We saw barns, cabins, stables…"

"And there's a coach house, and a big place for chickens!" Patty's bright blue eyes were dancing with excitement. "Mama, we shall all love it here!"

Kitty drew them to her in a big embrace. She too felt a rush of elation. They would be able to make their home here; all of them together at last.

George looked up at her. "Mama, aren't you relieved that this home, our plantation, was not destroyed during the war?"

Kitty smiled and glanced at Nat. "Indeed I am, son. We all must give thanks to God for that blessing."

Nat observed his son proudly. His intelligence was keen, and he exhibited an independent spirit. He quietly gave thanks for his family and for this home—a perfect place to raise his children.

That evening Nathanael wrote his impressions in a letter to a friend in Rhode Island.

We found the house and outbuildings more convenient and pleasing than we expected. We have a poultry house nearly fifty feet long and twenty wide, parted for different kinds of poultry with a pigeon house on top that will contain one thousand pigeons. We have a fine smoke house, a coach house and stables, a large out-kitchen and a magnificent plantation house.

After a long journey, they laughingly prepared bedding for the first night in their new home.

TWENTY SIX

1785–1786

The plantation house had not been occupied for years. It took the family more than a month to settle in and make it comfortable. They worked together and for the most part, enjoyed their tasks as they scrubbed down the rooms and furniture, restored the barns and the poultry house, and prepared the ground for planting. The garden was in ruins, but a great variety of flowers and fruit trees still survived. Kitty made gardening fun with creative games so even the children joined in the weeding and plowing. They chased the leaves out of the woods and into the tall grass, tumbling over each other with laughter.

All this outdoor work under balmy winter skies did wonders for Nathanael's health. In spite of his financial worries, his body gained muscle and tone and his deep laughter returned. Kitty and his children taught him to play "Puss-in-the-Corner" in the warm Georgia sun. In the evenings, he placed a child on each knee and taught them all to sing funny songs, mostly invented on the spot. This was followed by family reading.

Hard work was required to restore their dwelling and plant the rice fields. Nathanael wrote to Henry Knox that Kitty often switched from *"the gay lady to the sober housewife."* She was also in the early stages of pregnancy, and she felt anxious about the unborn baby's health.

Yet they persevered, and soon the rice plantation was up and running. Nat's hope was to have sixty acres of corn and one hundred thirty acres of rice planted by the spring of 1786.

They took family walks down by the river, enjoying the lush canopies of gnarled live oaks and their spectral gray curtains of hanging moss. The surging banks of azaleas and camellias that grew along the riverbanks seemed magical. Sometimes they caught glimpses of clusters of snowy egrets, or spotted the elegant blue heron. Even the thick, dank, shrimpy smell of the river gave their property an ethereal presence, certainly different from anything they had experienced in Rhode Island.

Out of the eastern forest, two deer leaped in tandem into the bottom of the meadow, a buck and a doe, and then raced across the corner of the clearing, disappearing into the trees.

"How many of you saw the deer?" cried out Kitty in delight. Everyone but little Louisa claimed to have seen them. Kitty and Nat exchanged smiles, savoring the strange, silken light rising up from the greening marshes. The breezes carried the aroma of jasmine and rosemary.

Phineas Miller taught the children five days each week, and in Nathanael's opinion, he was a very clever lad, much loved by the youngsters. Nathanael and Phineas purchased books together to include in their well-stocked library, whose dark wooden shelves, crammed with leather-bound tomes, lined the walls. Nathanael's desk was an outsized antique, carved mahogany piece inset with tulipwood. A matching serpentine sideboard stood in dark contrast to the light airy atmosphere, created by the buttery sunlight peeking through the windows.

Kitty yearned to give a party in their home, and Nathanael was pleased to indulge her. They were somewhat restrained in what she was able to spend, but their first party was quite a success, bringing together neighbors and even friends from Savannah and beyond.

"Look at pretty Mama," squealed Cornelia, pointing to Kitty as she arrayed herself in the bedchamber. All five children were stretched out on her bed beneath the fragile silk-brocaded canopy, watching as she arranged her hair. Turning to giggle at their animated faces, she rose and walked across the thick Oriental rug to sit beside them. Kitty's exquisite aqua-colored silk gown, trimmed in Belgian lace and set off by her sparkling shoes with diamond buckles, gave her the air of a princess. Around her neck she wore her gold, heart-shaped locket containing Nat's picture.

Little Louisa reached over to touch her raven hair, settling softly over her pale shoulders.

"Mama," she beamed.

"I love all of you, my little cherubs," Kitty said with laughing eyes. "Now, shall we go greet the guests? I will let you say hello and then it will be time for prayers and bed."

"Aw, Mama. I'm a big boy now," scowled ten-year-old George. "I should be allowed to dine with you." George had already planned to stay up late and spy on the party while they dined.

Pleasure danced in Kitty's eyes as she kissed each one tenderly. She turned to George. "Perhaps for the next party, dear. We might have an early dinner next time so all of you can join us."

The dinner meal, the largest of the day, was generally served at mid-afternoon, after the planter returned from riding and working his fields. But when a dinner party was given, the large meal was served about eight o'clock at night. Fashion demanded that a very large variety of foods, arranged on the sideboard in formally balanced patterns, be presented. Two full courses with wine were offered; the tablecloths were removed after each course. This evening Kitty had prepared turtle soup, pork and chicken, fish and meat pies—all accompanied by gravies and sauces. Her neighbors brought fresh and pickled vegetables, which were offered with bread, rolls, biscuits and butter. Finally, dessert appeared on the sideboards: pies, cakes, jellies, creams, tarts and fruit compotes.

"Kitty, your cooks are quite excellent," remarked Anthony Wayne, delicately wiping his mouth with an Irish lace serviette.

She grinned at her friend. "Just one, and the house servants and I helped her." A warm flush filled her chest and cheeks. "I am happy you enjoyed dinner, Anthony."

She rose to help the servants clear the table of the linens, exposing the beautiful polished wood. Over that they placed fruit, crackers, pieces of Gloucester or Cheshire cheese cut from eight or ten-pound imported wheels, and nuts, accompanied by more wine and cordials. They toasted absent friends, all the ladies at the table, and their future in Georgia.

***

In April of 1786, Nathanael shared his contentment in a letter to a friend in Rhode Island.

> *The garden is delightful. The fruit trees and flowing shrubs form a pleasant variety. We have green peas almost fit to eat and as fine a lettuce as you ever saw. The mocking birds surround us morning and evening. The weather is mild, and the vegetable world progresses to perfection. We have in the same orchard apples, pears, peaches, apricots, and nectarines, plums of various kinds, figs, pomegranates, oranges and strawberries three inches around.*

During her advancing pregnancy, Kitty read by the hour, sometimes with Nat, but more often with Phineas. In the evenings they all matched wits over word and card games.

Isaac Briggs, a Georgia politician, was a frequent visitor to the plantation. Kitty enjoyed discoursing with him about local issues, including slavery.

"I, unlike my husband, have no problem with owning slaves," said Kitty. "My Rhode Island grandfather made money from the 'Triangular Trade,' where rum was shipped to Africa and traded for slaves, who were shipped to the West Indies and traded for molasses and sugar. That was sent to Rhode Island and made into rum." She shrugged, glancing over at Phineas for his reaction.

"At this point I have not yet determined how I feel about slavery," opined Phineas.

"Then by all means make your determination. Living in

Georgia, you must have an opinion," said Briggs. "I would not be a slave myself, and if forced to be, I would liberate myself by any means in my power."

"As would I," smiled Kitty. "Does this not also apply to riding your horse, although you would not be willing to be ridden yourself?"

"There is a huge difference," snapped Mr. Briggs. "A horse has no soul, yet a Negro does."

"Sir, please prove that a horse or any other animal has no soul," chided Kitty.

"I believe," began Briggs, chewing on his lower lip and looking from Kitty to Phineas. "I believe it isn't as easy as I had thought."

Later, Isaac Briggs complimented Kitty in a letter to a friend.

Before meeting Miss Kitty Greene, I was told she had no more gravity than an air balloon and that she had no regard or affection for her children. I was told she cared for nothing but flirting, rattling and riding about. But they were wrong. Kitty is a lady who disdains affectations, acts and thinks as she pleases, within the limits of virtue and good sense. Because she does not consult the world about her actions, she is generally an object of envy. She confesses she has passions and her virtue would be in resisting; keeping them within bounds. Kitty possesses an unbound benevolence; she is honest, has an enormous share of maternal affection, and has formed a great basis of education for her family.

Kitty was now in the last stages of her pregnancy. She spent more time indoors due to bouts of dizziness. In early April she was working alone in the kitchen, which was unattached to the house. As she stretched to remove the rice spoon from the shelf, hanging just beyond her reach, she fell forward and landed on her side. Raw pain seared her flesh, and she knew she could not rise. Her cries for help went unheard for over an hour. Finally, Phineas heard her and rushed to her side.

"Oh, Phineas, thank God you've come. My hip must be broken," she cried out, tears of frustration streaming down her face. "And my foot as well, as I cannot bear weight on it."

Phineas covered her with his coat and went for assistance. When Nathanael returned from the fields, he found her in bed, tended by a neighboring doctor. Her hip was bruised, and the muscles in her ankle were swollen and strained, but not broken.

"I am worried about our baby, Nat. What if...?"

"Calm yourself, my love. We will give you rest and bring in help. I will assign the children to take turns reading to you," he said softly, his expression exceptionally vulnerable.

Her eyes softened. "That won't be necessary, Nat. Let them play. I'll get help from Phineas and the servants."

On April 4, Nathanael wrote to Sammy Ward. *This misfortune is the greater from her particular situation, being under hourly apprehension of the baby's birth and struggling with hopes and fears.*

The accident resulted in premature labor, and the baby died several hours after birth.

Nathanael drew his wife into his arms and held her as she wept. Stroking her cheek, he felt her tears on his shirt. Burying his face in her shoulder, they gave in to their loss.

"What else must we deal with? How much more can we take?" Kitty hauled in a shaky breath.

Nathanael pressed his lips together as an unexpected surge of anger caught him by surprise.

Wiping at her tears, he could see the anguish in her eyes. Compassion flooded his heart.

"Fate has dealt us some low blows, Kitty," he answered softly.

"And I don't trust fate to let go of us now." Biting down on her lip, she closed her eyes tightly. Tears burned their way from beneath her lids and she let them fall freely. "But together, Nat, we can survive."

Fate's next visit to the Greenes would shatter their world.

TWENTY SEVEN

1786

Social custom in Georgia called for visits back and forth among plantation neighbors. Kitty was frustrated with this system because she could not choose where she wanted to spend her free time. Several of the country neighbors bored her with their deficient educations and mindless small talk, but she was not a hurtful person and politely returned everyone's first call. Once that duty was fulfilled, she opted to spend time with her close female friends and select gentleman friends, like Anthony Wayne, described by Kitty herself as "an old and honest friend," who was a constant visitor at her home.

Nathanael approved of the close friendship between Kitty and Mad Anthony. He saw how his wife's grief and depressions evaporated in the presence of Anthony, and he trusted them. Riding across the meadows, lush with vegetation and painted with springtime flowers, they ventured down to the wild river, laughing, gossiping and joking about everything. Both were fervent gardeners and shared seeds for herbs and flowers as they planted side by side in their adjoining gardens.

The whisperers of Savannah watched and censured their time together, especially if Anthony visited Mulberry Grove in the evenings when Nat was away on travel. Kitty laughed at the scandalous hearsay. To those who mentioned the gossip to her, Kitty replied that they ask the busybodies if her five children, several servants and resident tutor Phineas Miller would not have been made aware of any *untoward activities* going on under their watch.

Kitty and Nathanael traveled to Savannah to visit Nat and

Susan Pendleton and other friends. Kitty was ready to entertain again and enthusiastically received these same friends at Mulberry Grove. Her women friends facilitated her settling into her new role of plantation mistress and assuming responsibilities she disliked—the demands of the plantation—including attending to the slaves' clothing and administering their medical attention. At times her exhaustion reinstated her depression, but in smaller doses. Yet Kitty steadfastly pursued the domesticity she knew was required of her.

Nothing had been resolved about the war debts Nat had accumulated by signing promissory notes for his soldiers' provisions. The merchants in Charleston pressed him for payment. He could not keep up with his expenses nor respond to their demands. He knew he must delay his intended visit to the North until later. His meetings with Nat Pendleton, the legal counsel for his affairs, distressed and upset him. After one of those meetings, Kitty went outdoors looking for him.

"Where is Nathanael?" Kitty asked Phineas.

"He's gone out, Miss Kitty. On foot. He didn't say where he was going."

Walking toward the river, Kitty found him sitting on the remains of an ancient oak stump. She approached quietly and stood behind him, watching his shoulders shake as he sobbed. She placed her hands over her mouth to stifle her own whimpers. After several moments, Nat turned around slowly.

"Oh Nat. What it is? Your health?" She tried to stop the hot, smarting tears stinging her eyes.

The face gazing up at her was that of a fatigued, gaunt former soldier who had given his life for a cause and signed away his future for his beliefs. Still, behind those tired eyes she could still recognize the striking young soldier with the dancing hazel eyes.

A slow smile trembled on his lips. He stood up and opened his arms, folding them around her. Kitty rested her head against his chest, listening to the quickened beat of his heart and breathing in the faintly woodsy masculine scent of him.

For a moment, he simply held her. His embrace undid her—the offer of comfort she hadn't asked for, the gift of affection she hadn't expected.

"Just my financial troubles, lassie. I've not been given any bad news on my health, and my wife and children—the loves of my life—are developing beautifully into true plantation ranchers." He rubbed his temple and Kitty noticed how the weariness revealed itself in the drooping slope of his shoulders.

She studied him with serious eyes. "Nat, maybe we'll never stop being afraid for our finances, but you certainly don't have to do it alone. I'm right here and together, we will make this work."

He dropped a kiss on the top of her head, then reached out and took hold of her elbow, guiding her home.

⸎

Kitty looked out the window at the Savannah River, watching her children at play. This simple act gave her such peace. She was beginning to lose her unreasonable fear of her children drowning, and with summer approaching, Phineas had agreed to teach them to swim. Kitty was a good swimmer, having learned as a child on Block Island.

Both Kitty and Nathanael were delighted with the floral beauty of their southern home. Their vegetable garden and fruit orchards were in full bloom, offering delicious additions to their daily meals.

"Oh Nat, these peaches are so juicy, and so sweet. And to think we've grown them here on Mulberry Grove," grinned Kitty, reaching for her serviette to stop the juices from running down her chin.

The plates were cleared from the dinner table. Kitty thought Nat seemed preoccupied, lost in thought. She placed her hand over his.

"I'm thinking about the journey home this summer. Although I detest the sea voyage, I am very much looking forward to seeing General and Lady Washington again. The children will adore returning to our family, and the summer heat is about to engulf us here, so it will be a perfect time to depart."

Nathanael looked at her, suddenly regretful. She admired his quiet strength and loved knowing she could count on him for guidance. Although he was iron strong, there was also a part of him that was flexible and tender.

"Did I say something wrong?" she asked, confused by the intensity of his gaze. Dampness shone in his eyes as he rubbed his hand over his jaw. His voice fell to a whisper.

"Kitty, we shan't be returning north this summer. Our finances simply cannot allow us to make that journey." He drew a deep breath. "In fact, I've been called to Savannah next week to meet with another creditor about payment on Banks' debts." He delivered the news with an air of solemnity.

Kitty smiled, looking hopeful. "Then I shall join you, and we will stop to visit the Pendletons."

That evening, after the children were in bed, Kitty reached for Nat's hand and led him to their bedroom. She knew his body was fatigued and offered to knead his weary muscles. With a deep groan of impending relaxation, he succumbed to her skillful fingers.

After a soothing massage, Nathanael pulled himself up and leaned close to Kitty. He inhaled her floral scent as he ran his fingers over her soft skin. They shared a lingering kiss, carrying passion and a radiant glow and lighting her up from the inside. His next kiss, deeper and stronger, propelled heat to her fingertips and toes, even to the ends of her hair. And it felt like rain, drenching her parched soul.

She came to him willingly, pressing her body to his, and when his tongue entered her mouth, she welcomed it, tasting, savoring, surrendering to a luscious carnality she had not felt in years. With that surrender, something seemed to unfold inside her like leaves unfurling, tight-budded roses spiraling open, or shoots pushing up through soil to reach the light. It was pleasure, and it began to hurt, but not like any pain she'd ever felt; it was a pain that came from deep inside her and spread through her body—sharp, acute, and sweet. She suddenly felt overwhelmed with joy.

It made her conscious of God's presence, and she knew it came through grace.

⊷◌⊶

When their Savannah business was completed, Nat suggested they stop at the Gibbon's estate before returning home so he could examine William's rice fields. She thought it was a great idea.

The afternoon was hot and muggy. The men headed out the door, hatless. "Are you not going to carry an umbrella, Nat?" Kitty asked.

Nat grinned at her. "Nay, Kitty. I've been too long a soldier to do that."

While the men walked over the vast fields of rice, Kitty remained in the cool house, entertained by his wife. When they returned two hours later, the four of them took refreshments together and then Nathanael and Kitty boarded the carriage for the ride to Mulberry Grove.

Nat slept through the ride, waking up with a scowl as they pulled into their lane.

"What's wrong, Nat?"

"I have a headache. Perhaps I took too much sun in the fields," he told her.

"Let's get you to bed. With a good night's sleep, it should vanish by morning."

The following morning Nathanael joined his family at breakfast but ate little. He rose to prepare his horse for a ride in the fields and promptly sank back into his chair.

Kitty's saucer eyes widened. "Do you still have pain, Nat?"

He nodded, closing his eyes. She helped him back to their bed and shut the curtains. "Sleep my darling. I shall summon the doctor." Leaning over his weary frame, she placed a soft kiss on his mouth.

Nathanael wanted to protest that it was simply sunstroke,

but found his mouth could not form the words; they came out shattered. He immediately fell into a deep sleep.

Dr. John Brickel arrived several hours later from Savannah, and saw that Nathanael's head was swollen. He applied the normal procedure of bloodletting and advised rest. Nat Pendleton arrived that evening with papers for Nathanael to sign regarding the sale of timber on Cumberland Island.

A few minutes later he went to Kitty. "I'm concerned about my friend. He does not look good." Nathanael's forehead was swollen and appeared to be inflamed.

Kitty nodded, alarm written all over her face. "No, he doesn't, and I know not what to do. The children want to go to him, and he asks for them, but I'm trying to give him as much rest as I can."

"Let me take them to Savannah for a few days. I'm sure Susan will entertain them with the city's charm," offered Nat Pendleton.

Kitty went to prepare the children's luggage, not knowing how long they would be away. Phineas offered to join them. Frightened by their father's swollen face and their mother's fear, the children cried when they kissed him goodbye.

George illustrated the Greene valor as he calmly took his father's hand. "Fear not, Papa. I will watch over my siblings. You must fight hard to get well, and then I shall bring them home to you." After leaning down to kiss his father's burning forehead, he respectfully saluted him before departing.

Kitty sent for Anthony Wayne and they took turns sitting by Nat's bedside. Anthony watched as his friend's condition deteriorated, noticing with alarm that the few words Nat was able to articulate were incoherent. His moaning stopped altogether as Nathanael lapsed into a state of unconsciousness.

"Anthony, I shall send for Nat Pendleton. We must get another doctor's opinion straight away!"

Dr. McCloud was called in as a consultant and taken into the darkened bedchamber. After bleeding Nat, he assured them that this was indeed sunstroke. "The only cure for this is total rest. Hopefully, he will come out of this and recover."

His candid words shattered Kitty, who had been remarkably resilient and courageous up to that point. Her eyes widened in genuine disbelief, fear stamped on her features. Her brain refused to engage the doctor's words.

Feeling like a butterfly trying to move through thick honey she moaned, "Oh, Anthony, I cannot bear this. "You must promise me he will recover." Her heart burst and flooded her eyes.

"We will pull him through this with our strength," he assured her. "I will rouse him with words of valor, reminding him of all he did in the war."

Kitty shook her head. She felt a dark wave of sadness slipping under the door and into her pores. It seemed so sudden and so private. Anthony wrapped his arms around her before the sob broke through. They didn't speak a word for the longest time.

Nathanael opened his eyes, looking directly at Kitty and nodding his head as if he were happy. He tried to speak, but the words would not come. Instead, his eyes spoke to her: "Kitty, you are all I ever hoped for." Then he sank against the pillow and slept.

"I do not want him to leave me, but I know he must." Covering her mouth to smother her sobs, she quietly left the room.

Nat Pendleton returned and the two soldiers stood at their friend's bedside. "How can this be sunstroke?" asked Anthony to Nat. "This man spent hours under the grueling sun, with little food, no sleep, fighting asthma, and never faltered."

"If only we had our surgeon Johnson here," General Wayne thought aloud. "He would know what to do for Nathanael."

"Nathanael is too young to give up. He's only forty-four years old, with an entire life to live," groused Nat.

General Wayne gazed at the still form of his dear friend. "Young? Our dear Nathanael sacrificed his youth and health years ago to the war. And after that, the ungrateful Congress never came to his support when he was in need."

Nat Pendleton swayed, tears clogging his throat. "And he sacrificed everything for the people."

"Do you think he has lost the will to live?" Anthony Wayne whispered, lifting his head to cautiously gauge his reaction.

Nat picked up one of Nathanael's hands as he looked down on eyes staring vacantly at him. "General Greene, squeeze my hand if you hear me," he implored.

There was no response. "Talk to me, Nathanael. Do this for Kitty and your children," he begged, his face shattering with heartbreak.

There was a long silence between the friends. Raw hurt gleamed in Anthony's eyes. "Perhaps Nat is convinced that Congress will help Kitty and the children if she became a widow."

"Nay, Anthony. I will not hear of this," whispered Nat. "Please do not speak that way."

"Our General Greene was a casualty of the war. He will never escape his internal wounds, and has already endured them for a lifetime." Sorrow ripped at Anthony's voice, leaving him helpless. His eyes were glassy with tears.

TWENTY EIGHT

JUNE 1786

Kitty sat in a chair, weeping silently. The tide of pain blocked her vision at the edges and caused the narrow tunnel of remaining sight to swim with spots. Her husband, her strongest friend and protector, lay still on the bed beside her.

Anthony Wayne had been with him, talking to him about their times together, ignoring the lack of response and the vacant eyes fixed on the ceiling above. He drifted off to sleep, but was suddenly awakened by the sound of Nathanael's erratic breathing. Glancing over at his friend, Anthony watched as he lifted his fingers from the bedding in a gentle gesture—a weak wave that said thank you and good-bye. Still holding his hand, Anthony watched in dread as his dear comrade gently slipped away.

A heavy shock settled over the room. Grief, floating through the air, came down to sit beside him. Tears ran down his face. Trembling, cradling his friend's hand, Anthony gently placed his fingers over Nathanael's eyes to close them. Then he left the room to find Kitty.

Leaving her alone with her husband, Anthony returned to the parlor, picked up Nat's quill and began to write to the many friends in Savannah.

> *My dear friend, General Greene, is no more. He was great as a soldier; greater as a citizen; immaculate as a friend. Pardon this scrawl; my feelings are but too much affected, because I have watched a great and good man die.*

That afternoon, Anthony Wayne and Nat Pendleton dressed General Nathanael Greene in full uniform, the one he had worn on formal occasions as major general of the Continental army, and covered his hands with the gloves the Marquis de Lafayette had given him. Kitty's hands trembled as she placed her gold chain and locket over his heart.

In Virginia, Martha Washington had just finished setting the supper table when George walked through the door. She remarked that he had mail in the parlor and wrapped the warm bread in a covered basket, lingering a moment before setting it on the table.

"Oh dear Lord, nooo," moaned George a few moments later. Dropping the basket, Martha rushed to his side. His face was ashen, his eyes dull and expressionless as a slow stream of tears trickled down his cheeks.

"What is it, George?" She took the letter from his shaky fingers.

Colonel Harry Lee's words blurred after she read the first sentence.

Your friend, and second, the noble General Greene, is no more. Universal grief reigns here. How hard is the fate of the United States to lose this man in the middle of life. Irreparable loss! But he is gone. I am incapable to say more!

"Why Nathanael, Lord? Why not me?" George Washington, doubled over in misery, scolded his God through his own grief. His pain would not be denied.

Martha slowly lifted his body upright and laid her head in his lap. Their anguished tears ran unobserved, and in the privacy of their home they mourned Nathanael.

༄

Nathanael Greene was dead at the age of forty-four; Kitty was thirty-two. On June 20, the day after his death, his body was placed in a coffin and carried by boat down the river to Savannah. Approaching the Savannah harbor, lines of anchored ships dropped their colors to half-mast. Business in Savannah was suspended for the day. A military guard of honor stood at attention before the large crowd gathering in front of the Nat Pendleton house. All watched in silence as the casket was lowered and carried up the steps of the bluff to the Pendleton home—where Kitty and her children were waiting.

General Nathanael Greene had helped to preserve the nation's freedom, and the nation mourned its loss. His body lay in state in the parlor until late afternoon. The funeral party carried him to the old colonial cemetery belonging to Christ Church as the band played the solemn "Death March of Saul" and artillerists on the bluff fired guns at one-minute intervals. In the absence of a clergyman, Judge William Stephens read, his voice trembling with emotion, the funeral service of the Church of England, followed by thirteen rounds of musketry. The casket was then locked in a vault. The mourners slowly withdrew.

Kitty was alone with her children, and fought valiantly to give them what little strength she still possessed. Incredibly, she did not fall apart. She was devastated, but would not expose her collapse to her children. Sleep, her defense mechanism, had always been her refuge, but she could not afford to fall back on that now. Her children needed her awake.

Her first impulse was to leave Georgia forever and return to Rhode Island, but her close friends advised her against it.

"Give yourself some time," advised Nat Pendleton gently. "It's all too sudden and we must go through Nathanael's papers and journals before making such a drastic decision."

"We never discussed the possibility of widowhood." Her voice fell to a whisper. "We never knew he would go so quickly... at least I did not. Perhaps he knew when his head pain wouldn't subside, but he couldn't tell me. And I"... Her lips trembled as she worked at words that would not come.

Susan Pendleton comforted her as she wrapped a shawl around her shivering shoulders. Kitty tried to eat but had no appetite. She felt constantly chilled as her tiny frame became more fragile. The Pendletons did everything they could to keep her from succumbing to illness.

Phineas offered to return to Mulberry Grove with the children, but they did not want to leave their mother. She forced herself to push forward and soon was strong enough to make the journey with them. Returning to the plantation, she began to prepare for the enormous task of facing their future.

Late one afternoon she set out alone, strolling through the forest toward the riverbank. The afternoon sunlight pierced holes in the evergreen canopy in rich golden shafts of angled beams. The gray carcasses of decaying trees, clumps of ferns, mats of moss, and red-capped Russula mushrooms made the woods look like a primeval place where humans were strangers.

She thought sorrowfully of the upward climb that lay ahead of her. *Oh, Nat, what would you want me to do? Please help me. I'm so frightened. Give me your strength. Show me the right words to comfort the children. This is so terribly hard for me.*

Kitty sat down on the same old oak stump where she had found Nat weeping. She knew she would have to limit her inner battles and not wrestle with demons she couldn't see. *Focus on what is in front of you,* she advised herself.

Giving in to her grief, fatigue fueled her intermittent sobs. An emotional storm rolled within her: frustration, grief, and heartbreak formed a whirlpool of contending winds.

"I have nothing to give you, God, but my own deep pain, and my own empty soul," she whispered. Tears formed rivulets down her dirt-dusted cheeks, and she wiped her nose with the hem of her skirt.

The calm arrived with such tenderness that she could only know it had come by the sudden absence of her sorrow. One moment she was trapped in suffering, and the next she was at rest in the hands of God. A gift from the invisible realm.

Kitty bowed her head. "Thank you, Lord. I can feel Your peace flowing from the well I've been digging." Sucking in a deep breath, she inhaled the briny smell of the river: ferns and lilies and rich black mud.

She rose, feeling light and comforted, and began her slow walk home. Before her sprawled a bucolic bouquet of color, with the deep green of live oaks in the distance blanching to the newer green of the wild summer grass. The darkness was gone and the boundaries she had asked for became clear.

⌍⌎⌏⌐

Kitty placed Phineas Miller in charge of the plantation's management, and began planning her late summer trip to Rhode Island. Her friend and confidant, Anthony Wayne, became the most outspoken of her advisors.

"Anthony, we're not leaving forever. I need to return to speak with the estate's co-executors and see what we can do to get Nathanael's war monies reimbursed."

"Yes, I know Kitty. But will you return? We all adore you here, and could not bear the idea that you will abandon Mulberry Grove."

She grinned. "Silly Mad Anthony. My children and I will be back in no time. Pray come by and make sure the plantation is running well. I shall leave Phineas in charge, and he will appreciate your assistance."

Anthony scowled, uncertain. He too had suffered the loss of his former commander and friend, and was mourning his loss. He begged her not to leave. In defeat, he agreed to drive her and the children to the Savannah dock and waved a dispirited good-bye as the ship set sail.

Landing in Newport, Kitty immediately found a place for them to stay. Nathanael Greene's will had been made out nine months before he died, in which he bequeathed all his real and personal property to Catharine Greene and his children on an equal basis. He appointed his wife and two close friends, Jeremiah Wadsworth of Hartford, Connecticut and Edward Rutledge of South Carolina, to be the executors of his estate. Nathanael also chose Nat Pendleton as his attorney, and as he was in Newport, he was able to meet with Kitty and Jeremiah on the following afternoon. They were forced to tell Kitty the unfortunate news.

"Sadly, Kitty, Nathanael died before beginning to pay off the huge debts he owed to his three principal creditors, one being Jeremiah." Pendleton looked over at Wadsworth before continuing. "Although your husband left behind a potential fortune in real estate, most of it was pledged as security against his indebtedness."

Kitty listened quietly, hands folded on the tabletop. After a long moment, she spoke. "Could we sell off all the lands but Mulberry Grove?"

Jeremiah shook his head. "It would not be advisable at this time. Land values are so low that whatever you received would not provide you and your family with security."

"What about the money the government owes Nathanael that he borrowed to equip his Southern army?" Kitty's shoulders tightened and she bit down on her lip.

Nat Pendleton reached over the desk to place his hand on hers. "Kitty," he said gently, "that could take years, but we will help you. I shall find a contact person in the Congress." Meeting Jeremiah's gaze head-on across the table, he added, "We both advise you to return to Georgia and support yourselves by the proceeds from the plantation crops."

Kitty closed her eyes tightly. Tears burned their way from beneath her lids. Thanking her friends, she rose smoothly and walked away, dignity gathered around her like a cloak.

Catharine "Kitty" Littlefield Greene (1755–1814). *Courtesy of Telfair Museum of Art.*

Nathanael Greene (1742–1786). *Courtesy of General Nathanael Greene Homestead Association.*

Block Island, Rhode Island. Birthplace of Kitty Littlefield Greene. *Courtesy of Rhode Island Historical Society.*

Greene home in Warwick, R.I., Nathaniel Greene's birthplace. Built in 1684 and remodeled in the 1860s. *Photo taken by author with permission from Thomas Casey Greene Jr.*

House of Governor William Greene, Warwick, R.I., built in 1680. Kitty and Nathanael Greene were married here in July 1774. *Courtesy of the Governor William Greene family.*

Wedding invitation of Nathanael Greene/Kitty Littlefield, penned by Nathanael. It hung for years in the room where they were married in the Governor William Greene home. *Courtesy of the Governor William Greene family.*

General Nathanael Greene home (Spell Hall) in Coventry, R.I., built in 1770 for his future wife. *Courtesy of the Library of Congress.*

Interior of Spell Hall in Coventry, R.I. Fireplace wall in dining room. *Courtesy of the Library of Congress.*

Earliest life portrait of George Washington, age 40. Painted by Charles Wilson Peale, 1772. *Courtesy of the Library of Congress.*

Nathanael Greene (waving hat) at the Battle of Eutaw Springs, S.C., September 8, 1781. The battle marked a decisive victory for his troops. *Courtesy of the Georgia Historical Society.*

Equestrian statue of Nathanael Greene, by Henry Kirke Brown (1877), Stanton Park, Washington, D.C. *Courtesy of the Library of Congress.*

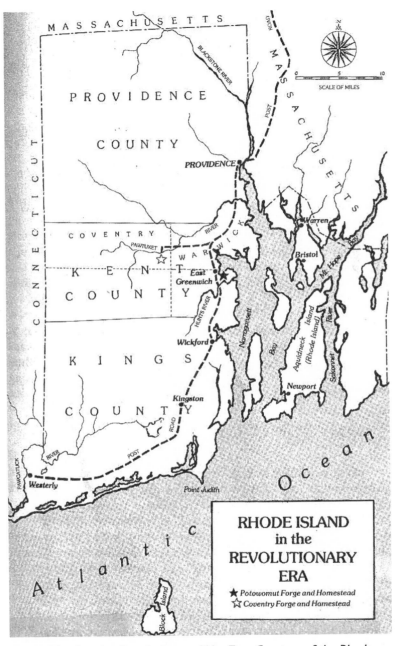

Rhode Island in the Revolutionary War Era. *Courtesy of the Rhode Island Historical Society.*

Ruins of Mulberry Grove, Savannah, GA. The plantation was gifted to Nathanael Greene for his services during the Revolutionary War. *Courtesy of the Georgia Historical Society.*

Eli Whitney (1765–1825). From an oil painting displayed in the main banking room of the First Company of Georgia. *Courtesy of the Library of Congress.*

The original Dungeness on Cumberland Island, GA. Built in 1802, measuring 76 feet tall. It burned down in 1867. *Courtesy of CUIS/NPS.*

Part 2

TWENTY NINE

1786–1787

Kitty Greene and her children sailed to New York and went on to Philadelphia to visit friends of Nathanael's. She welcomed these distractions; his friends made her feel closer to her husband. Several of them shared "Nathanael stories" that she had not heard, offering her laughter and tears. This was therapeutic and necessary for her healing.

Kitty requested a horse-drawn carriage in Philadelphia to travel to Mount Vernon and spend time with George and Martha Washington. She desperately wanted to see Martha. Taking eight-year-old Cornelia with her, Kitty drilled her daughter in etiquette and proper behavior along the way.

"Darling, remember to rise from your seat when you meet General Washington. Then curtsy, which you do so well, and stand quietly and modestly when he asks you questions."

"Yes, Mama," responded a timid Cornelia. She wondered why this was so complicated when her parents were already good friends with the Washingtons.

As always, Martha Washington welcomed them effusively and graciously, hugging Kitty to her bosom and kissing Cornelia's cheeks as she embraced her. They sat talking quietly while they waited for the tea service; soon the click of George's footsteps rang through the hall and General Washington entered the parlor, his huge smile reflecting his delight in seeing them.

Cornelia took several tiny steps toward him with the intention of making a curtsy and voicing the words her mother had taught her. But in her flustered state, the little girl dropped to her knees at his feet and burst into tears.

With a tenderness reserved for children, George picked her up and smiled warmly. "Oh my child, are you well?" he asked softly, wiping her cheeks with his own handkerchief. Within moments, he soothed her fears and led her to the seat beside her mother as if she were a princess.

Kitty related the story to many people, always with a renewed appreciation of the kindness of Nathanael's close friend.

"Why, he made her feel perfectly normal, laughing with her and telling funny stories about Nat. He rescued Cornelia from humiliation and composed her—even with my disapproving eyes scowling at her from across the room—which I thoroughly regret. Then he sat her next to him at the dining table and heaped delicious food on her plate. At that point I was beaming with pride for both of them."

Here Kitty always paused for effect. "After dinner he invited her for a walk in the garden, and she happily accepted. Later she told me he drew her into conversation about her daily life, her hopes and even her fears. They talked a lot about Nathanael, something she hadn't done much with me." Kitty had always been very fond of General Washington, yet felt humbled by his concern for them.

Martha and Kitty spent several days catching up on their lives. They discussed many subjects, including the schooling for her children, especially George, who was now eleven. George Washington had his own ideas about the boy's studies, which Kitty politely listened to, but did not finalize anything. She wanted to keep her eldest son at her side, and put the discussion out of her mind.

On the eve of her departure to Mulberry Grove, George Washington sought her out.

"Lady Greene, I want you to know that if ever you think it proper to entrust my namesake to my care, I will give him as good an education as our country could afford. I promise you I would bring him up to either of the genteel professions that his friends may choose or to those his own inclinations would lead him to pursue, at my own cost and expense."

Kitty was speechless—completely taken aback. This offer, from a man who had neglected his own affairs during the war and was already burdened with several fatherless children in his own family of nieces and nephews, was truly an act of friendship and love.

They sailed for home from Philadelphia, and Kitty spent the time mentally preparing herself to employ the role she understood so well from the war days: raising her children without the assistance of their father. She knew she needed to be a stern, yet loving, disciplinarian.

Anthony Wayne and Nat Pendleton were waiting at the landing and covered them with hugs. As they pulled up to the mansion, Kitty raised her eyes and saw the servants on the porch, grinning broadly and waving their arms as they welcomed them back home. Kitty was surprised and touched, and as she returned the wave, she felt the warm allure of optimism opening up her heart.

❧❦❧

"Phineas, please tell me honestly. Do you believe we shall make a profit this year?" asked Kitty casually, over a cup of afternoon tea.

He nodded, and sent her a slow smile. "You've been reading my mind again, Miss Kitty. I was about to tell you it looks like the rice fields will produce sufficient crops, and we shall actually make money this year."

She smiled at him. "Good. By the way, I believe the time has come for you to call me Kitty. Are you comfortable with that, Phineas?"

He met her gaze. "Yes, Kitty, I am. Thank you for your faith in me."

Phineas Miller had worked hard and capably as plantation manager. He would eventually turn the first year's loss into a profit by the end of 1787. Kitty observed him beneath her lashes and wondered what she would have done without his knowledge and assistance. Unlike Anthony Wayne, who was flamboyant and boastful, Phineas was reserved, humble and quietly strong. He seemed to be a man she could count on. His slightly crooked nose, the firm jaw line and his astonishingly blue eyes gave his face a rugged appeal.

In addition to his plantation management, he continued tutoring the children. When they read the classics, Phineas invited Kitty to join them, knowing that reading was her favorite pastime.

Although General Wayne visited frequently, Kitty was beginning to lose patience with him. *I'm getting weary of Anthony's rumored affairs, and I disdain the way he treats his wife Polly,* she thought. *It is good that he is nearby and can accompany me from time to time to social functions, but I prefer the stability of Phineas, who is kind and good with my children. What a pity he is eleven years my junior. But then again, does that really matter to me?* She giggled aloud.

Phineas looked up, puzzled. "I beg your pardon. Did you say something?" he asked.

Kitty grinned. "Lost in thought, and it was quite an amusing one." She suddenly became quiet, feeling the presence of Nathanael. Her heart felt like a soft, damaged piece of her chest, like a bruise on a peach. An immediate wave of sorrow rose from her stomach and tightened her throat.

His intense gaze made her feel as if her mind were being probed. Could he read it?

"You've built a hard shell to protect your soft heart," he told her. She gave him a quick, assessing glance, and glimpsed a flicker of compassion in his expression.

Somewhere, an owl hooted, and the rich note seemed to stretch, endlessly, like the call of a score of hunter's horns, sounding together and making the sweetest harmony. She let out a breath—a single breath so deep he thought she had held it inside for a long time.

Phineas placed his hand on top of her forearm and squeezed gently. "It is time for their lessons," he murmured, rising up from the chair. "Are you joining us?"

She shook her head. A warm flush filled her chest and cheeks. He glanced over his shoulder at her as he walked away. She was sitting perfectly still, her head bowed.

❧◎◇

Kitty wrote a series of letters of petition to the United States Congress for indemnity to recover the funds that Nathanael had paid to Charleston merchants. She kept in close contact with Edward Rutledge and Jeremiah Wadsworth, who were speaking to their Congressional contacts on her behalf. She knew that General Washington was acutely aware of her circumstances, yet she felt uncomfortable asking him about his progress, knowing he was waiting for her answer about her son's education.

Unexpectedly, she received another generous offer for the education of her son. The Marquis de Lafayette, who also had a son named after General George Washington, suggested that George be educated in France as the guest of the Lafayette household. Kitty was embarrassed by this, knowing that her estate was heavily in debt to the Marquis. But Lafayette told her he had promised Nathanael he would educate George in France if anything happened to him. The Marquis, hearing nothing from Kitty, went to Henry Knox and asked for his help.

It was early autumn and Kitty knew she must make a decision. She talked it over with Mad Anthony, who agreed she should send George to France. Surprisingly, so did Phineas, who promoted the value of living in another culture and learning French. Kitty decided to speak directly to her son.

On a warm afternoon she asked him to walk with her to the river. A breeze stirred the yellow-tipped marshes and playfully rattled the brittle brown fronds of the palms on the shoreline. Kitty and George sat on the sun-warmed wood of the dock, ground down as smoothly as marble. A dozen ducks floated atop the gentle rolls of the Savannah River, without a single quack to disturb the stillness.

"Look, Mama. Watch them bobble one by one under the water and reappear to shake themselves off." George loved the wildlife. While he loved to fish with his friends, he refused to hunt.

"It's unusually quiet on the river, isn't it, George? Except for the hum of insects and the plop or splash of a fish." Kitty closed her eyes to feel the warmth of the sun on her face, savoring the almost erotic sensation.

"George, do you remember when we moved here and I was so frightened you children would fall into the river? Yet none of you seem to harbor that fear. Has Phineas taught you to swim yet?" Her remarkable saucer eyes grilled him.

"He has certainly tried, and Patty and Cornelia picked it up quickly, but I'm such a stooge. My body is too clumsy to learn." Turning to her with a grin, he kissed her cheek. "Let not your heart be troubled, Mama. I shall eventually grasp the concept."

She turned her face toward him with a cautious smile. "I want to speak with you about a grand opportunity, my son. Our friend the Marquis has offered to send you to school in France, at his expense, for the next few years. What do you think?"

George let out a long, weary sigh, and then glanced at his mother. "What do you think, Mama?"

A new sadness took hold of her, a sadness she had to shake roughly from her body as she stood up and walked down to the river's edge. George watched her from the dock, counting the ginger-colored reeds surrounding her ankles.

Turning unexpectedly, she spoke. "I want you near me, George, but I think you should take advantage of this opportunity. Your namesake, General Washington, has also offered you an education here in America, which would keep you closer to me. Of the two offers, I believe your father would have wanted you to go to France," she said quietly, hoping to lend him encouragement.

George tried to smile, but his mouth couldn't quite manage it. "I've known about General Washington's offer, Mama, and I knew it would be around for awhile. The offer from the Marquis is a new one to me. Shall we take time to think it over? I would like to discuss it with Mr. Miller before I make a decision."

As she walked back up to the dock, she sent George a crooked grin. Taking his hand and holding it between hers, she gave him her response. "That is the answer I had hoped to hear, son. You are as wise as your father at this young age. He would be so very proud of you."

THIRTY

1788

George would be living with the Knox family in New York while the final preparations were made for his passage to Europe. He spent the last week in Georgia leaving orders about his personal belongings.

"Cornelia and Patty, you can both ride Beaux, but be careful. He gets spooked easily and can buck you off." The girls listened solemnly, taking his advice seriously.

"Natty, stay with your pony for another year and then the girls will show you how to ride the horses. I would have liked to have taught you myself, but I'll be away learning French and warfare and..."

"You shall certainly not be learning warfare," interrupted Kitty. "Not at twelve years of age!"

Louisa ran to him and threw her arms around his waist. "I want to go with you, George. Take me please," she pleaded.

Kitty knew George would leave a huge void in their home. It took all her will, and Phineas' gentle persuasion, to follow through and send him to France. Henry Knox arranged for the twelve-year-old boy to travel with a diplomat, Joel Barlow, who would leave for France in May. Henry gave him fifty dollars and saw him off at the dock, after which he wrote to Kitty.

Your lovely son embarks with all the intrepidity of a hero. I have watched the emotions of his mind on various occasions and the result is that he possesses certain traits of greatness which will anon be the pride and solace of your life.

Both Kitty and her son wrote to George Washington explaining their decision. Young George believed he would receive a better education in Europe, and his tutor agreed. Kitty, knowing France was in the throes of political upheaval, set aside her worries and deep sense of loss and supported his decision. Martha and George Washington did the same, wishing him well.

Mulberry Grove was thriving, and Kitty credited Phineas with the successful management of the plantation. He had become indispensible to her, not only in their rice business, but also as her companion and friend. She knew that tongues were wagging, especially when they decided to take the four children to Connecticut for a consultation with her adviser, Jeremiah Wadsworth. Anthony Wayne, already jealous of Phineas, learned about the trip and rushed over to Mulberry Grove to admonish her.

"Anthony, I am a free woman and will choose with whom I spend my time," she snapped back, after his covetous remark.

A muscle jerked in his jaw and his lips whitened. "Does it not bother you that you and Phineas are the subjects of gossip? Everyone believes he is your lover, and some are saying you are a loose woman. They say you pay him as a male companion as well as a business partner." In his frustration, his voice rose to an irritated shout.

Kitty was livid. Her heart thudded painfully against her rib cage, and she felt as if some kind of explosion were building up inside her. Her eyes flashed flames of anger. "I care not what they say! They have been saying the same things about you and me for years, even when Nat was alive. And that would have made me an adulteress, would it not?"

A flash of something close to pity moved quickly across her face when she read his expression. "And now, they still talk about us. You, a married man, and I? What am I? A strumpet?"

He looked stricken, and reached out for her. "Forgive me, Kitty. I speak as a spurned man. I have no right to make any demands of you." His tender gesture broke down all defenses.

Kitty knew she had just deliberately smashed the bridge that had been built between them. Deep sorrow twisted violently inside her. She shuddered under the weighty boundaries she had just drawn around herself. "Excuse me," she said in a choked whisper as she rose. He let her walk away.

৩৯৩৯

Jeremiah Wadsworth was in New York attending a session of the Congress, of which he was now a member. During the summer of 1788 Kitty took her four remaining children and Phineas to Wethersfield, Connecticut, where they rented a cottage. Relieved to be free of the southern humidity, they found the heat up north to be almost as stifling. Wadsworth was her only ready source of income until her Mulberry Grove crops were harvested in the fall. Also, as principal creditor and co-executor of Nat's estate, he held a great deal of power over Kitty and her children. She turned to Phineas for advice.

"Phineas, he may not be here to help us with our immediate problems, but he is in a position to personally present my indemnity position to the Congress. On Jeremiah's back depends our future: whether we will live like common beggars or live comfortably in the style I've known and desire. I intend to earn his devotion and generosity through my letters, since I am unable to speak to his face."

Phineas knew she had already sold her phaeton and most of her furniture to pay her creditors a portion of what they owed. She was beginning to lose heart. He could not bear to see that, so he traveled to Hartford to procure a bill to send to New York. If that failed, she would be forced to ask Jeremiah Wadsworth to send her some spending money.

Kitty had not heard from her son George since he left for France. She used that excuse to ask Jeremiah Wadsworth to write to her when he knew that George arrived safely, including her veiled plea for "just a bit of money" in that same letter.

I would thank you to send me two or three hundred dollars by some safe conveyance. I wish to have the money to get us a little furniture…the children are delighted with the books you had the goodness to send. I have thought it best to set them up one by one as a prize in the school room in hopes it will have a better effect than acquiring what they want so easily. Natty says if he had a bag of marbles he would study hard for them.

When Wadsworth did not travel to Connecticut to see her, she told him she had thoughts of going directly to New York to argue her case before Congress, and that she would meet him there.

You do know that Nathanael, realizing his soldiers were without proper protection from winter, risked his fortune and future, and his family's happiness to relieve them. Can Congress know this and be deaf to the miseries of the widow? No, I will not believe mankind so ungrateful, so unjust—I ask no favors but justice. It shall never be said of me that I set myself down quietly and waited for my ruin. I am a woman—unaccustomed to anything but the trifling business of a family. Yet my exertions may affect something. We should do very well, I feel, if our land on Cumberland Island were sold and if my appeal for aid to the Congress is heard. If not, and if I sacrifice my life in the cause of my children, I shall but do my duty, and follow the example of my illustrious husband.

Jeremiah encouraged her visit to New York, but advised her not to appear personally before Congress. He was not willing to be publically associated with her because he was already implicated in one scandal. One of his "so-called" lovers, Elizabeth Whitman, was found dead in a hotel room along with her deceased newborn baby, a pair of forceps and a probe. Besides Jeremiah, several other men were suspected of having relations with Miss Whitman, and the father was unknown.

Jeremiah Wadsworth would not take any chances, and met Kitty secretly at his quarters to discuss her business affairs. At the end of the meeting, he took her to dinner, after which he invited her to stay with him.

"Kitty, I want you to stay the night here with me. I have your best interests in mind at all times, and would do anything for you." His warm voice gave her confidence.

Kitty vacillated. She knew he held remarkable control over her family and her life and resented it. At the same time, she realized her feelings for him were strong, and she yearned to be desired and cherished by someone.

She studied him with serious eyes. He saw a spark of fire, then a flicker of acceptance. He held her gaze until he could see the slow rise of heat that turned her cheeks a becoming shade of pink. Her expression softened and she sighed heavily, sinking back into the sofa.

When Jeremiah lifted her chin to look into her eyes, she arched her back and drew him to her.

⁕

Kitty and Jeremiah spent nearly a week together in New York. He was extremely jealous of both Anthony Wayne and now Phineas Miller, simply because they had traveled to Connecticut together. Kitty finally convinced him that they were not having an affair, but Jeremiah wanted sole possession of her, to the point of requesting her to give up her male friends. She told him she would not do that.

They compromised when Kitty agreed to leave Natty, now eight years old, in the Wadsworth household with the understanding that Jeremiah would oversee his education. This would give them legitimate occasions to spend time with each other. Wadsworth also agreed to pay the school fees for Patty and Cornelia in a fashionable school in Bethlehem, Pennsylvania—The Moravian Young Ladies Seminary. The school had a reputation for fostering moral growth and self-discipline in addition to intellectual development, and this was enough to convince Kitty to leave her young daughters there. With a heavy heart and a brave smile, she kissed her three children goodbye, and sailed south with only her youngest child Louisa and her business manager Phineas.

Kitty disembarked at Charleston to attend to estate business while Phineas and Louisa sailed to Mulberry Grove. She was a guest in the Edward Rutledge house, and for three weeks held daily conferences with Edward, the estate's co-executor. Kitty admired Edward and his brother John as political figures of eminence. Because they had received their legal education in England, the brothers had fought hard against the radicals who wanted to sever all ties with their mother country, but Edward eventually changed his position and voted for resolutions favoring the Declaration of Independence. He was the youngest man to sign the document, signing his name just below the "J" of John Hancock.

Edward appeared older than his forty years. He was of medium height, a little heavy and partially bald. His snow-white hair was curled over his neck, and he limped painfully because of the arthritis he acquired during his year's captivity by the British. Yet even though he suffered, he was a cheerful man—pleasant and serene. Kitty liked him very much, and often said he was the one man she knew who best bestowed sympathy and relief to others.

What Kitty especially liked about him was the fact that he was never in awe of her. Charmed by her personality, he regarded her as a friend, and understood his job was to advise her. He was also totally in love with his wife Henrietta Middle-ton. He knew about Kitty's conflicting interests with regard to Wadsworth, and often disagreed with Wadsworth's counsel because of that.

Kitty wrote to Wadsworth about the "ladies of rank" who visited her; most of them belonged to the city's tight society who seldom visited anyone outside their own noble families. She mentioned they had snubbed Lucy Knox during her visit to the city. Understanding his jealousy of Phineas Miller, she wrote him: *Do not be unhappy. Pray do not. You have not the reasons you suppose. I wish you a Merry Christmas and send you a kiss to convince you of it. Kiss the dear children for me whom I love so. God bless you again and again.* Only Kitty knew the pain she suffered knowing he would spend Christmas with his wife, and her children, but not with her.

THIRTY ONE

1789

The last week of 1788 was not pleasant for Kitty. She spent it alone aboard a schooner, on her return voyage to Georgia. Greatly relieved to finally reach Savannah by the first of 1789, she stepped off the ship and embraced the balmy weather. Nat Pendleton invited her to rest in their home, but she declined, anxious to see her child and Phineas.

Unpleasant news awaited her in the form of a letter from Edward Rutledge. Disgusted by Jeremiah Wadsworth's recent letter to him, he enclosed it in his letter to Kitty.

Wadsworth is very anxious about the estate, and not a little about his own situation. He requests a payment for what he advanced to you... We shall prevent his being called on in the future, to advance any more for the children.

The following day Kitty received her own letter from Jeremiah stating that his wife had been questioning his correspondence from her. Barely averting disaster and coming up with a feeble explanation to give her, he told Kitty he would burn all her letters.

Kitty had a swift response prepared for him.

My Dear Friend,   *January 31, 1789*
I am grieved to find you are so distressed in your circumstances—and hope by the time this reaches you, you will have received such remittances as will relieve you. I have sent you the very first of the crop as you desired. I hope you have

nothing to fear from the advances made for the children—
for while I live you cannot possibly suffer. I will take care
that you are paid every farthing due you. I have property,
and power, sufficient to secure you—and you know my pride
would not permit me to suffer you or your children to be
wronged for mine...

You say in your private letter that you were nearly
involved in a serious misfortune...I thought my letters were
burnt long since. You say you are unhappy because you never
expected to see me again. I told you before I left you, that it
depended on yourself alone. I still consider myself as a kind
of ambassador—liable to be recalled by my sovereign—but
tell me seriously, did you for one moment of your life think of
coming to Georgia to see me?

Tell Natty his Mama will write him as soon as he can read
her letter—and tell him also that his heifer had 3 calves—all
marked for him as shall be the increase. You have no reason
for the jealousy you mention—I give you my word.

Kitty Greene

The deep attachment Kitty felt for Jeremiah had begun years ago, during her isolated months in New England while Nat was fighting in the South. This same connection inspired Rhode Island rumormongers to call her an adulteress. Isaac Briggs quietly investigated this gossip and found it to be false. Now she feared she was losing Jeremiah, as she had lost the blind adoration of Mad Anthony, due to her own impertinent actions. While Nathanael was alive, she told Isaac that her one redeeming virtue was keeping her passions "within due bounds." At this point in her life, she saw no reason to exert her prior restraint, and decided to apply the full powers of her charm to achieve her means.

Analyzing the situation, she studied the four men closest to her. Three were married, and Nat Pendleton was a friend and advisor. Kitty admired his wife Susan, but also envied her, at times seeing her as a formidable rival. When Nat paid loving attention to Susan in Kitty's presence, she felt jealous because she did not have a man who displayed such admiration to her. The other married men, Anthony and Jeremiah, did not bring their wives into society with them, yet still could not act out their feelings for Kitty publicly, and this upset her.

That left Phineas. Kitty knew he had harbored strong feelings for her for a while. Perhaps it was time to act on those feelings.

⌒☉⌒

It was a cold and dreary February afternoon when Kitty invited Phineas to join her on a walk to the river. As they entered the forest, she was acutely aware of the bare trees against the landscape—more conscious of them than ever before. Intrigued by their exposed and intricate lines, she pointed out to him that they had taken on a beauty of their own.

"Phineas, look at the fine details in the color and formation of the branches, only recently hidden beneath lush plumes of leaves," she said. "Look how they stand out against the sky."

They stood in silence and watched through the stark branches as the sunset slid down to the water. Phineas took her arm and led her to the bank overlooking the river—shining in a moss-green tint. Depending on the time of year, Kitty saw color changes from brown to gray to green, even silver—subject to the light framing it. A fine column of mist rose over the river, as thick as the smoke of a fire.

Kitty shuddered, wrapping her cloak tighter around her shoulders. Phineas smiled softly and drew her small hand into his.

"Would you like to return to the hearth?" he asked thoughtfully.

Kitty shook her head. "No, this is lovely, and I enjoy sharing it with you." She tipped her head back and smiled up at him. He cautiously lifted a hand to her face. Through the mist, her blue-green eyes seemed to flicker. Then she looked away, eyes downcast.

"Do you consider me extremely complicated?" she asked

hesitantly. "I realize I have not adapted well to this transition from having a family and money to losing both."

Choosing his words carefully, he answered. "Kitty, your ability to adapt is far more dangerous to you than to any of us. Take heed that you do not continue adapting until nothing of you remains."

Kitty nodded, gazing at him. "I want to see a balance between doing and being in my life. Someone told me to quiet myself frequently to store food for my soul. Do you believe that, Phineas?"

He brought his hand around the back of her head and bent down. She saw sadness and earth in his eyes—a man far too deep to be concerned about surface thoughts—and she understood he wanted her as she was. His hands tilted her chin up and she studied his strong face. Her eyes fluttered and closed as he dropped the lightest of kisses across her lids, causing her to tremble when she realized he was kissing away the traces of fallen tears.

Then he found her lips. Kitty sensed his deep moral reluctance giving itself up to her more powerful need for him. Her lips were moist and slightly parted in surprise. At the first gentle touch of his mouth, the ground beneath her feet fell away. She felt both of them being swept away together and held on for dear life, as if only the contact of their mouths could keep her in this time and place. Kitty kissed him back, passionately, greedily, feeling as though she were stealing the kiss.

Hearing her soft gasp, Phineas' heart raced. He dug his fingers into her hair, kissing her again, stroking her hair with a gesture that was at once protective and gentle.

Searching his eyes, Kitty broke into a soft laugh. "Oh Phineas, I am so happy we have finally taken this step. It will make the rest of the evening much more relaxing."

He enjoyed hearing her laugh, liking the unfettered energy of her laughter. It felt contagious.

They strolled back to the house, hand in hand. Kitty felt the soft, velvety air on every inch of her skin and shared with him that it was as if a great, airless white calm had settled over her, like a canning jar over a lightning bug.

He nodded and grinned, squeezing her hand. "Kitty, I believe great changes in our lives happen so deeply and silently we don't even know when they occur. I too am feeling timeless, almost suspended in air." He stopped and pulled her to him, holding her face between his hands. "And the dream I've held for so long has finally been fulfilled today."

ↄ◉ⵙ

Kitty followed the news coming out of Philadelphia. The members of the Constitutional Convention had signed the United States Constitution there on September 17, 1787, and shortly after, the Constitutional Convention convened in response to the dissatisfaction with the Articles of Confederation and the need for a strong centralized government. After four months of secret debates and many compromises, the proposed Constitution was submitted to the states for approval. Although the vote was close in some states, the Constitution was eventually ratified and the new Federal government came into existence in early 1789.

During the previous summer, Martha Washington wrote Kitty she knew her husband's involvement would not end with the ratification. The Federalists, adherents of the Constitution, wanted General Washington for president—an office to be held for four years. Both he and Martha believed it should be for someone else; he had certainly done his share for the new country and was happy taking care of his Mount Vernon. George dreaded the notion that some would say he supported the Constitution to gain the office of president for himself; every part of him despised self-interest. Kitty selfishly wanted George to hold the position, knowing that with her friend as president, her pleas to Congress for Nathanael's overdue funds were more likely to be heard.

The states began selecting their electors for the first presidential election in November, 1788. Martha wrote that the reports were overwhelming in her husband's favor. When the votes were counted on April 6, 1789, Martha's dreams of them "growing old in solitude and tranquility together" were no longer possible. General George Washington officially became President George Washington on April 14, 1789 and headed off to New York City, the temporary capital of the United States.

Martha sent Kitty a copy of President Washington's inaugural prayer.

Almighty God, we make our earnest prayer that Thou wilt keep the United States in Thy Holy protection. That Thou wilt incline the hearts of the citizens to cultivate a spirit of obedience, and to entertain a brotherly affection and love for one another, as fellow citizens. May we be pleased to do justice, to love mercy, and to conduct ourselves in charity, humility, and gentle temper of mind, which were the characteristics of the Divine author of our blessed religion, and without whose humble example we can never hope to be a nation. Grant us our supplication through Jesus Christ our Lord. Amen.

The first president of the United States wrote in his diary: *About ten o'clock I bade adieu to Mount Vernon, to private life, and to domestic felicity.* He was inaugurated on April 30, 1789—ready to begin the next season of his life.

THIRTY TWO

1789

Anthony Wayne missed Kitty and their formerly close relationship. He continued to champion her cause in Congress, and even though he was living away from his Georgia plantations, his heart remained in Georgia. He had heard the rumors of Kitty's new love interest—Phineas—and although he had expected it, it pained him greatly.

Addressing the House of Representatives, General Wayne fought for her petition, telling them he was "a witness to the pressing necessity that compelled Nathanael to become the surety for the debts at Charleston and that Nathanael would never have offered in a claim to Congress but upon the purest principles of honor and justice."

Two years later, when his election from Georgia to the House of Representatives would prove to have been the most fraudulent in the history of the new republic, Kitty did not desert him as many others did. In a letter to her attorney Nat Pendleton, she wrote of Mad Anthony's downfall.

And I can tell you this for a truth—that had your wishes not been successful, I would have been, with my children, an object of charity. Thank God General Wayne kept his seat long enough to do me the most essential of services...it is to his exertions, that I owe my small amount of independence.

Phineas and Kitty lived together in harmonious ease. He loved her deeply, but realized the time for marriage had not yet arrived. He knew she would not marry him until she received

Nathanael's debt payment from the Congress. He also understood that her compelling infatuations with other men were a part of her spirit. It was he who welcomed her home each night with kind words and open arms.

Jeremiah Wadsworth, still married, was in no position to pursue a competitive courtship, and found the situation of his involvement with Kitty intolerable. He knew he could see her only a week or two each year, after which she would return to Mulberry Grove and to the youthful Phineas Miller.

There were other men who found Kitty's charms and beauty irresistible, and she made sure that Phineas and Jeremiah were aware of their interest. An aristocratic French planter, the Marquis de Montalet, moved to a nearby Savannah River plantation and quickly found his way to the lovely Lady Greene's home. When he began to make serious propositions to her, she decided he was seeking another fortune and rebuked his efforts, telling him she loved another: Phineas Miller.

Still Kitty led Wadsworth on, writing him that she would return to New York and appear personally before Congress. He discouraged her, but this time Edward Rutledge firmly disagreed.

Wadsworth may think the business can be done as well by a petition whilst the humble petitioner is a thousand miles off, but he is mistaken. The effects of personal application, with justice, humanity, and gratitude on your side are wonderful. They ought to be irresistible.

Rutledge suggested that Alexander Hamilton draw up her new petition. He offered to accompany her to New York, but later withdrew his proposal when his wife Henrietta objected. In mid-summer Kitty, accompanied only by little Louisa and a nurse, sailed north. Her son Natty and Jeremiah Wadsworth awaited them at the dock in New York. Natty welcomed her with enthusiasm; Wadsworth offered her a chilly reception, confirming her suspicion that their relationship was drawing to an end.

☙⊙ᘐ☙

Kitty divided her time between her cousin Sammy Ward's home on Broadway and Henry Knox's home a few blocks away. President and Martha Washington were living in a rented house on the corner of Cherry and Franklin Streets and Kitty was invited to dinner several days after she arrived.

A stream of visitors, wanting to catch a glimpse of the former commander-in-chief crowded the home, but George always made time for Kitty and Natty. She liked watching him attend to the public as she and Martha sat in the parlor, talking over tea. Always dressed in a dark black velvet suit, a pair of immaculate white gloves and a polished sword at his side, President Washington struck an elegant figure. Kitty noticed that his powdered hair was now gathered in a silk bag on his neck.

Martha enjoyed having Kitty on hand for the Thursday state dinners. Lady Washington sat at the head of the table, her husband on her left and Kitty on her right. Kitty was the belle of the ball with her outlandish stories of Revolutionary camp days, and provided laughter and levity to the guests.

After dinner the ladies would retire to the drawing room on the second floor while the president conversed with the men in the dining area. George preferred to spend the last part of the evening with Lady Greene, Martha and the other female guests.

One evening President Washington lingered until everyone departed and turned to Kitty. "Stay a moment, Kitty, if you will. I would like to ask you some questions."

Kitty nodded and smiled, anticipating information on her petition to Congress.

"I've read your latest appeal—the one Henry Knox and Alexander Hamilton assisted you with. It is well-written and the legal acumen is excellent." He smiled gently and added, "And your feminine charms steal through your words, but I am afraid you do have a number of deaf subjects to preach to."

"But Mr. President, I am certain your words would give it a boost, or in the very least, grab their attention. Am I correct?" Kitty was confused by his statement.

Martha interjected. "He can and has helped you, dear Kitty. But we do not want to give you false hopes. This petition may take some time and try your patience."

Kitty shuddered. Her silky thick hair swayed as she shook her head. "Time and patience I have not," she countered. "My family must pay our enormous debts, we must eat, and . . ."

"There is another issue I should like to address, Kitty." George Washington reached across the table, placing his fingers lightly on her forearm. "It has to do with your living with Phineas Miller as a married woman, without the benefit of marriage."

Her eyes flickered; someone not knowing her well could have missed the shock that widened her pupils for just a fraction of a second. She felt raw. She still had wounds.

"People talk. Tongues wag about you and your flock of infatuated men." Martha considered her next words. "Kitty, you know we truly care about you and your family. We only wish you happiness and security, and as your older friends, we feel an obligation to advise you," added Martha kindly.

Kitty felt the sadness bubble up in her spirit. "I love Phineas, and the others do not matter," she whispered. Finding her strength, she added. "But I cannot marry Phineas until Nathanael's debts have been paid to me by the Congress." Seeking their eyes, she continued. "You know as well as I, that as a married woman I would receive nothing. It would all go to Phineas."

"Do you not trust him? Would he betray you with Nathanael's money?" George's face was closed; his thoughts unreadable.

Kitty nodded her head. "Yes, I do trust him. But this is Nat's battle, and should be fought by his widow." After a moment she looked up. "Then, and only then, will I turn to Phineas and hope for the privilege of accepting his marriage proposal." A hint of a smile flickered on her face.

President Washington lifted his fingers from her forearm and smiled as Martha pressed Kitty into an all-inclusive embrace. Then he wrapped an arm around her shoulder and guided her to her carriage, handing her over with a warm smile and a sweeping bow.

THIRTY THREE

1789–1791

Kitty and Lucy Knox rekindled their thirteen-year-old friendship, bonding in the social whirl of New York City. Both women loved the theatre, and were thrilled when President Washington invited them to enjoy the plays from his presidential box at the Johns Street Theatre. His personal secretary, Tobias Lear, became a new admirer and a devoted friend, captivated by Kitty's intellect. Lucy hosted a sizable Saturday night dinner party at her four-story mansion on Broadway, and Tobias Lear was seated at Kitty's left. The evening was a consummate success, and after the guests departed, Kitty and Lucy lingered at the hearth, sharing memories of the first time they explored the city together.

"Do you recall how excited and shocked we were at our early discoveries in New York?" asked Lucy. "What year was that, do you remember?"

Kitty nodded. "Yes, it was 1776, and your husband's headquarters was just down the street. We would sneak out during the late afternoon, slip through the alleys and doors where we had no business, a bit frightened because it was during the course of the British siege, but we thought we were immortal. Imagine our cheekiness!" They giggled together at the enjoyable reminiscence.

"Lucy, do you ever tire of the social whirl?"

Her friend nodded. "I do. But with you here, it has taken on a new light. And you?"

Kitty dropped her eyes. "To be perfectly truthful, I no longer revel in the things I did before. I require more peace and less activity now." She smiled placidly. "Due to my continuous fear of the future, I find my frivolity has been diminished. Please forgive me, because I will always remain grateful for your friendship."

"Now now Kitty. This too shall pass. Your petition will be resolved, and soon Henry and I shall visit you in Georgia at your lovely plantation."

During the course of this visit, Kitty felt humiliated and then angered by Jeremiah Wadsworth's indifference. He not only neglected to help her get her petition into the right hands, but he totally ignored her in social situations. She spent her time doting on Natty, taking him with her to visit Patty and Cornelia in Pennsylvania—a journey that brought her renewed sadness at the realization of the state of her crumbling family. She hastily decided to leave her son in the same neighborhood where his sisters lived, enrolling him in a nearby school, so the siblings could spend time together. Alone and unhappy with societal amusements, she made her preparations to return to Georgia. But she resisted actually booking her vessel without collecting more information on her status with the Congress.

In late November she received a letter from Nat Pendleton urging her to stay up north. But Kitty could no longer bear to be away from Phineas and the others who encouraged her, and finally set sail for Charleston. She needed to speak with Edward Rutledge and was surprised to find Nat Pendleton also in the office when she arrived. Her two advisors boisterously differed in their advice, and finally Nat insisted that she and Louisa return to Georgia with him in time for Christmas.

Phineas was thrilled with her return, showing her how much he missed her with his loving attitude. One day later, a letter from Jeremiah Wadsworth arrived with new bills attached. In her anger and frustration, Kitty wrote him her feelings.

I am extremely hurt by your recent behavior. It is not all fair play between you and myself. Or you are not the man I have taken you for. Some persons, I suspect, have poisoned your mind against me—pray tell me. Something whispers to me that I shall live to convince you I have acted honestly to you and that you will repent your unkind suspicions of me. To describe to you the continued torments I feel on account of my debts is impossible. To reflect that my friends are suffering inconvenience on my account makes it doubly cutting.

In early 1790, Kitty Greene, who hated sea travel, was on the high seas once again, sailing northeast to renew her efforts for Nathanael's claim and visit her children. She was also impatient to bask in the society of New York. Implausibly, she made up her mind to once again become involved.

"Darling Phineas, I hate to abandon you and Louisa here in Georgia, but this shall be a fast visit. She is doing well with her studies and I can leave assured that all will go well in your capable hands."

Kitty now considered the ordinary in Phineas beautiful: the curved shoulders now looked muscular, and the wave of black hair on his collar was not too long but followed the contour of his ears. She stroked his face. "I will miss you, Phineas. Your soul has made you unique and very dear to me."

A slow smile spread across his face. He opened his arms and folded them around her as she rested her head against his chest.

"Go in peace, Kitty. Surely you will return with excellent news from the Congress, and we will celebrate your victory."

⊷⊙⊛⊶

On February 4, 1790, Mad Anthony Wayne penned a letter to Kitty, now on her way to New York, from his plantation in Georgia. He had returned to Georgia for an extended stay, and was now forced to watch her leave him again. Although deeply hurt by her actions, he had a favor to ask of her.

I am making my arrangements to leave the plantation, from a conviction that we shall have a very serious Indian war

soon. I have solicited the President for a commission. I must
therefore ask you to become my advocate with the President
and your other friends in power when a favorable opening is
offered, and you will well know how to time it.

When Kitty received the letter, she knew she would respond
and make the proper recommendations to her friends. Sadly,
she also realized she must end the friendship, and wrote him
her reasons.

Kitty was staying with her cousin Sammy Ward in Manhattan, but even her family members were unable to cheer her
up. Seemingly in a constant state of grievance, she wrote letter
after letter of complaint to her friends and allies. To her advisor and attorney, Nat Pendleton, she grumbled that she had
only received two short notes from him in several weeks.

> *I could tell you many things, but not one word will you glean*
> *from me, nor would I write you now but from the ill-natured*
> *hope that I may interrupt you in some favorite reflection or*
> *amusement. I know not whether I ought to send my love to*
> *Mrs. Pendleton, who no longer treats me well. The President*
> *has given me his picture, with his and Mrs. Washington's hair:*
> *the most flattering proof of their friendship and affection. Oh,*
> *I forgot momentarily my anger, or I would not have told you*
> *this, but do not take it as a mark of forgiveness. Give my love*
> *to your son, 'tho I care not about the rest of you.*

Kitty's emotions surprised her at a party when she encountered Nat Pendleton's wife Susan, who was in town visiting
her father. Susan showed her a loving letter she had received
from Nat, causing Kitty to feel that her heart had been pierced
by a sword. Kitty wrote him that same night.

> *I have reflected some time to determine what I should write to*
> *you—when I tell you that Mrs. Pendleton this very evening*
> *has shown me your letter, you will account for this contention*

of passions—yet what right have I to have any passions about it? I have the strongest wish that you were here in my room. We should have an uninterrupted tete-a-tete ... I should look disdainfully at you, quarrel with you, and perhaps complain a little. I am rambling.

The papers containing additional evidence in the claim against Congress have not arrived and I shall lose every advantage this session—and another evil I shall suffer by it is that you are not here. I shall not see you, the Lord only knows when. I will write again tomorrow if the vessel does not sail. God bless you,

Catharine Greene.

Kitty returned to Mulberry Grove via Charleston in November. Edward Rutledge advised her to sell the Cumberland Island property. He reminded her that her property continued to be vandalized and trespassers were taking over her lands, yet she refused, stating that one day she would live there.

While in Charleston, just before her return to Georgia, she wrote to Jeremiah Wadsworth, encouraging him to take action on her claim. He would not budge. When she complained to Rutledge, he was furious and told her to insist that Wadsworth fix a specific date to open the proceedings.

Alexander Hamilton wrote her that he learned General Greene had not notified Congress when he endorsed the notes of John Banks in South Carolina. He feared this might present a problem, and signed off the letter with the words: *I love you too well not to be very candid with you.*

In May of 1791, Kitty and everyone else at Mulberry Grove were in a state of excitement. President George Washington was on his way to Savannah, on the last leg of an extended southern tour, and would make a stopover at Kitty's plantation. On May 12, shortly before dinner, word reached them that the President had embarked on the Savannah River at Purysburg, South Carolina, several miles above Mulberry Grove. He was expected to arrive within the hour.

Little Louisa, now seven years old, rushed down to the landing, with Kitty and Phineas following close behind her. As soon as Louisa sighted the vessel, she jumped up and down, waving and shouting, "Hello Mr. President. We are waiting for you!" Kitty's heart swelled at her daughter's happy spirit.

Kitty was dressed to receive royalty and stood tall and elegant, her face flushed with contentment. Phineas, standing to one side, held on to Louisa's hand. The servants stood a few feet behind them. Inside the barge-like vessel, rowed by nine ship captains, sat the President and his staff—all eminent Patriots of the Revolution—including the Honorable Noble Wymberly, Colonel Joseph Habersham, the Honorable John Houston, General Lachlan McIntosh, the Honorable Joseph Clay, and General Anthony Wayne. No one realized the moment might be awkward for Kitty or Anthony.

The oarsmen were dressed in light blue jackets, black satin breeches, white silk stockings, and round hats with black ribbons, bearing the inscription *"Long live the President."* The President stepped ashore, into the affectionate embrace of the widow of his strongest officer in the Revolution. For sixteen years they shared their common love of Nathanael, and now they would honor him at his home.

President Washington and his staff were treated to an elaborate dinner banquet—a long-awaited respite from his arduous schedule of interminable speeches and state dinners. Kitty noted with pleasure that Phineas' conversation was sought out by the President, and she saw that General Wayne was polite and respectful to him as well. When the meal was finished, the President and Kitty retired to the parlor, where they spoke privately about their lives, their hopes, and her indemnity claim.

"I can only opine, dear Kitty, as I have no resolution to share. In my judgment, you will win this petition. I only wish I could tell you when."

Kitty answered with a smile in her voice. "Will you stay on in New York, Mr. President? I have heard word that the seat of government will be transferred to Philadelphia."

"It is in the process of determination, but I believe it will come to fruition before the year's end."

He met her eyes without flinching. "Kitty, I cannot tell you how much it has meant to me to come to your home, meet your Phineas, and see little Louisa again. I only wish our Nathanael were here to show me around his property, as he once told me he would do."

Biting down on her lip, she closed her eyes tightly. Tears burned their way from beneath her lids. "He is here, George, with us in this very room. I can feel it." Kitty spoke with a quiet conviction.

The President looked upward and through the windowpane. "So can I, Kitty." His voice cracked. He stood up, straightened his shoulders, and saluted General Greene's memory. "You have kept your word, Quaker preacher."

THIRTY FOUR

1791–1792

George Washington promised Kitty he would return to dine again with her when he left Savannah. The President and his party arrived early Sunday afternoon by land. The lead chariot of the caravan was pulled by four horses and held the President, his valet de chamber, two footmen, four saddle horses, a coachman and a postillion. The chariot was white with ornate designs of the four seasons painted on the doors, the front and the back; the framework and the springs were gilded. Following this carriage was a two-horse baggage wagon, bordered by four outriders dressed in their gay livery of red and white.

Kitty and her small family welcomed George Washington at the front door of her plantation.

Grinning broadly, George embraced her and exclaimed, "The drive through the arch of moss-covered oak trees was delightful. The afternoon sun enshrined your home in streams of majestic light. It was a vision of glory, sent to us from the Master above."

Suddenly Louisa appeared at his side. "I have a gift for you, Mr. President," she grinned. Opening her small hand, she presented him with a tiny frog.

His eyes twinkled as the frog leapt from her tiny palm. "Splendid! I like frogs ever so much," George beamed, scooping it up from the ground. "Let us put him in a small container with holes to breathe, shall we?" Louisa nodded and dashed away to find a small jar.

The entourage stayed for the mid-day dinner and rested

several hours. When they departed in the direction of Augusta, Georgia, the hosts and servants lined up to wave good-bye. The silent isolation of the wilderness pervaded once again over Mulberry Grove.

⌾⌾⌾

Kitty sailed to Philadelphia, now the seat of government, in December, 1791 to resume her plea for Nat's estate. She went directly to the Washingtons' dwelling, a large home on High Street, as their guest. It was the same house where she and Nathanael had visited the Benedict Arnolds years ago.

With the President's assistance, Kitty was granted an audience with the State House. For several hours she stood before Secretary Alexander Hamilton and his subordinates, defending her petition. There were dozens of affidavits, including a sworn statement by John Banks (that Nathanael had forced him to sign) officially stating that he had never been in partnership with the general. There were also several of Nat's letters, statements signed by Henry Knox, former South Carolina Governor John Mathews, Generals Anthony Wayne and Benjamin Lincoln, Colonel William Washington and others. Many of these certifications were witnessed by Nat Pendleton, and all were in support of Kitty's cause.

Hamilton approved the petition with the following statement: *Although Nathanael Green technically erred in signing his promissory notes without the government's authority, his family must not be allowed to suffer poverty in consequence.* He forwarded this to the House of Representatives for congressional action.

Kitty formulated a new plan. Her long-time friend Anthony Wayne was a member of Congress as a representative from Georgia. She had seen him only once since her final letter to him, but had since learned that he was a very unhappy man, unable to rise above the terrible darkness that settled over his spirit. This despair began with Nathanael Greene's death, intensified when he lost Kitty's friendship, and progressed to a state of heavy despondency. Learning of the depth of his misery from George and Martha Washington, Kitty decided to make amends, beginning by asking for his forgiveness.

She went to him and they spent an entire afternoon in conversation.

"Anthony, what about your family?" she inquired.

"I've severed ties with them. I chose not to attend my daughter's wedding here in Philadelphia," he answered. "I no longer write to or see my wife."

The fire was dying. Anthony rose to put a couple of logs on the embers, stirring it with a poker.

"I am so sorry, Anthony. After all you've been through, I am truly saddened by your words." She reached over to take his hand. "What has happened to your son?"

"Ay, Kitty. I saw him and raked him over the coals for not finishing his education. He's gone from my life now, too." The reflection of the flames danced in the depths of his eyes.

She shook her head as her eyes filled. "But your friends helped you pick up the pieces when they elected you to Congress. I am sorry I was not one of them." Wiping away a tear, she told him, "When you needed me, I was not there for you. Forgive me, my dear Anthony."

Her words brought a smile to his lips, tinged with sadness. "Why are you here, Kitty?" he asked, vulnerability portrayed in his eyes. Kitty could not bear his expression of unhappiness.

"First, to ask for forgiveness.Secondly, to ask for your help."

Taking both of her hands in his, he smiled. "You are forgiven, my friend. For Nathanael, for you and for me. Now tell me how I can help you."

She told him. She gave him something worthwhile to fill his time, and consequently, he was able to crack his apathy. He now had a purpose to fulfill. He proposed a resolution in her behalf, speaking in favor of her and Nat's family, and spent days rounding up votes in her support. This was the one distinguishing feature of his career as a congressman. Singlehandedly, Anthony

Wayne did for Kitty in several months what Jeremiah Wadsworth should have done years before.

During this time, a movement in Georgia, instigated by her own lawyer Nat Pendleton, was underfoot to unseat Wayne in the House of Representatives because of the fraudulent nature of his election. James Jackson, the man who lost his congressional post to Wayne, appeared on the floor of the House to plead his case and lead the impeachment proceedings against Wayne.

Kitty watched in sorrow as this unfolded. Jackson was known to oppose her appeal, and if he brought Wayne down, she knew her cause was doomed. Her heart ached for Anthony, who had worked so hard for her and would now certainly succumb once again to depression.

In mid-March the resolution to unseat Wayne was brought to a vote, and by unanimous acclaim of all fifty-eight members present, was passed. A resolution was offered that, if voted upon, would give Wayne's vacated seat to Jackson. For five days, arguments were heard. Kitty was too distressed for solace. She and Anthony waited out the verdict together; it was the least she could do for him.

On March 21, word came that the House was deadlocked, twenty-nine to twenty-nine. The tie would be broken by the Speaker's vote. Kitty prayed, alone and with Anthony. She prayed with Martha and George Washington. She could hardly breathe when the final message arrived that the deciding ballot was against Jackson. A new election would be held in Georgia to replace the unseated Wayne.

There was hope, but Wayne was no longer there to call for action on her petition. Nothing was done, and time dragged by slowly. On April 17, Kitty received a letter from Edward Rutledge, heartbroken over his wife's fatal illness. He tried to encourage her, but his tears smeared the words on the letter.

My time is much occupied. My dear little girl is on the eve of her departure. I must therefore bid you adieu. God grant you success.

Kitty remained in her quarters, her spirit deadened by one catastrophe after another. Flooded with grief for Ed Rutledge's loss, and for Anthony Wayne, she wrote to Phineas that she could not eat nor sleep. She told him there was no safety anywhere, and tucked that into her grief.

Martha came to her with the news that a bill for indemnification was finally before the House. Kitty did not want anyone with her while she waited. Finally, the President himself knocked softly on her door. Folding her in a tight embrace, he told her that her claim had been approved by a margin of nine votes: thirty-three to twenty-four.

"Oh God, oh Lord. Praise to you God," she sobbed into the arms of her dear friend, who held her like a baby. "Ten long years of fighting have ended." The color had fled from her cheeks and the words caught in her throat.

After a few moments Kitty heard the door open and felt Martha's warm palm on her shoulder blade. Turning toward her, she allowed Martha to rock her, swaying to the sound of cicadas, like blissful music in the background. A deep sense of gratitude flooded her heart.

"It is finished, my dear. The victory is yours." Martha's words radiated compassion.

A smile rose from the warmth of Kitty's heart and spread across her face. Her eyes searched both of their faces. "Can you feel him here?" she asked, choking on her words.

They nodded solemnly. Then George's familiar grin surfaced. "He has given you the strength and the power of his love. Now you are free to live your life as you will."

"What is the next step?" she asked hesitantly.

"My signature," he answered. "And that is assured."

Kitty felt a sigh escape her throat, and with it she expelled all the distress, the grief, and the anguish. The inner peace had arrived with such tenderness that she could only know it had come from above. One moment she felt trapped in suffering, and the next she was at rest in the hands of God.

"May we pray together?" she asked serendipitously. Bowing

her head, she expressed her gratitude silently, while George Washington prayed aloud. Each one of them prayed to God, and then Kitty whispered her gratitude to Nathanael.

THIRTY FIVE

1792

O n April 29, 1792, Kitty Greene sat in the gallery of the House of Representatives waiting for word from the President. Tobias Lear, his secretary and her personal friend, stepped through the door and approached the rostrum, handing over the message from George Washington: *This day I have approved and signed an act for indemnifying the estate of the late General Nathanael Greene.*

Kitty Greene was awarded the first installment of the approximately $47,000 involved in the South Carolina indebtedness. The rest would be paid within three years. The check, included with the letter, was signed by Alexander Hamilton.

On May 25, 1792, Kitty penned a letter to her lawyer Nat Pendleton.

> *I am in good health and spirits and I feel as saucy as you please—not only because I am now independent, but because I have gained a complete triumph over some of my friends who did not wish me success—and others who doubted my judgment in managing the business—and constantly tormented me to death to give up my obstinacy, as it was called. They are now as mute as mice—not a word dare they utter. O how sweet is revenge!*
>
> *In an earlier letter to you I expressed more resentment in it than you would have pardoned for your shabby conduct to my friend General Wayne. I heard of all the proceedings. I confess I felt your opposition to General Wayne was personal, to him and to me. I can tell you this: had your wishes been*

successful, I would at this moment have been, with my children, an object of charity. Thank God General Wayne kept his seat long enough to do me the most essential services, and however insignificant you may think him, it is to his exertions that I owe my independence.

This letter was written with intended malice on Kitty's part, provoked by her anger toward her friend, Nat Pendleton, and his movement to unseat Anthony Wayne. This letter reached him, but a rash of prior letters she had written him was stolen in her outgoing mail by some of her new political enemies. Realizing this, she felt gratitude and relief that he remained unaware of her spiteful remarks.

Even in her elation Kitty did not forget Anthony Wayne, now living in dishonor. Turning her energies to helping him obtain a commission in the new army to prosecute the Indian Wars, she spoke of his skills that helped save the country during the Revolution. His successful attacks against Indians who fought for the British proved he could manage the intricacies of warfare against them. She reminded the politicians of his brilliant surprise at Stony Point, of his cunning and astuteness on a par with the Indians themselves.

Kitty took her campaign for General Wayne to the President himself.

"My dear friend George, you have always been so gracious to me and to my husband. Now I come to you for one final favor." Kitty lowered her eyes and peeked up at him through her lashes. "You must understand the pressure and disgrace that Anthony Wayne has suffered due to his crooked election, which, as you know, he was for the most part unaware. Be that as it may, I am here with you to plead for his future. He is a soldier above all else, politics included."

The President raised his brows as his face broke into a puckish grin. "And what are you saying behind those eloquent words of praise, Lady Greene?"

Kitty dropped all pretenses. Her face fell, and the raw

pain was palpable. "He needs us, Mr. President. He needs his friends so badly. We cannot abandon him now. I have failed him again and again, and it breaks my heart to see what he has become."

President George Washington took a long moment in reflection. Finally, he sought out her eyes and declared his decision.

"He is a true soldier, and has never failed me. I shall appoint him commander-in-chief of the army. He will go west with his soldiers, and he will do well by both of us, his true friends."

He saw the tears shimmering on her lashes. "You are a great leader, my friend."

Kitty and the President knew that this new post would take their friend far away, and they wondered if they would ever see him again. But he deserved this responsibility, and neither one of them was willing to permit their selfishness to thwart his desire to return to the military.

Neither Lady Greene nor President Washington expected the impact Anthony Wayne would make. He defeated the British-inspired Indians in the Great Lakes regions and opened up a vast territory for peaceful settlement. This final assignment marked the end of General Wayne's long romance with Kitty. He died at his post four years later. Kitty mourned his death as if he were a close family member.

∾⊙⊙⊙∾

Kitty and Phineas drew up a legal agreement in 1791, concerning their relationship and prospective marriage, and told no one. It was recorded in the county court house in Savannah, and specified that Phineas would disclaim any property that might result from a disposition of Nathanael's estate. They knew that Kitty's status as his widow was of great importance in her petition to Congress.

Now that she had received her compensation on Nathanael's behalf, Kitty was hesitant to follow the next step in her love for Phineas. Married women became property of their husbands and forfeited all personal rights, including jurisdiction over their own children by previous marriages. She had no problem allowing Phineas to assist her in these decisions, but felt offended that she would no longer be able to transact business, retain her earnings, or make property settlements. She would be granted those rights only as a widow. She knew she wanted to make the final decision on Nat's property on Cumberland Island, and this weighed heavily on her mind.

Kitty was also reluctant to relinquish the title of "Lady Greene." Having spent years fighting for the justice of her cause, she was not ready to disqualify herself from the esteem accorded to the wife of a fallen hero. In the back of her mind, and in spite of her victory and her professed love of Phineas Miller, she enjoyed being celebrated as an influential widow.

She and Phineas decided to visit Savannah together, telling no one of their plans. They wanted a weekend away and selected a lovely inn hidden behind the main avenues, registering under false names. A grand old tabby home with pink walls and a tiled roof, it sat between the sycamores and the branches of an old weeping willow. The trees and the walls afforded privacy and a shady enclosure. The house faced inward, all rooms opening to a large central patio. A rough-hewn bench sat in the courtyard; red clay pots with petunias, African daisies and sweet alyssum were situated around it.

"Isn't this most romantic?" she asked him. "I feel frisky. I want to sing and play, as if I had no concerns."

"My darling, what are your concerns at this point? You have your monies from Nat's estate, with more arriving shortly. Your children are doing well. Your latest letter from your son George informs you that he is splendidly happy in Europe. The girls are enjoying their lives up north, and they both know we shall be visiting them shortly. Why do I feel that you are not at ease?"

She studied him with serious eyes. He remembered that the

first time he saw her, those wild blue-green eyes had sized him up like he were a cut of beef.

A furrow formed between her brows. She dug deep for restraint. "What I want," she continued, her fairy eyes drawing him in, "and what I need right now, is you."

Phineas gathered her in his arms. His mouth found hers before she could turn her head. She felt his lips, his teeth, his tongue. She opened her mouth to his as the intimacy of the kiss increased and experienced a strange helplessness in her limbs, as if he were absorbing her very being.

His lips became more demanding, and hers parted under them, submitting. "I love you, my heart." The murmured words were barely coherent, thickly groaned into her ear as he kissed the bare warm curve of her neck, following it to the hollow in her shoulder. He cupped a hand behind her head, thrusting strong fingers into the disarray of her hair, and drew her flushed face into his shoulder.

The only sound she made was a quiet sigh that tasted of surrender. His lips brushed against hers and she melted into him, moaning his name as his hand curled around the back of her neck. Her own heart was drumming as she whispered her approval. Her lips trailed over his jaw to his throat. On a shuddering breath, she wrapped her arms around his waist, and then ran them up his back.

"My darling," she whimpered. "I want to gather the broken pieces of my heart together, pull them into my lap, and study them. Maybe then I could find the missing piece that will allow me to accept the absences of those I love."

She couldn't erase the last ten years. She couldn't escape the truth. Her mouth curved into a sad smile, and her soul ached for all those loved ones lost to her.

"Kitty,the world is full of regrets and times where you think of 'if only.' Be content with what you have now, with what we have." The room grew darker. The moon had yet to rise. He saw the glimmer of her eyes as she gazed up at him.

He lowered his mouth to hers with all the fire, and the force, and the fury that he had previously held back. He wanted to save her, and himself.

Kitty closed her eyes, battling a wave of helplessness. Her heart cracked open like an egg.

THIRTY SIX

1792

In late September, Kitty, Louisa and Phineas traveled to New York. This trip would be much more pleasant than recent trips Kitty had taken, since the main purpose was to pick up Natty and Patty and take them back to Georgia. Louisa was eager to see her siblings; Kitty was overjoyed that most of her children would be together again. George was still in France finishing up his studies, and Cornelia, now fourteen, was invited to spend winter in Philadelphia at the presidential mansion with the Washingtons.

There was another reason for this voyage. A neighboring family, living across the Savannah River, needed a tutor for their children and asked Kitty and Phineas for advice. Kitty wrote a letter to Ezra Stiles, the president of Yale and the man who recommended Phineas to her family. He proposed contacting a twenty-seven-year-old Yale graduate from Connecticut named Eli Whitney.

Eli and Phineas negotiated a contract by mail, agreeing to meet in New York. After Kitty's business and family responsibilities were completed, they would sail to Savannah. Mr. Whitney replied he did not have the funds to make the voyage, so Phineas advanced him the money for his passage.

They met at Kitty's quarters in New York, where Eli told them a frightening story about his sail from New Haven. His sloop had run aground and could not be freed for many hours. Eventually, five of the men onboard requested to be rowed ashore and hired a wagon to take them into New York. Two days later, Eli ran into an acquaintance from Connecticut, whose face was so broken out with smallpox that Eli feared he might be contagious.

Phineas and Kitty sent him to Dr. Coggswell's hospital to have him inoculated. Fortunately, the process caused him little inconvenience and he finished his quarantine period in the described time. Once released, Kitty Greene and her family showed him the city, insisting he join them for meals and pleasurable activities. Eli Whitney wrote to his father that he considered himself *very fortunate indeed.*

The party set sail in late October and the voyage lasted nearly eight days, due to terrible weather at sea. Kitty discovered that Whitney also suffered from seasickness. They both stayed below, sleeping as much as they could. During their time in voluntary confinement, she was able to learn a great deal about him.

Eli was the oldest of five children, born in Westborough, Massachusetts. Left motherless at an early age and reared in a rigid Puritan atmosphere, he had developed meticulous manners. Moreover, he had been left in charge of his younger siblings, and quickly became proficient at manufacturing skills when his father added a forge to the family shop. They produced nails—in great demand during the Revolution. After the war, when nails were no longer needed, Eli used his tool-making skills to create hatpins for ladies' bonnets, walking sticks, farm products and even a fiddle for his sister.

But Eli wanted a college education, and knew he needed proper preparation for his goal. Through a schoolmaster post obtained in an adjacent town, he was able to save enough money to attend three summer terms at Leicester Academy. When his father remarried, he advanced his son $1,000 for entrance fees and expenses at Yale. Still, Eli felt unprepared for college and requested to spend a term under the tutorship of Elizur Goodrich, one of the country's famous mathematicians. Mr. Goodrich took him under his wing and shared knowledge that Eli would not have gained anywhere else.

Ezra Stiles, Yale's president, was impressed by Goodrich's

recommendation of Eli Whitney. He allowed him to enter Yale in the middle of the year, and then became Eli's most inspirational teacher. Stiles—an avid reader, a curious information gatherer, and a genius in collegiate studies—was knowledgeable in everything an eighteenth-century scholar needed to know.

At the end of his years at Yale, with no money in his pockets, Eli Whitney heard about the teaching position in the South. He loathed teaching and detested travel, but knew he must accept this opportunity presented to him. Just before his departure to Georgia, he wrote his brother Josiah that *he was traveling to the end of the earth and most likely would never be heard from again.*

Phineas and Eli were the same age and got along well. Whereas Phineas was handsome in a slender, elegant way, Eli was taller, well-proportioned yet clumsy, and not as good-looking. He possessed a rather long nose and a delicate mouth, but his lustrous black eyes exuded intelligence. He was quiet and unassuming, polite and interesting, and quickly befriended Kitty's children.

Soon Eli, like every other man who spent time with Kitty, was totally smitten with this elegant lady. A gorgeous woman at thirty-seven, she was now the "finished" lady Nathanael wanted her to be. One of her new Savannah friends described her to her circle of women as *inimitable.*

"In conversation, Kitty seems to appreciate everything spoken on just about any topic, and often astonishes the others by the ease with which her mind grasps the ideas presented. She possesses a retentive memory, a spirited imagination and a great facility of speech. She is one of the most brilliant and entertaining women I have met."

Kitty became quickly aware of the dexterity and skill that Eli displayed in creating things. Astonished, she watched him mend objects, build tools and devise solutions to problems. She handed him her broken watch and within moments, it was running. Her children had several discarded damaged toys that Eli found and repaired. He also built new toys for them. Within the first week of his arrival to Mulberry Grove, she knew she could not let him go across the river to tutor the neighbor's children.

"How will we tell them?" she asked Phineas. "They trusted us to get them a tutor and are willing to pay him well. But he is so useful here at Mulberry Groove."

He nodded. "We will tell them the truth. He came to us and said he did not want to teach. Besides, he has a good head for figures and an uncommon aptitude for arithmetical calculations."

Kitty listened impatiently while struggling to find the proper words. "But we need to replace him with someone, Phineas. We cannot go to them empty-handed," she said with sincerity.

Phineas grinned impishly. "Would you like me to offer my tutoring services to their children? After all, they've seen how well I've done with yours."

She shot him a dismissive smile. "Do not speak of it! I could not spare you, dear man." She drew a deep breath. "Do you think Ezra Stiles would be able to find another Yale graduate who could arrive quickly? Perhaps we can stall the neighbors for a week or so."

He smiled at her concern. As often as she had shown him her self-centered side, she had equally displayed thoughtfulness and compassion. Phineas knew her better than anyone else, and her empathy for others was one of the reasons he loved her.

Phineas and Kitty rode together to the neighbors' plantation to convey the news: Eli had decided to stay on as an employee at Mulberry Grove, and they had arranged for another Yale graduate to sail to Savannah and tutor their children. Everyone was pleased with the new arrangement, and no one seemed happier than Eli.

One thing baffled Eli: the relationship between Phineas and Kitty. He admired and liked Phineas, and found him to be extremely intelligent and kind. Although he enjoyed watching their naturalness together, and their obvious tenderness and concern for each other's happiness, he was puzzled by the way they lived openly and traveled as man and wife. Eli expressed his bewilderment in a letter to his friend Stebbins. *I find myself in a new world, and I believe the moral world does not extend this far south.*

⚜

Kitty loved to entertain, and felt she had the means to do so. In November of 1792, she invited a group of gentlemen from Augusta, Georgia to her home. Several of these men were officers who had served under Nathanael. They were accompanied by Major Pendleton, Major Forsyth and Major Bremen. As the night wore on, the men fell into conversation about the state of agriculture, and the subject of growing cotton came up. They expressed regret that there was no proper way to clean the green seed cotton or even separate it from the seed.

"We could turn to farming the cotton if we simply had a faster way to produce it," stated Major Pendleton. "Our soil could certainly do with an alternative crop."

"Many of us do not even have soil suitable for rice cultivation," opined Major Bremen, glancing at his hostess, "although you and Mr. Miller have done well here."

Kitty smiled warmly as the wheels of her mind turned. "Gentlemen, you should apply this concern to our young friend, Mr. Whitney. He can make anything. He has the mind of a genius."

All eyes turned to Eli, listening uneasily from the chair next to Phineas.

"Why, just yesterday he made a tambour frame for my embroidery. And he's invented some ingenious toys for my children! Come with me and I shall show them to you." She rose smoothly, leading them into the small room he was using as a workshop. While the gentlemen inspected the toys and the tambour frame with interest, Kitty noticed Eli was uncomfortable answering their questions, modestly disclaiming all pretensions of being a "genius."

"Mr. Whitney, would you consider helping us find a way to separate the seed from the fiber?" Major Pendleton was intrigued. "The way it is being done now is very clumsy and slow. With a new machine, the Negroes would be given a boost, affording them the means to work faster. Perhaps we could turn the river valley into Eden?"

Eli shifted from one foot to the other. "I would like to think about this project for a while," he answered softly. Looking up, he smiled at Major Pendleton. "But thank you for your confidence."

Kitty added, "Mr. Whitney is studying law at the moment, with my encouragement. Let us give him time to see where his brain can be best used."

Several months later, Eli wrote a letter to his father.

I heard much said of the extreme difficulty of ginning cotton, that is separating it from the seeds. There were a number of very respectable gentlemen at Mrs. Greene's who all agreed that if a machine could be invented which would clean the cotton with expedition, it would be a great thing both to the country and to the inventor.

Phineas Miller encouraged Eli to mull over the idea to see if he were even interested. He also told him that he and Kitty would subsidize the expenses, and if Eli were successful, they would offer him a partnership. Those were the words that enticed Eli to seriously reflect on this breakthrough invention.

THIRTY SEVEN

1792–1793

E li Whitney held the white fluffy cotton boll in his hand, closely examining it. This was the first time he had seen cotton. He tugged at the fiber, struggling to separate it from the green seeds.

"What do you think, Eli?" asked Kitty, holding another cotton plant in her hand.

"These seeds are covered with a kind of green coat resembling velvet," he replied, impatience manifested in his voice. "I must figure out a way to separate these."

After Kitty's encouragement, yet still frustrated with misgivings, Eli turned his mind to working out the framework of a machine to assist the cotton planters. He studied the laborious task of removing the seeds by hand—how it took the workers over ten hours to separate one pound of lint from three pounds of seeds. At this rate, he realized that cotton would never compete with wool and flax.

Kitty and Phineas took Eli to the cotton fields to analyze the hand motions of the slaves cleaning cotton. Squatting down beside them, he questioned them about their method, and they showed him how one hand held the seed as the other filtered out the short strands of lint. He tried to visualize a machine capable of duplicating the manual process, but much more quickly.

Retreating to his upstairs workshop, now converted into his laboratory, Eli took a few bolls of cotton and some tools and lost himself in the world of mechanics. Brainstorming, he drew out his plans, and soon was so absorbed in his work that he stayed in the room night and day, coming out for his meals only when Kitty insisted. To test his drawings, he employed the tools he found on the plantation, or made new ones to suit his purpose.

Kitty and Phineas were impressed with his original drawings, and immediately agreed to furnish the funds for the construction and experimentation of the machine. Kitty pledged money from her recently gained fortune, and Phineas drew up a contract to make them partners.

After ten days, Eli came downstairs to speak with them. His expression told Kitty and Phineas that he had overcome the challenge.

"Tell us what you have, Eli." Kitty asked eagerly. His face reflected his doubts.

He showed them his crude model with wooden teeth that did not work well. "I've tried and fussed over this, but I am not satisfied," he groused.

"Let's have a look," encouraged Phineas. "Give it a go."

Eli pressed the bulk cotton against the wire screen, which held back the seeds while the wooden teeth jutting out from an adjacent rotating drum teased the cotton fibers out through the mesh. The model jammed.

"I cannot get this to flow smoothly." His eyes clouded with defeat. "I must find new wires, or give it up completely."

Kitty walked over to him and placed both hands on his arms, detecting the weariness in the drooping slope of his shoulders. "You are working too hard on this, Eli. Take a break. Select a book from our library and go to the river. Turn off your mind for a day or two. After that, have another look at your model, and you will find the solution."

Phineas nodded. "She is right, my friend. You have labored too long on this, and the problem will work itself out if you give it a rest."

Eli, dispirited and exhausted, accepted their advice. During his time away from working on the project, he wrote a letter to his father.

I involuntarily happened to be thinking on the subject and came up with a plan of a machine, which I communicated to Mr. Miller, who was pleased. He said if I would pursue it and try to experiment to see if it could work, he would be responsible for the whole expense. I should lose nothing but my time, and if I succeeded he would share the profits. I have made a little model that is not perfect, but is a start. I shall now turn my attention to perfecting this machine.

After writing the letter he felt relief, trusting that somehow he would make it work. And he concurred that he needed time away to relax. Taking a book from the library, he headed down to the riverbank to enjoy an afternoon of warm sun and reading pleasure.

At the day's end Kitty went to the river and sat quietly on an old tree stump overlooking the water. The sun was low and buttery; a breeze wafted through, smelling of honeysuckle. Eli, absorbed in his book, was unaware of her presence. After a while he looked up, startled to find her watching him.

"This is the stump where I often found Nathanael, contemplating his problems or giving thanks for his blessings." She leaned forward, elbows on her knees. When she turned, her smile was radiant.

Eli set down his book and met her gaze, wondering how often she thought about her husband.

Arching her neck, she looked up at the sky, feeling a momentary sensation of floating, of becoming unmoored.

"I don't suppose you much like it here, do you, Eli? Coming down from New England, like I did, you certainly can see the contrasts." She shook her head slowly and then laughed. "But I hope you will come to appreciate, and maybe even learn to love this strange land of marshes and swaying moss, of ancient fortresses, crumbling and lichen-covered."

The woman never ceased to intrigue him. She seemed to have the ability to read his mind.

"Yes, Kitty. I do miss my home and my family. But I am

opening my attention to new possibilities, and believe me when I say that I am grateful to you and Phineas for taking me in and giving me opportunities to grow." His eyes were drawn to her finger, now pointing to the sky above the river. They watched, wordless, as the sun painted the river with broad streaks of pink and orange. The day's final light turned the skyline into sheets of solid gold.

She broke into a wide smile and abruptly changed the subject. "My son, George Washington Greene, will be coming home very soon. I'm looking forward to your meeting him, and I know you two will get on well."

"He is returning from France?"

"Yes, and I have missed him every day for five years." She grinned impishly. "I would never tell any of my children, but George is my favorite. He and I weathered many trials together, mostly when he was too young to remember." Her eyes clouded over as a hint of a smile flickered on her face at the memory—the night of the Boston bombardment of 1776—when the warmth of his little body gave her strength and comfort.

"Has he been with the Lafayettes all this time?" asked Eli, hoping to satisfy his curiosity.

"He lived with them at first and then they sent him and their son, also named George Washington, to a boarding school. Recently he wrote me requesting money for the passage home. Phineas and I have been very worried these last months, after hearing the dreadful outcome of the French Revolution. We immediately sent him money and expect him home within a fortnight."

Four days passed before they received word that George would be arriving in Savannah on the weekend. Cornelia had just come back from Philadelphia, and Kitty would finally have all five children home together for the first time in five years.

George returned, in full health and thoroughly educated. He regaled them with stories of the events of the French Revolution, unfolding on all sides during his time in France. He told of how Madame Lafayette paid daily visits to him and her son at the boarding school until it was no longer safe, at which time she urged him to return to America. Murderous mobs were surging through the streets, and by the time he left France, the Lafayettes had been captured and were languishing in separate prisons, while their son—his best friend—was rushed away to a mountain hideout.

There was a constant flow of visitors to the plantation and Kitty was in high spirits. Eli fit in well with the family, but realized he needed to get back into creative mode. Within a few days he and Phineas had dug out a large space in the basement—his new laboratory—where he moved his tools, plans and models. Eli was now ready to go back to work.

THIRTY EIGHT

1793

Eli had given up. Turning slowly to face Phineas and Kitty, he no longer hid his frustration and embarrassment and mumbled dejectedly, "I have reached the end of my road; I am prepared to abandon this machine altogether."

All three of them stared at Eli's invention, willing it to spring into action.

"It is not such a difficult task," Eli said to the cotton engine, as if to a lazy child. "The teeth I have set into the wooden cylinder pull the cotton fibers away from the seeds, and the seeds drop away…"

Feeding a handful of fluffy cotton into the machine, he turned the crank. Wheels studded with wire teeth caught the lint and ripped it from the seeds. The seeds fell to the bottom of the machine. Up to this point the engine worked perfectly. But Eli had found no way to remove the accumulated lint from the teeth, which impeded its passage between the slats. It took only a few moments before the machine bogged down. Again.

With the mood as somber as a wake Phineas studied his friend, trying to find encouraging words.

But Kitty's thoughts were elsewhere, her blue-green eyes darkening with concentration. Finally she spoke.

"Eli, do you remember on the vessel coming to Savannah when we talked about the giant? How if we let him, he'll take away our peace?"

Eli nodded reluctantly, wondering what she would say next. She seemed to have a way of getting him out of a rut.

"Please retain your focus," she continued. "You are so close. Just keep the giant at bay."

Phineas' hand was firm on Eli's shoulder as he agreed. "You are almost there, my friend."

Seeking a solution, Kitty continued. "Eli, have you considered replacing the wooden pegs with different wire hooks?"

Her question was met with silence. After a long moment Eli responded. "I have drawn my own wire, but I will take another look at it." His words came out splintered.

Rising slowly, he reclaimed the model and headed for the door. Kitty watched him solemnly.

Just as he grasped the door latch, Kitty's eyes widened with an insight. She startled her companions by throwing back her head and laughing delightedly.

Dashing to the door, she stood before Eli. "What! Would you allow such a trifling problem to change your resolve? Trust it to a woman's wit to find the cure—prepare to turn the cylinder once again!" Her eyes filled with mischief.

Hurrying across to the fireplace, she picked up the hearth brush and came back to wave it over his model, now sitting on the table. "Perhaps this brush's stiff bristles would help you remove the lint from the teeth!" She flicked the hearth brush at the cylinder, still clogged with cotton fibers.

After a few flicks of her wrist, the cotton fibers lay in a pile on the table top.

Eli stared at her in shock and amazement, struggling to understand how such an elegant solution could be so simple.

Then he cried out, "Kitty, thank you for the cue! I do believe that's it!" Brown eyes ignited with inspiration, he rushed out of the room with his model.

Alone in the basement, hands trembling in anticipation, Eli went back to work. He painstakingly added another cylinder that turned in the opposite direction of the picker and forced it to move faster. As the short stiff hog's bristles combed and removed the cotton, the fibers were thrown off away from the gin, making them easier to retrieve. The cotton filaments fell away in small, white, downy clouds.

Sinking into a chair, Eli wearily massaged his shadowed eye sockets and pushed back his disheveled hair. He sat quietly, rubbing his palms against the tops of his thighs. Time passed, and he looked down at his hands, pressed together in front of him as if in prayer. Staring vacantly at the floor, he kept trying to sort it all out.

Eli felt his fingers wiping away a slow stream of tears trickling down his cheeks.

"Kitty has solved the puzzle. We have done it. My machine is complete." A small smile gradually blossomed into a joyful grin.

Pulling himself together, he staggered upstairs to inform his friends, who waited anxiously for him by a window. Eli's face radiated triumph as his fragile voice shared his news.

"If my calculations are accurate, this machine will turn out in one hour what several workers cleaning cotton by hand now do in a day." His grin spread.

Kitty was startled by her overflowing sense of pride in this news.

Her lower lip quivered as she reached up to hug Eli. She turned to Phineas, flinging her arms around his neck and kissing him soundly. She let out a whoop of delight.

Thunderstruck, they could only stare at each other as the room became wrapped in peaceful silence. Outside, a night bird cooed to its mate, who answered with a seductive warble. Palm fronds rattled in the rising wind.

The world had just changed forever.

Eli Whitney constructed a full-sized cotton gin, powered by one man and a horse, and gave a demonstration for the planters of the region proving that his gin could clean as much cotton as fifty slaves working by hand. The planters raced to sow their fields with green-seed cotton, anticipating their future success. Eli was immediately offered one hundred guineas for title to his gin, but wrote his father that *he was now so sure of success that ten thousand dollars, even placed down before him, would not tempt him to give up his rights or relinquish the model.*

Phineas urged Eli to take out a patent quickly, before anyone else could copy his machine. Kitty teased him about her role in the invention.

"Eli, you know perfectly well that we invented the gin together, do you not? Why, without my brush suggestion, you may never have finished it."

He gave her a crooked grin and nodded vigorously. "Indeed I do. However, as a woman you cannot get a patent. 'Tis a pity, isn't it?" He didn't even attempt to look apologetic.

She had the grace to laugh. "As long as Phineas has a partnership with you, I will remain content. This is such a joyous time for us here at Mulberry Grove. All my children are home, you will change the future of the cotton industry, and Georgia will soon become the Empire State of the South."

In June of 1793, Eli sailed to New York and took a stagecoach to Philadelphia to get his cotton gin patented. There were several steps involved, which Eli completed, and then carried the paperwork to Secretary of State Jefferson, who assured him it would be a great success. Finally, on March 14, 1794, the patent was issued for a term of fourteen years, beginning on November 6, 1793.

While Eli was away there was a break-in at the outhouse at Mulberry Grove where the original model was stored. The locks were broken and the machine was stolen. In very short time, hundreds of copies were made, and subsequently, larger gins were constructed to run by horse or water power.

THIRTY NINE

1793

George Washington Greene was idolized by his younger siblings. Louisa, who had barely known him before he left for Europe, was constantly at his heels, begging him to build her swings, forts, and even a little boat. Natty, his younger brother, now thirteen, was thrilled to have his big brother home again, and told him so.

"Please stay with us in Georgia. Mama and Mr. Miller want to send me back up north for my schooling, but I just want to be here at the plantation. Can you help me convince them?"

"I'll do my best, Natty. We'll get them to agree to keep you here with me."

They took long hikes and horseback rides through the valley. George assured him that he would be around for a long time. He understood that Natty needed a brother. They both liked Phineas very much, but knew he was not their father. He wasn't even their step-father.

"George, why will Mama not marry Mr. Miller? It would be nice to have another father, now that ours is dead."

George grinned. "Have patience, Natty. I believe she will. Once this cotton gin patent gets squared away, I imagine we will have a grand wedding here at Mulberry Grove."

"What is left to do, George? Miller and Whitney Company is already set up. They built a ginning house here to demonstrate the machine. The patent is being drawn up. Why is Mama waiting?"

George laughed and gave his brother a poke. "You are asking me about women? I probably understand them less than you, my brother. I have just begun to find the time to socialize."

Kitty took much pleasure in her favorite role—illustrious hostess. She loved inviting neighbors she favored and friends from Savannah to dine at her splendid plantation. George was now meeting the eligible young women of the area, and his sisters were basking in the attention of the local gentlemen.

George's down-to-earth, boyish personality made him popular with many in Kitty's social circles. Nimbly identifying the key point of any discussion, he would add some witty, insightful pleasantry—usually designed to make the speaker feel more intelligent than he might actually be. Many young women returned home after one of Kitty's soirees feeling certain they had met their future beau.

This charm was only strengthened by his unpredictable, candid style. A tendency to impulsively improvise in his speech and actions intrigued people, even as it caught them off guard.

One day George was straightening up the tool shed when his new friend Stits poked his head around the door.

"Is what you're doing there quite as interesting as it looks?" he asked George mischievously.

"More or less," George replied, around his well-known grin.

"Then by all means join me in an afternoon outing on the Savannah River!"

Before he'd finished the invitation, George had begun untying his stiff leather apron and grabbed his hat from a nail on the door. Stepping outside, he glanced at the sky through a thatch of billowing Spanish moss; a huge slate-colored cloud shaped like a chisel was moving toward them.

"That looks a bit threatening," George murmured. "Let's decide when we reach the canoe at the dock if we want to risk taking a ride this afternoon."

They both knew that spring rains had been heavy, making the river high and swollen. But Stits already guessed that the possible danger only whetted George's appetite for the unexpected.

There was no further mention of the weather at the dock. Stits untied one of the canoes kept there for pleasure jaunts and stepped carefully into it. George stepped into the front and sat down, pushing his hat jauntily over his forehead.

"Off in a cloud of camel dung to see the great Sahara!" he proclaimed, obviously pleased that their leisurely canoe ride held the promise of excitement and a good story for his friends.

Within ten minutes, his gaiety had faded. Rough currents churned by suddenly strong winds beat at the side of the boat. When Stits asked nervously if they should head back, George fretfully laughed off his friend's question and rowed them directly into the forceful waters. After several frightening moments, a ferocious wave took them by surprise and slapped hard against their canoe.

Horrified, as if in slow motion, Stits saw George grasp one side of the boat, and then the other, desperately trying to stabilize them.But in mid-decision, the canoe overturned and sank vertically into the muddy water, George's arm slapping futilely as he went under.

Stits, gagging and heaving, struggled to break the surface. Gasping and winded, he pulled himself to the bank and collapsed. In a few moments he felt strong enough to stand and search the river for George and the canoe. There was no trace of either.

Hurrying as best he could, Stits staggered back to Mulberry Grove, sounding the alarm as he approached.

"Come quickly," he hollered. "Help me find George! The canoe flipped over, and I've lost him!"

Kitty shrieked, "He cannot swim! Oh God, he's drowning!" Grabbing Phineas by the arm she bolted toward the river, pulling him helplessly behind her.

Patty and Cornelia rushed to the neighboring plantation to find people who could help search for their brother. A frantic search commenced. Darkness finally forced them back to the house.

Phineas managed to keep them hopeful. He settled the children down with prayer, held Kitty as she wept, and consoled Stits in his misery, assuring him that he was not to blame. He put together a meal that no one ate. Kitty was beside herself, alternating between sobbing uncontrollably and attempting to assure them that George was about to walk through the door, whistling and announcing in his cheerful voice that he was home.

Leading Kitty into the bedroom, Phineas promised to hold her through the night. He could barely endure the low keening sounds rising up from her soul. Drawing her head to his shoulder, he physically felt her sobs, as if he had taken her shoulders in his hands and shaken her.

"My son was not supposed to die today," she cried, sorrow splitting her voice. "I want to remember him as he was this morning. His face was so happy." Her beautiful emerald eyes were feverish, her skin nearly translucent.

"Please don't lose your faith, my love. He may be out there, disoriented and making his way home," offered Phineas.

"No," she insisted, "I know he's gone. My grief is drowning me, sweeping me away. My son is calling out to me."

"Hush now, darling. Come morning, we will take up the search again. Let's wait until then and sleep a while."

Kitty shook her head forcefully. "You do not understand, Phineas. My darling son is no more."

∽⊙⊙∾

The following morning the lifeless body of George Washington Greene was washed up on the edge of the river—at the point closest to Mulberry Grove. When Kitty saw George, she threw back her head, ripping a cry from her soul to the Heavens.

The next day his body was carried by boat down the river, as his father's had been, to a Savannah dock. A hearse took him to the colonial cemetery.

The small chapel blazed with candles and smelled gloriously of the pine and cedar boughs decorating the altar and edges of the pews. Kitty shrieked when Phineas pulled her away so they could close the casket. She sobbed, "My heart feels they should bury us together."

For months the family mourned George's loss, and each one grieved differently. His siblings visited the river's edge, as a way to feel closer to him. Kitty could not return for the longest time, and when she did, the anguish was fresh and heartrending. With all the transformations her life had already taken, she found this one too harrowing to even contemplate. Moments of overpowering grief came unbidden, alighting so fleetingly that they felt like tiny birds swooping down on her. And Kitty learned these moments were incapable of being blotted out, however passionately she wished for that closure.

Phineas grieved through song. Kitty had no idea he had such a lovely voice until he lifted it in song on their walks together. He would close his eyes, throw back his head and release a voice like a great bronze bell, dark and strong and filled with power. The first time he sang she stopped and held her breath, mesmerized as his tune spilled out into the waning afternoon.

"Oh, Phineas, your voice is like fire, wind, and earth. It reminds me of smoke."

He laughed, tucked her head under his chin and held her close. After a long moment, he resumed singing the hymn.

"Why did you not share this with me before?" she asked, puzzled.

"I did not want you to know all my secrets," he responded softly. "Little by little, my dear. That's how we acquire patience, and that is how love deepens."

After a month had passed, Phineas asked her to accompany him to the river. The rains had pelted the land all afternoon, but now they rested. Kitty was edgy and needed a respite from the house.

"Come with me for a ride," he urged, hoping that riding horseback would give her pleasure. She smiled and followed him to the stable.

They heard the steady fury of the Savannah River as they approached. The day was overcast and cool, but even at a distance they saw the water through the mist—an even deeper gray than before—and she made out the rocks and bushes and trees. She pointed out a single swallow, fluttering toward a willow tree.

Lowering themselves onto a log, they watched the water pattern change as it made its way past a rock jutting from the river. The river kept flowing, parting, foaming and then became whole again after it passed the rock, leaving its impact on the rock. All at once she felt as if she were the river, swirling in an ever-changing design around the rock, separating and coming together again without letting herself get snagged into scummy pools. It was the nature of the river to be both turbulent and gentle; to be abundant at times and lean at others; to be greedy and to yield pleasure. It gives and takes life. She knew the spirit of the river would always remember the dead.

Kitty had hoped that by going to the river, she could alleviate the agony of death. Now she knew the pain would not be denied. "Phineas, he has not only disappeared from our lives, but from our future." She swayed, fresh tears clogging her throat.

Briefly stunned into the blackest kind of silence, they sat together on the old log, each wrapped in the vicious senselessness of it all. Taking both of Kitty's hands in his, he said, "George lives on in our hearts. He's with his loved ones gone before him; he's with his father. He is at peace, dear one."

When he looked over at her, her eyes were filled with tears. Then it came to her: her sweet, sad familiar sorrow. And today, almost gratefully, she bent under it. She was not alone.

FORTY

1793–1795

Eli Whitney's reports from New England brought encouraging news to Mulberry Grove. After arriving in New Haven, Eli scouted out workmen to manufacture his full-scale cotton gins and stayed close by to personally supervise each detail of the process. By mid-winter, a few dozen cotton engines, "gins," were either under construction or already completed.

Meanwhile, Phineas arranged the sales and contracts from Mulberry Grove, where he set up a large ginning house to demonstrate the machines. He knew Kitty and the children needed him close by. George's tragic drowning was still very present in their hearts.

In the spring of 1794, Kitty placed an ad in the *Savannah Gazette,* announcing that the gin would soon be available for sale at Mulberry Grove. A proposition was offered: instead of a cash-fee to purchase the machines, two-fifths of the ginned product would be charged by the company, while the planters could keep three-fifths of the yield.

Eli returned to Georgia and proudly handed over the patent to Kitty and Phineas. "It's finally ours," he announced, excitedly assembling one of his gins for them to see. "I now feel energized and ready to show off our product to the scores of interested planters."

Eli offered Phineas half-interest in his patent for $1,000. They both understood that Kitty controlled the bank strings. In June, the money was made available to her by the government and the *official* launch of the Miller and Whitney firm took place. Kitty asked to remain unnamed in the legal papers, so Phineas would have faith in her private, unwritten, yet unbreakable bond of love. She always knew he would give her equal share in the enterprise.

Eli was wracked with chills and a high fever the night before his scheduled return to New Haven.

"I cannot travel, Kitty. Would you or Phineas be able to travel in my stead?" he asked in despair.

"Absolutely not. Neither Phineas nor I would leave you like this," she told him, pulling up a stool to wipe down his brow with cool water. Eli was comforted by her affectionate maternal skills, and with rest, he recovered quickly. In less than two weeks he left on his journey north.

Kitty and Phineas ran the business from the plantation, and finally found a peace and tranquility they had not known for a long time. They figured out a system that rewarded them credit through portions of Nathanael's estate, pledging that as collateral.

The cotton gin at Mulberry Grove heralded the launch of a new era in the South. Industrialists came from as far away as New England to reap the promised cotton harvest. John C. Nightingale was one of these representatives. Twenty-four years old, from a renowned mercantile family in Providence, Rhode Island, he was sent to Mulberry Grove to enter into a cotton planting enterprise with Phineas Miller. Several months after his arrival, he realized he had fallen in love with Patty Greene.

"Sweetie, what do you think of John?" Kitty asked her oldest daughter, who appeared oblivious of his attentions.

Patty looked at her mother in a bemused manner. "He seems quite nice. He is very interested in the gin, isn't he, Mama?"

Kitty laughed pleasantly. "He is very interested in *you,* my girl. I would say he's *besotted.*"

Patty's face flushed a vivid shade of red. "Oh, Mama, how can you even think that? I'm a mere seventeen-year-old girl, and he is worldly."

"Patty, he is drawn to your bashfulness, your modesty, and your sweet timidity. Just give him a little encouragement, and you will see what I'm talking about."

Phineas also encouraged Patty to get to know John, and told her how much he liked and respected him. Then he went to Kitty and offered her his advice.

"Patty feels overshadowed by your beauty. You must find a way to let her know how lovely she is. I know you do not compare yourself to your daughter, but you should realize that any woman who knows you is aware of how men react to you."

"Oh no, Phineas. Not Patty. She is so pretty and sweet in her own right."

"Encourage her, my love. Make her feel special. Tell her how attractive she is. It will be easy for you, because I know how much you love her."

Kitty took the time to develop a close bond with all three girls. Phineas was right: it came naturally and she now was able to see them as friends as well as daughters; even little Louisa, now eleven years old.

The courtship prospered under the family's encouragement, and a spring wedding was planned.

Louisa was the one who asked her mother the question that was on everyone's mind.

"Mama, since we are having a wedding anyway, why don't you and Mr. Miller get married as well?"

Eliza looked at her fondly and smiled graciously. "Darling, a wedding is a special moment for every woman. This is Patty's time. We should allow her that significant day, don't you think?"

Cornelia chimed in. "But when, Mama? All of us want you to marry him. Why haven't you?"

Kitty looked her daughters in the eye, her expression softening. "It is almost time, my darlings. It will happen because we love each other." Reaching out to embrace them, she added, "Thank you for caring so much."

In the spring of 1795, Patty Greene married John C. Nightingale in the parlor of Mulberry Grove. This event was the most gala affair at Mulberry Grove since the colonial days, when the wealthy Tory, John Graham, had entertained his Savannah friends in the same house. Their friends came from as far away as Rhode Island, New York and Connecticut. Mulberry Grove was transformed into a fairytale dwelling, decorated with fresh May flowers from the garden and verdant greenery from the plantation grounds. Well-wishers from all over Georgia and South Carolina were in attendance. A shy and very lovely Patty Greene sparkled on her wedding day, and Kitty fought tears as she thought how proud Nathanael would have been to stand at her side. This blessed festivity helped unify a family so recently torn apart by grief.

∾⟨⊙⟩∾

Only two weeks after the wedding, Kitty and Phineas received news of the cotton gin firm's first disaster. Eli wrote them that his shop in New Haven had been destroyed by fire, and he lost all his tools, his materials and a good number of cotton gins under construction. Eli was so distraught that he feared this could put an end to the total cotton gin enterprise.

Kitty wept at the report. Phineas kept his calm self-control and penned Eli that this was a setback, but it was not lethal. He told him they would persevere since they were both in the prime of their lives and well-informed about the world. They would be able to sustain such a misfortune.

Eli Whitney went back to work and rebuilt his factory. He made more tools. It had taken him two years to make the first twenty gins. Now, without his papers and drawings in front of him, with only his astonishing memory, he reported that twenty-six machines were ready to be shipped to Georgia, just seven months after the fire.

"God bless Eli," whispered Kitty in relief. "What an extraordinary man. God has given us the perfect partner."

It was time for them to travel north. Kitty, Phineas and the three girls, accompanied by Patty's husband John, sailed to New England.

Their first stop was to visit Natty, who was studying in Connecticut. They stayed a week, enjoying themselves completely. Then they sailed to Block Island to visit Kitty's aging father and other family members. Kitty could not remember when she had relaxed so much, surrounded by so many who loved her. She felt like she was constantly repeating just how grateful she was for each one of them.

Finally, they met Eli in New Haven, where they inspected the gin factory and marveled at the production of the cotton gins, already beginning to revolutionize the economy of the South.

While they were visiting in the north, some of their friends from New England devised a land development plan and called it the Yazoo Company. This was an investment scheme that promised to pay huge dividends in just a few months. Their plan was to buy up cheap land in Georgia and sell it at a later time for a great profit to prospective cotton planters relocating to the state.

"I am not in favor of this," objected Eli. "It's all come too quickly, and we've had no time to study up on it."

"But we must strike when it's hot," reasoned Kitty. "Surely you agree, do you not?" She turned to Phineas for support.

"Let us review it a little more, and when we return home, we can make our decision," he suggested.

The company Yazoo became a name none of them would ever forget.

FORTY ONE

1795–1797

The Yazoo Land Company was promoted by a group of New England industrialists. One of the officers in the company was Kitty's son-in-law John Nightingale, who urged Kitty and Phineas to invest in the company, promising great returns. Eli Whitney was also asked to join, but he balked.

"This plan sounds too good to be true," he told them. "My father taught us that if investments sounded too good, they generally were not reliable."

"Very well then, Eli," smiled Kitty. "Phineas and I will put a portion of our investments in the plan, and hope for the best."

John Nightingale was enthusiastic. "The Yazoo Land Company will buy 35,000,000 acres of undeveloped land from the Georgia legislature for $490,000. This property extends as far west as the Yazoo River, a tributary of the Mississippi. So this amounts to one and a half cents per acre, or seventy acres per dollar!"

Phineas and Kitty visualized large profits providing them with a permanent working capital for the cotton gin firm. They bought a hefty amount of shares with promissory notes, signed by Kitty and secured by the assets of the Greene estate.

The state government agreed to the operation and the terms were made public. Swiftly and unexpectedly, an enormous cluster of outraged citizens descended upon the legislature, screaming for justice. They had a clear sense that something was wrong. It was soon discovered that dozens of lawmakers and other key officials had been bribed across the board to approve the scam. Members of the Georgia House and Senate were given free shares in the land company. The enraged and resentful citizens dubbed the land scheme the "Great Yazoo Fraud," crying out for its repeal.

Many innocent families in Georgia and in New England were caught up in the affair, having invested a great deal of their money in the Yazoo Company. Kitty and Phineas believed John Nightingale was innocent and had not known of the corruption. Kitty felt differently about Nat Pendleton, their personal friend and lawyer, and Georgia's chief justice.

"How could he not have warned us?" wailed Kitty, suddenly comprehending their tremendous monetary loss. "Nat had to know about the bribery."

"Kitty, he would have told us if he knew," consoled Phineas. "You saw how he publicly supported it. He staked his political fortune in Georgia on the plan's success."

Kitty shook her head hopelessly. "Perhaps he too was bribed. How can you trust him, Phineas? After all the things he's done to us?"

Phineas tenderly cupped her face in his hand. "I trust him because he bought some shares in partnership with me," he answered quietly, his eyes fixed on hers. "We've all lost money here, Kitty."

"Not only money, Phineas," she whimpered. "We've lost friends from New England. We've lost face with so many others, including our dear Eli, and now we must fight to rescind this horrid plan."

James Jackson, the man who had opposed her indemnification claim and led the proceedings to unseat Anthony Wayne in the House of Representatives, fronted the anti-Yazoo movement. Kitty and Phineas understood that his position regarding the Yazoo issue was morally correct, and they quietly involved themselves in supporting the fight against it.

The stormy ex-congressman fought fiercely to rescind it, including participating in several duels. He was stabbed in the chest with a knife that barely missed his heart. As governor of Georgia in 1796, James Jackson was extremely influential in voiding the Yazoo Act through the state's Rescinding Act. Standing in the central plaza before Georgia's new capital building in Louisville, Governor Jackson drew "fire from Heaven" through a magnifying glass, and then dramatically set the flame to the Yazoo papers, destroying all state records of the legislation and land sales.

Phineas Miller and Kitty Greene lost all their ready cash. Their estate property was pledged for collateral; they unwittingly compromised the cotton gin firm's credit. Eli listened as they apologized to him, his heart melting with sorrow while they berated themselves, and he forgave them.

Kitty and her family grieved for John Nightingale's reputation in Georgia. It had become public knowledge that he was an officer in the Yazoo Company. He and Patty were humiliated. Kitty and Phineas showed them compassion, in spite of their own losses, and never held it against him.

Nat Pendleton, with renewed hatred in his heart for Georgia, and knowing that his relationship with his beloved Kitty was now ruthlessly damaged, moved to New York with his wife.

A backlash against the cotton firm was beginning to unravel. Even Eli Whitney's name became suspect, since it was attached to the Miller and Whitney Company. The farmers took advantage of the firm's humiliation and lobbied to have the company's patent rights set aside, calling the partners "greedy monopolists." They brought up as evidence their exclusive control over the machines, costing the growers two-fifths of their crop to gin their cotton.

Eli was devastated by this turn of events. "Pirating will reign unbridled," he lamented. "And already rumors abound that the cotton ginned by us is inferior to that processed by other machines."

"Pay them no heed," advised Phineas. "We will carry on as before."

Eli bowed his head. "No, Phineas. We've just received word that the proposed trade to Great Britain is no longer secure.

The rumormongers have made certain that our tribulations have reached the ears of our British partners."

New gins had sprung up, built from the plans of the stolen machine, and now Eli and Phineas were forced to begin legal efforts to protect Eli's rights. More than sixty drawn-out lawsuits would eventually be fought to sustain Eli's patent—another expensive burden for Eli, Phineas and Kitty.

⁊⊙⊙⊙⊱

On the last day of May, 1796, in a Philadelphia ceremony witnessed by Martha and George Washington and several other intimate friends, a radiant Kitty Greene kneeled beside Phineas Miller as the clergyman pronounced them man and wife. Everyone in the room except the clergyman wept for joy. The affair was so private that it did not make the local papers, even with the President of the United States giving Kitty away.

"After eleven years, Mrs. Miller, you are finally my wife." Phineas' eyes shone with adoration. The children, their friends and the family members were notified shortly after the wedding. Eli was in Connecticut when he heard the news.

After returning to Mulberry Grove, Kitty remarked to Phineas that she was concerned that they had heard nothing from Eli.

"Do you think he is indisposed? This is not like our Eli. Let us send him another letter about our nuptials. "

Phineas gently shook his head. "My darling, I believe he has taken this hard. Give him some time."

Kitty's mouth dropped open. "Taken our marriage hard? Do you mean…?"

He nodded. "I think he's always been a little in love with you. This must have been a crushing blow to his heart."

Phineas, perceptive to men's reactions to Kitty, had guessed the reason for Eli's silence. Eli was hurt, even though he had no personal aspirations with Kitty. As long as she lived, she would be his only emotional tie to womanhood. There was a covenant of affection between them, based on common interests, intellectual stimulation, a deep understanding of each other's needs, and mutual respect.

Eli eventually explained his feelings in a letter to them, while also wishing them happiness. His explanation was worded to include his special feelings toward her, and his belief that prior to the wedding, he was able to envision himself and Phineas as members of a three-way partnership, with Kitty as their common inspiration in life's great adventures. He told them how lonely he felt.

Eli's words troubled them both, but more pressing trials required their immediate attention. Their ginning company was virtually bankrupt, and their credit was used up. Pressed to liquidate more land, they sold the South Carolina property awarded to General Greene, for just half its value.

The first patent suit finally came to trial in Savannah, Georgia in May, 1797. Phineas, dejected after so many months of hope, explained the outcome to Eli in a letter written on May 11.

The tide of popular opinion was running in our favor and the Judge was well-disposed towards us, and many friends were with us who adhered firmly to our cause... The Judge gave a charge to the jury pointedly in our favor; after which the defendant himself told an acquaintance of his that he would give two-thousand dollars to be free of the verdict. And yet the jury gave it against us after a consultation of about an hour. Thus after four years of assiduous labor, fatigue and difficulty we are again set afloat by a new and unexpected obstacle. The actual crisis has now arrived which I have long mentioned as possible—our insolvency as a partnership.

These months weighed heavily on Kitty and Phineas, but their love remained unfaltering. Kitty helped Phineas in every aspect of his life, including taking on the role of encourager under new burdens and anxieties. When they received his letter of October 7, 1797, they understood that Eli was experiencing the strains of adversity even more heavily than they.

The extreme embarrassments which have been accumulating upon me are now becoming so great that it will be impossible for me to struggle against them much longer. I have labored hard against the strong current of disappointment, which has been threatening to carry us down the cataract, and I have labored with a shattered oar. I am now far enough advanced in life to think seriously of marrying. I have looked forward with pleasure to an alliance with an amiable and virtuous companion, as a source from whence I expected one day to derive the greatest happiness. But my own unremitted attention has been devoted to our business. It is better not to live than to live as I have for three years past. Toil and disappointment have broken me down in my perfectly miserable situation.

Kitty cried openly as she read her friend's words. She felt determined to help Eli in some way, but what could she do? Phineas consoled her by writing Eli an uplifting response.

It is very true that I have the advantage of you in partaking with a beloved partner of my life the sweets of domestic felicity, but you will remember, my dear Whitney, that this is not my fault. I have borne my proportion of the burdens occasioned by our failure. Although we have lost money, I shall be tolerably well-satisfied if by prudence we can be preserved from ruin and able to preserve our integrity and character. Kitty and I wish you would contemplate the same for your life, as we hold you in great esteem.

Eli pulled himself together and entered into a contract with the federal government for the manufacture of firearms. He deliberated the decision, knowing he would be forced to live in the Northeast. Yet he wrote them of his plans, adding that he would *constantly long for Mulberry Grove, where I have enjoyed a society I had never known before. I will sorely miss the new social freedoms I discovered under Kitty's guidance, and the stimulation of Phineas' friendships with the eminent gentlemen who flocked to the plantation.*

FORTY TWO

1798-1800

All of their money was gone. The post-Revolutionary boom was followed by a period of depression which began in 1790. On October 17, 1798, Phineas was forced to place a notice in the Savannah paper advertising the sale of Mulberry Grove.

Property is remarkably well-adapted to ornamental improvement and profitable culture. There are 400 acres of river swamp, under good care and well drained, and 200 acres of upland in good order for cotton or provisions. The remaining 2,000 acres consist of oak, hickory, and well-timbered pine land.

They had been able to hold on to Nathanael's property on Cumberland Island, and after hours of discussion, Kitty and Phineas decided to move there with the children. They would revise Nathanael's plan to sell live oak to the navy. They also hoped to grow Sea Island cotton on Cumberland Island, well-aware that the New England states and Great Britain were clamoring to buy it.

Eli Whitney continued living and working in Connecticut, yet remained in correspondence with the Millers. Kitty wrote him that they were virtually living in poverty, save for the food they could grow on the plantation. She told him that when the creditors and tax collectors bore down on them, they were forced to sell twelve slaves from the rice plantation in order to raise the necessary money.

There were no buyers for the plantation. Times were difficult in Georgia, and nobody had the money or the inclination to spend it on such a large property as Mulberry Groove.

In early 1799, Phineas wrote Whitney a dismal letter.

> *There is no relief in sight, my friend. The prospect of making anything by ginning in this state is at an end. Surreptitious gins are erected in every part of the country; and the jurymen at Augusta have come to an understanding that they will never give a verdict in our favor, even though the merits of the case be as they may.*

An update even more distressing than their personal news arrived in a letter from Mount Vernon, written by Martha Washington. Her beloved George was dead.

"Oh no! Not George! Dear God," howled Kitty. Phineas heard her anguished voice and charged from the patio into the parlor. Kitty turned to him with a dazed expression.

"My God, what does the letter say?" He reached for her hand.

"I can't take any more bad news. I simply cannot," she keened, her heart slashed with pain.

Phineas took the letter from her hand and read through it quickly. He felt his own tears burning their way from beneath his lids. Martha's words, so tender and loving, expressed the incredible bond they shared, a bond that would continue beyond George Washington's death.

> *Together we had enjoyed reorganizing Mt. Vernon to make it more easily manageable, for us and for the grandchildren...On December 12, George returned from his dusty, cold ride wet and shivering, yet refused to change his damp clothes before dinner. The next day, he went out in the snow to mark the trees to be cut, even though he clearly exhibited symptoms of a bad cold. That evening, he read the newspaper to me and a friend—his throat was congested and his voice muffled. In the middle of the night, George experienced great*

trouble breathing, but refused to let me go for help until the morning came. At dawn I arose and sent for three doctors, who alternately bled, purged and blistered him, but to no avail. They said he had contracted quinsy, a severe throat infection. They told me that it would progressively close his windpipe until he suffocated.

Phineas could not continue. He turned away, his expression unexpectedly vulnerable, letting the letter float to the floor.

"Dear Martha composed the most tragic sentence," murmured Kitty. "I cannot even imagine how devastating it was for her to watch him suffocate." Sobbing, she picked up the missive. "She said *that his dying was prolonged by his strength.* Oh my Lord; my poor Patsy," she whimpered, referring to Martha by the pet name she had used so many years back.

'Tis well that it is over. I shall soon follow him. I have no more trials to pass through. His body lay in state in its lead-lined mahogany coffin for three days, according to his death-bed wishes. The night he died, December 14, 1799, I moved into a small third floor bedroom. I closed off his study and our bedroom forever. I shall never sleep again in the large bed we happily shared.

"I cannot believe her strength. I could never have stood up so well under such tremendous grief."

Phineas tenderly settled her under his arm. "But you did, my love. Several times. I was there." A slow smile crossed his lips.

She had become quiet. After a long pause, she spoke up. "Darling, do you remember how George was never too busy to listen to my personal problems? That man, who held the country together during its most hopeless days, always made time for me."

"He was indeed your friend, as is Martha. What will you do?"

"I must go to her as soon as I can. In spite of our financial difficulties, I must find a way."

The next letter to arrive was from Edward Rutledge's son. He informed them that Edward, currently governor of South Carolina, had died a few days ago. He had been in bad health and depressed over political misfortune. Within three weeks Kitty had lost two of her closest friends.

There was one piece of good news for the Millers. Phineas won a contract in late 1799 to supply live oak frames for six 74-gun ships in Georgia and another contract to supply two 74-gun ships to Colonel Shubrick of South Carolina. This would be a promising beginning for their transition to Cumberland Island.

The new century was dawning. Kitty tried to keep an optimistic outlook, in spite of their many problems. The economic depression of 1800 grabbed hold of the South and made it nearly impossible to sell the plantation. Yet Kitty and her family struggled on.

"Phineas, notwithstanding our financial problems, we still have each other and the children," she said, during one of their customary afternoon walks to the river.

"We are blessed, my lady. We have food, beauty around us, and a great affection for each other." He stopped suddenly, twisted off a garland of wisteria, and placed it in her hand.

"My favorite," she giggled. "We shall adorn the supper table with the fragrance of wisteria, known also as the nectar of the gods." Breathing in the aromatic sweetness, they laughed as the gentle breezes teased the bouquets into a sensuous sway.

"I believe wisteria, like love, defies description. Words are inadequate to convey the quality of its fragrance, just as they are inadequate to portray my love for you." Phineas' voice and expression were gentle. She slipped her hand through his and squeezed tightly, and then turned to face him.

Reaching up, Kitty cupped the back of his neck with one hand and brought his lips to hers, kissing him deeply and urgently. He saw a sparkling invitation in her eyes. His gaze traced her nose, lips and down to the smooth line of her jaw, and he sighed, a shiver of desire snaking its way through his veins.

Laughing, he leisurely released her. "Kitty, I've just realized the source of our passion."

She arched her eyebrows and giggled. "You have?"

"It has occurred to me that the lack of fulfillment is the most precious gift we have. It is the source of our passion, and also our search for God. 'Tis even the source of our creativity. Do you not believe that the best of life comes from our human yearnings, and from being unsatisfied?"

Kitty took a deep breath before answering. "Are you saying that by suffering financially now, we appreciate each other more? And we search more earnestly for God?"

He grinned, looping an arm around her waist. "Indeed I am. And we will find our creativity as we release our control to Him. He will guide us, and turn our yearnings into blessings." Their eyes met as they laughed quietly at the wonder and absurdity of appreciating their weakening circumstances.

They walked back home, holding hands. The wisteria was clasped in Kitty's other hand, and she swung her arm in contentment. The sun wasn't quite down yet, but the light was gray. The days were marked by this protracted twilight, darker shadows gathering among the trees while the sky remained the color of dark blue steel.

"Papa often told us that miracles fill the space that is given to them," Kitty told him. "And unlike dreams, miracles do come to life."

FORTY THREE

1800-1802

Mulberry Grove was put on the auction block in August, 1800. On August 6, Major Edward Harden paid $15,000, an amount far below what the Millers had expected. Fortunately, Kitty and Phineas were not present for the humiliating transition since they had already moved to Cumberland Island several weeks before.

The Millers, Kitty's children, John Nightingale, and the household staff and slaves arrived together to the virtually uninhabited island. The Lynch family, co-owners of the island, ran an indigo plantation attended by slaves. Separated from the mainland by tidal waterways and marshes, this large barrier island offered a warm refuge for the displaced family from Mulberry Grove. Almost eighteen miles long and three miles wide, Cumberland possessed a seventeen-mile white sandy beach, and it was situated only two miles from the mainland.

"I love the little bluffs here," Kitty said to the family. "They are much lower than the craggy bluffs where I grew up on Block Island, but they are sandy bluffs nevertheless. And here we have warm breezes, wild cattle and boar, and several varieties of turtle."

Fourteen years earlier, on the southern tip of the island overlooking the sea, Nathanael Greene had begun construction on his family's future home. Now only the foundation stones were in place, so Kitty and her family moved into a humble dwelling two miles north of the site. They knew that with time and money, they would build their home on the same spot Nathanael had chosen for them.

They all worked together. The slaves cleared the land for sugar cane and cotton fields while the family planted vegetable and flower gardens. Years ago Nat planted magnolia trees, now blossomed into glossy leaves and huge, fragrant white flowers. Kitty remarked that few trees could match the magnolia for year-round beauty.

The work was financed through a contract specifically drawn up with permission to cut down a certain quantity of live oaks. Eli Whitney's brother Josiah, an agent of the Millers in the lumber business, helped secure government contracts when needed. To get the job done, they employed a work gang of over one hundred men; all of them met daily at the humble Miller dwelling for their meals.

Kitty's main interest was to prepare the fields for cotton. She supervised the cutting and burning of trees in the island's thick maritime forest, and soon rows of snowy white cotton bolls were visible throughout the fields. They hoped to begin construction of their mansion on the south end with their profits in both cotton and timber. They would call it *Dungeness*, after a rustic lodge by the same name that General Oglethorpe built for himself on Cumberland around 1736.

"Why did he call it Dungeness, Mama?" asked Cornelia.

"Your father told me that General Oglethorpe named it for his friend, the Duke of Cumberland, (for whom he named the island) and his castle in England. Castle Dungeness was situated on the Cape of Dungeness in the county of Kent. We both liked the name and the history behind it."

"Are we going to follow Papa's plan for the house? Will there be thirty rooms, as he proposed?"

Kitty laughed. Cornelia, at twenty-two, reminded her so much of herself at that age. "Let's wait and see what the new architect thinks of your father's drawings before we commit to that."

There were many debts still pending on Nathanael's estate, and near the end of 1800 a federal marshal came to the island to sell portions of Nathanael's Cumberland properties. One buyer was Lucy Stafford Spalding, a widow who purchased one hundred twenty-five acres. Her son, Robert Stafford, would later become Cumberland's largest landholder.

Kitty and Phineas remained optimistic as they envisioned great profits from both the cotton and lumber sales. They brought in architects and craftsmen to commence the construction of their home. It would have a tabby foundation six-feet thick below ground and four-feet thick above ground. Tabby was a mixture of limestone, water, oyster shells and sand, and was easily available on the island. As far as they knew, their house would be the largest house ever built of tabby.

The house would be nearly ninety feet tall. It was designed to have four stories over a basement, where the servants would live. The first two stories held the lofty tall-windowed rooms for entertaining and dining. The third and fourth stories contained the bedrooms. A massive flight of steps climbed up to the front entrance, laced with hewn granite. The roof was covered in copper and included four brick chimneys, from which sixteen fireplaces would expel their fumes.

On the outside, there were to be six Doric-crowned columns, running from the basement to the roof. A colossal flight of stairs led to the doorway, flanked with granite. Kitty knew her elegant garden had to be as magnificent as her home, and spared no expense in making it so. She and Phineas laid out over twelve acres of intricate, detailed gardens, surrounded by a tabby wall. Then they built terraces descending to the salt-water marshes, and Phineas made certain that trees and shrubs of tropical fruits were included among the flora.

One of the early visitors to Cumberland commented in a letter: *The garden and the grounds seem quite a paradise with hedges formed of lemon, groves of orange trees, roses and other flowers in full bloom, even though it is only January.*

During the duration of the construction of Dungeness, Kitty lost no time in making sure her two single daughters were introduced to a number of eligible males. She invited Dr. Lemuel Kollock, who had been their family physician in Savannah for several years, to visit them in their humble dwelling. Kitty and Phineas had known him in Newport, and eventually persuaded him to move to Georgia. He was about fourteen years older than Cornelia, and had earned a reputation for his romantic conquests in Savannah, but Kitty hoped Cornelia might find him interesting and attractive.

Cornelia was having no part of the plan. "Mama, please do not insist that I entertain Dr. Kollock. I do not much like him, and his reputation for sowing wild oats is disgusting."

Kitty smiled perceptively, knowing that her daughter resembled her character more than the other children did. She was pretty, popular and had already captured the interest of several men in Savannah while living at Mulberry Grove. One of her suitors was so smitten that he asked his father, explorer John McQueen, to name a mountain after her. *Mount Cornelia* is the highest point in Duval County, Florida.

Eli Whitney was lonesome, and ready to return to Georgia. He missed the children, Phineas and the southern hospitality, but most of all, he missed Kitty. He even considered courting young Cornelia, but changed his mind when he realized that neither Kitty nor Phineas would help him with his plans. They wrote that he would need to come down and accomplish this himself, but Cornelia gave him no encouragement. Sadly, her mind had been poisoned against Eli by a mutual "friend" from Newport, importer Ethan Clarke. Learning of this, Eli decided to remain in New Haven.

During the late summer of 1800, Kitty and several of her children became ill and decided to move closer to the curative sea air on the southern part of the island. This put them near the site of Dungeness, which was slowly taking shape. They moved into a small cottage, with easy access to the orchards and fields. Even after recovering, they decided to stay there.

Kitty and Phineas continued their late afternoon walks together, and now were intrigued by the secrets of the changing beach and ocean.

"I love the feel of the salty breeze sliding across my face," said Kitty. "And listening to the squealing of gulls and the pounding of the surf on the shore."

Phineas laughed. "I've always found this island entrancing and seductive, with its moss-laden trees almost as ancient as the surf itself." Lifting his head, he began to sing in praise.

At other times they walked to the sunset end of the ocean, searching for the silent places far down the beach where they heard absolutely nothing. They walked until the sea became soundless and unmoving. Sometimes they found it, and the ocean's silence amazed them. The beach turned flat and smooth, like shiny ice, and the water was so still that it looked like glass shimmering in the pink haze just before sunset.

"Kitty, I never knew the ocean had non-moving parts. The birds are quiet here as well."

She nodded. "I love the silence of this spot." Squeezing his fingers, she added, "We should come back often."

❧⊙❧

Kitty held up a letter and read it with excitement in her voice. "We're invited to a house party in St. Marys," she enthused. "It will be a long weekend for us, and the first time we've been off Cumberland since we arrived."

"Whose home is it, Mama?" asked Natty. "Who will be going?" Natty, now twenty years old, found life on the island to be dull and unexciting at times and looked forward to social activities.

"It will be at the home of James Seagrove, from New York, who has now moved to Georgia. Many of our New England friends will be in attendance. I believe a grand time will be had by all of us. Let's begin our preparations." St. Marys was a port on the Georgia mainland opposite Cumberland, and quickly reached by boat.

Phineas was unable to join them because he had business dealings on Cumberland that same weekend. He saw them off at the dock and wished them a wonderful time.

The second day of the visit, Kitty playfully accepted a dare to walk from one end of a scaffold to the other. When she reached the end, the host told her she had to pay a toll to come off, so she decided to turn around to escape in the opposite direction. Her foot slipped and she fell hard to the ground, brutally twisting her ankle.

Kitty was unable to walk and had to stay in her room for several days. She was frustrated and fought to remain in good humor, but her children were happily surprised to have unexpected freedom to interact with the guests and do as they wished. They made new friends and left the mainland with promises to visit each other.

The Millers and the Nightingales remained on Cumberland for an entire year, and Patty and John began building their own dwelling on Tract 3, calling it *The Springs*. They were all invited over Christmas to Savannah, as guests of Dr. Kollock. Kitty had been feeling poorly for over a month, but the festive parties and gathering of friends lifted her spirits and she quickly recovered. They also visited their Mulberry Grove Plantation, meeting the family that now owned it.

"Do you feel sad, Mama?" asked her kind-hearted daughter Louisa after they left.

Kitty smiled, reflecting on so many memories. "A little, darling, but we have a new home now on an island we love. And one day soon, we shall be able to move into our new mansion."

Louisa nodded pensively, deciding not to tell her mother how much she missed her childhood at Mulberry Grove.

Cornelia socialized with the young men on the mainland, and soon found herself particularly captivated by a young Virginian, Peyton Skipwith, Jr. Raised in a prominent family in Richmond, he came to Georgia looking for an opportunity in the quickly expanding cotton business. He settled on Cumberland Island as a land investor and a planting partner of Phineas Miller and John Nightingale. He and Cornelia had a lot in common and several months later, realized they were in love.

"Cornelia, should I ask for your hand from Phineas or your mother?" Peyton wanted to follow protocol, but more importantly, wanted to please his beloved.

She laughed. "Why don't you ask both of them? Mama always has a say in every decision, as you well know."

In April of 1802, Skipwith and Cornelia were married on Cumberland Island. Phineas, as the island's justice of the peace, officiated the sunset wedding on the white sandy beach, just as the sun submerged into the horizon. The last light reflections over the undulating waves appeared as sparkling stars, breaking off into brilliant speckles as the groom angled the bride's face to kiss her.

"Phineas, it's been almost two years since we moved here, and tomorrow our dear Cornelia will leave us for her new life." Kitty was trying to smile as she swiped the wetness from her lower lashes. She loved her children and wanted them to be happy, yet knew they would leave her one day. That day had come for Cornelia, the daughter who most resembled her. Cornelia and Skipwith left Cumberland the following day to their new home on the mainland, just a few miles from St. Marys.

"We shall see them often, love. They will come and go, as will we. It will not be as hard as you believe." Phineas lowered his arm to encircle her waist. His other hand slid to the small of her back, drawing her lower body close.

FORTY FOUR

1802-1803

Phineas Miller struggled to save the firm of Miller and Whitney, bringing lawsuits against Georgia businessmen who infringed on the patent rights with no regard to the law. He and Eli finally agreed to sell the patent, and the state of South Carolina was interested. Because of his own connection with the Yazoo scandal, Phineas asked Eli to travel to Columbia, South Carolina, to handle the transaction.

Eli completed negotiations with the South Carolina General Assembly, and quickly sent word that he was on his way to Cumberland. Stepping off the boat at the dock on Cumberland Island, he wrapped the Millers in a bear hug, beaming from ear to ear.

"What? You are so jovial! What good tidings have you?" asked Kitty, suspiciously.

"Indeed I do! I have, on my person, the agreement we've made with the legislature."

"Say your piece, old chum," encouraged Phineas, holding his breath.

"They have agreed to pay us $50,000 for the rights to the gin!!!"

Kitty grabbed Phineas' arm and let out an ecstatic whoop of joy right there on the dock. The workers turned around and grinned. The Miller and Whitney Company, after years of maligned and discriminated treatment, now found themselves solvent.

When they finally settled down back at the dwelling, Eli told them his story.

"You both know how I detest water travel, so I came south on a sulky—a lightweight cart having two wheels and a seat for the driver only—pulled by a horse I employed for the journey. I spent nearly two weeks in Columbia attending the sessions of the legislature, begging the support of the lawmakers in my bid to sell the patent rights. Believe me when I say that was more frustrating and time-consuming than making the cotton gin."

Turning to face Phineas, he grinned. "I can now surely appreciate the exhausting nature of the legal work you have done for years on behalf of our partnership."

Kitty broke in. "And what did they tell you?"

"They finally said 'Aye,' and an hour after the vote, I commenced my journey to see you."

"Oh Eli, how long have we hungered for this news! God is so good, and you are our angel," declared Kitty, deep affection shining through her eyes.

Eli spent several weeks on Cumberland, resting and relaxing, surrounded by the family he loved. He helped them prepare Dungeness for their upcoming move, and relished time spent on the twelve acres of tropical gardens, where he discovered countless varieties of semi-tropical and tropical fruit trees. There were flowers and shrubs mixed in; all the foliage was surrounded by a high tabby wall separating them from the fields of cane and cotton.

At the rear of the main house he discovered terraced gardens bordered by eight hundred silvery olive trees, leading down to the boathouse and landing on a nearby stream. At the front of the four-storied structure was a beautiful magnolia tree-lined avenue.

Kitty approached Eli, standing at the edge of the garden. "Do you like the magnolias?" she asked him.

He nodded. "They are beautiful."

"Nat planted them about sixteen years ago. He must have known they would draw me to this avenue again and again. Remember our tree-lined entrance at Mulberry Grove? Perhaps he wanted to duplicate it, but with magnolias instead of oaks."

Eli turned and looked a long moment into her face, as if it were a mirror and he were looking at himself in her eyes. "Are you happy, Kitty? Do you have all that your heart desires?"

She seemed to consider that. "I have all I need. I may still want things, but they are not necessary to fulfill my serenity." Placing her hand softly over his forearm she added, "And I hope the same for you in life, my dear friend."

A shadow passed over his face. "Sometimes I feel my life is running through my hands like water."

Kitty gave him a gentle smile. "Remember Eli, we all must look for the good still to come."

The sky groaned and cracked, and suddenly the cold, shrill needles of rain pierced their hands and the backs of their necks. Lightning sang and hissed around their shoulders, and thunder bellowed. The rain came straight down, striking the ground hard as a slap. Laughing together, Kitty and Eli raced toward the mansion, watching the trees roar and dance as if they were on fire.

🙂

Cumberland Island was made up of forests and marshes and had no villages, so dwellings and farms were scattered everywhere. The inhabitants agreed to build a road to connect the north end to the south, a distance of eighteen miles. They called it *Grand Avenue* and cut it through the dense forest that covered the interior of the isle. Kitty thought it looked like a fairytale tunnel, with its intertwining branches of live-oak trees covered by Spanish moss. Grand Avenue became the line of communication for everyone on the island.

Eli returned to Connecticut, and the Millers finally moved into their ninety-foot-tall dwelling, Dungeness. Kitty invited her younger sister and brother-in-law, Phebe and Ray Sands, and their children to live with them. She and Phineas, Louisa and Natty, and the servants made up the rest of the family inhabiting the beautiful mansion. Kitty was thrilled to share

Dungeness with everyone, and began planning long weekend visits for friends and family.

Always the gracious hostess, Kitty offered meals that were excellent and healthy. The fields and orchards provided quantities of vegetables and fruits. The streams and ocean yielded fish and shellfish, and the game abounded. Giant sea turtles trapped on the beach gave her the opportunity to create a soup that made her famous in the coastal region. Venison became a staple, as the island abounded in deer. The Millers were completely independent of the outside world as far as their culinary needs, and the well-managed plantation soon yielded generous cash income as well.

Phineas returned from a business trip to Savannah and handed her a newspaper article. *Dungeness, on Cumberland Island, is the Most Elegant Residence on the Georgia Coast* was the story title. She hugged him and then read the review, basking in the glory of her newly-earned trophy.

"And we've not even finished many of the rooms yet," she giggled. "It's a good thing they only asked to see a few of them when they visited."

Phineas chuckled at her delight. "Well, you've always said that once you finish a house, some misfortune would befall it and its occupants. You asked me to stop construction for that reason."

She gave him one of her sweet-eyed smiles, and then she raised her eyebrows at him. "Possibly because we were also running out of money, darling. But this is exactly what I wanted and you have given it to me." She tightened her arms around him. "I love you so much, Phineas."

"And I love you, my dear Kitty. I am a fortunate man to be your husband." His expression brightened. "Would you like to take a dip in the ocean?" he asked, with the enthusiasm of a child.

"Of course. And I'll prepare a basket of food to eat by the water to celebrate our good fortune."

The ocean was cool and dark green in its depths, with sunlight dancing on the surface. They immersed themselves all the way under the small waves and rode them into the beach, dunking each other, shouting and laughing and tumbling like puppies at the water's edge. Shaking the salt water from their bodies, they settled down to a meal of cold meat, cheese and biscuits, accompanied by Kitty's specialty—watermelon-rind pickles.

The white beach was empty, and the tall, half-dead palm trees rustled in the breeze. After a short rest in the shade, they stood up to walk again. Phineas pulled Kitty close into the curve of his body as they strolled slowly, kicking the glittering foam, arms wrapped around each other's waists. Languor surrounded them like the warm water.

"Darling, have you noticed that when we started out the air and water were almost alike, so still and thick and warm that it was like wading in warm blood?"

Phineas looked at her, a question forming on his lips as she continued. "But now a little wind has sprung up and it's all changing. The gentle surf creaming in around our ankles is now charged with bubbles, and the sun pouring over our bare heads and shoulders has mellowed."

"You are correct. Why, even the palm trees are clattering in the wind."

"Do you suppose this is a forewarning of the changes crossing the threshold of our lives?" Kitty stared at him and he saw the lively sparks disappear from her eyes.

Opening his arms, he folded them around her. "We have been blessed, Kitty dear. But we have worked hard, and now we have the lives we want," he told her, with a smile in his voice. " This will not be taken away from us."

"Nor will our love," she whispered. "That will endure as well," she added, with absolute conviction.

Looking over her shoulder, she took a last glance at the gray-blue Atlantic, now glittering in the hard sun, as if a handful of diamond dust had been tossed down upon it.

FORTY FIVE

1803–1804

Kitty and Phineas savored this harmonious season in their lives, filled with family, weekend events, and a successful harvest. The Sea Island cotton grown on their land was considered among the best that could be raised, and the lumber from their live-oak forests was shipped to ports all over the world. They signed on to a contract with the federal government to build the man-of-war ships. Cumberland oak, used in building the famed hull of the *U.S.S. Constitution,* was responsible for its nickname, *Old Ironsides.* The wood was so hard the British shot merely bounced off the sides.

After a year of entertaining and enjoying their life at Dungeness, Kitty experienced the peace she had always longed for. Her family was growing: Patty, living only a few miles north of Dungeness, had a baby boy she named Phineas. Cornelia, with her husband and young son, lived close by on the mainland, and often spent weeks on the island with her family. Rhode Islanders came to visit and stayed for a month; her Savannah friends stopped by regularly, and Kitty and Phineas occasionally hosted a gala dance event. This was the existence Kitty had always dreamed of, and now it was hers.

She offered her guests extravagant dinners of shrimp, crabs, oysters, and fish. There were courses of turkey, chicken, duck and geese. Pork, mutton, beef and venison completed the heavy main courses, which were always accompanied by a variety of vegetables, jellies and preserves. For dessert she loved to make her own brandy-soaked peaches recipe, certainly a crowd-pleaser. She insisted that her wine cellars be well stocked for everyone's individual preferences.

The Millers' guests enjoyed hunting, picnicking, fishing and carriage rides on the beach or through the wooded trails. In the evenings, they played cards and charades, or held musical performances and dances. Dungeness became the heart of the social activities in southeast Georgia.

In 1803, Phineas was elected to the State Senate from Camden County and also named Justice of the Interior Court.

"How will you ever find the time to work our fields, cut the timber, and assist me with our social affairs?" asked Kitty, grinning broadly. She knew he would manage it all.

Phineas traveled to St. Augustine, Florida in the fall to procure more tropical plants. In one of the gardens where he shopped, he carelessly punctured his finger on a thorn. On his return to Dungeness, he showed his sore finger to his wife.

"What do you make of this, Kitty?" he asked. "It has been more than a week, and the pain doesn't lessen."

"I will send for Dr. Kollock," she told him. Panic had replaced the concern in her eyes. She applied hot poultices— soft moist masses of herbs and cloth—to bring down the swelling. It grew worse.

Dr. Kollock examined Phineas and took Kitty aside.

"He has blood poisoning. There is not much we can do. His body will either fight it off, or it will succumb to the infection. I am so sorry, Kitty."

Her face crumpled with shock. "Surely there is more you can do. You have been educated in saving lives, not losing them," she moaned, tears springing to her eyes.

"You can continue the poultices if you wish, but we have not discovered a cure for blood poisoning. It is simply bacteria in the bloodstream, which in the medical world is known as *bacteremia*."

"What will happen to Phineas?" Kitty asked, closing her eyes and battling a wave of nausea and helplessness.

"He will have high fever, chills, nausea, vomiting and eventually delirium."

Kitty swallowed hard, containing her tears. "Dr. Kollock, I've known you for years. Please give me all the options. Should I call in more doctors? I cannot just sit here and watch him die," she cried out, her words edged in grief and fear.

He leaned forward and took her hand. "Kitty, I truly wish I could give you better news. I have none. We have no cure for bacteremia. I am very sorry." Kitty would later remember this moment as being so large it filled up the whole room and pressed her down into a chair.

"Make him as comfortable as you can," he urged. "He knows how much you love him."

Kitty gave up all her other duties and nursed Phineas hour after hour. Each day she examined his face for signs of improvement. She prayed fervently, begging God to spare his life. She watched him growing weaker, and did everything in her power to comfort him.

He leaned on her for strength. She held his hand, willing him all of her energy.

"My love, are you in pain?" she asked.

"No, Kitty," he smiled, focusing his eyes on hers. "I am dreaming about our new life together. I can barely stay awake."

She sat still for a moment, lips slightly parted, breathing through her mouth. Turning to him in the dark, she stroked his shoulders slowly, lovingly, urging him back from sleep to be with her.

A slow stream of tears trickled down her cheeks. "Please wait for me, Phineas. We shall all be together soon," she whimpered, gripping his burning hand in hers.

She read him stories from his favorite books and the poetry he loved.

"My sweet lady unveiled," he whispered to her late one evening. "I am standing in the room our Father has prepared for you." His voice broke, and she could not understand his next words. She thought he said, "I see you clearly—all of your heart."

"Phineas, are you dreaming?" She turned away, hiding the rush of tears gathering in her eyes.

Reaching for her trembling fingers, he held them to his lips. "You have so many crowns for your loving works. They are in your Heavenly room," he wheezed. "So tired…"

Lady unveiled? What did he mean by that? Memories rushed up, filling the room, holding her in place; the riverbanks with their sweet citrus scent of jasmine; his touch; the clearing of his throat; the sunlight of a lost afternoon moving in patterns on the wooden floors.

Phineas slowly opened his fingers as fatigue overcame him, releasing hers to the bed covers. "I go with Him now, love." She bent her head to his chest, corrosive tears pouring from her eyes as she prayed for his journey home.

Unexpectedly, Kitty sensed her pain as a part of beauty. She became aware that love, moonlight and sunlight are all shafts of pain, and that we are all meant to bear it.

Death came to Phineas on December 7, 1803, demolishing Kitty's world and bringing the island's inhabitants to their knees. A cloud of despondency hovered over Cumberland. Kitty withdrew into her cocoon, knowing what to expect. Her mind knew the pain would ease in time. Her heart felt they should be buried together. Her sad, sweet familiar sorrow had returned to sit down beside her.

∽⊙⊙⊙∾

The gentlest of men had died, only thirty-nine years old. He was buried in a garden at Dungeness. Eli Whitney was in North Carolina at the time of his death, negotiating the sale of the rights to the cotton gin. He headed to Georgia, understanding the adversity he would face because of the lawsuits Phineas had filed. Driven by fierce resolution, he had prepared his evidence to fire against his enemies, knowing that with Phineas' help, he would prevail. Arriving in Savannah in January, 1804, he was stunned by the shocking news of his partner's death the month before.

Eli rushed to Cumberland to share in the grief of Kitty and her family. He felt somewhat responsible for his death.

"Kitty, do you think the misfortunes of the cotton gin and the heavy burdens of the legal and financial affairs aged Phineas beyond his years?"

Kitty shot him a sideways look. "I do not understand, Eli."

"Did that weight on his shoulders weaken him, allowing these bacteria to end his life?" he asked her, agitated.

She went to him. "Look at me, Eli. He died of blood poisoning. None of us, nor his past, had anything to do with it. Please do not take responsibility for his death."

The heavy gloom of his passing continued over Dungeness. Eli left them and traveled to the mainland to face the struggles of the cotton gin enterprise alone.

They quickly received news of another tragedy—a fatal duel in Savannah between two of Kitty's family friends: Dr. Horatio Senter, son of her former Newport physician Dr. Isaac Senter, and John Rutledge, Jr., nephew of Edward and son of her former hosts in Charleston. She had known them both since boyhood.

Young Rutledge's wife was under the care of young Dr. Senter during a trip to Newport, and fell in love with him. Senter later moved to Savannah and set up practice under Dr. Kollock, perhaps to be closer to Mrs. Rutledge. When Senter visited his beloved in her country home near Charleston, they were surprised by the unexpected arrival of Rutledge. He fired on Senter as he ran from the home, but Senter suffered only a flesh wound in the hand.

Jealous and angry, Rutledge followed Senter to Savannah and issued a challenge. They met with pistols at dawn on the Strand above the Savannah River. Senter was hit in his left leg, just below the knee. His limb was amputated, yet he died of tetanus several days later. Sadly, this episode in their lives destroyed Mr. Rutledge's peace of mind and ruined his wife's character forever.

As if this were not enough for Kitty to bear, the shocking news of Alexander Hamilton's violent death reached Cumberland during the summer of 1804. He encountered Aaron Burr, vice-president of the United States, in a duel at Weehawken, New Jersey. Hamilton was killed, and Kitty went into mourning again. She remembered well how Lady Washington had named a tomcat in Hamilton's honor when they were all living in Middlebrook. She knew how much Alexander had helped her in her petition to Congress.

Kitty was appalled to learn that her old friend and lawyer, Nat Pendleton, had served as Hamilton's second in the fatal duel, and read the rules to the duelists, giving the ominous signal to fire. He held Hamilton in his arms as the dying man was rowed back across the river to New York. Grieving for his friend, Pendleton returned to the spot of the encounter and brought back a bullet-pierced limb from the treetop to prove Hamilton purposely fired into the air, consequently sparing Burr's life and sacrificing his own.

In the late summer of 1804 Aaron Burr, now a fugitive from justice, sent word to Kitty from his hiding place on St. Simons Island that he wanted to spend some time at Dungeness. Because she was a close friend of Alexander Hamilton, and aware that Cornelia once had a crush on him, she faced a huge dilemma, where her manners were put to the test. Kitty knew she could not deny a request from a former aide on George Washington's staff, but she had been Hamilton's dear friend.

Conferring with her children, she realized that she could not receive the man whose hands were tainted with the blood of Alexander Hamilton, even though he had been Nathanael's friend.

"Follow your instincts, Mama," said Patty. "Worry not about the others' opinions."

Cornelia shook her head. "Mama always thinks her viewpoint is the only one, don't you Mama?"

Kitty looked away. It seemed that she and Cornelia were at odds lately, and she wanted to resolve that. "Perhaps you are right, dear. I must be more tolerant of others, mustn't I?"

Unusual weather was coming and this gave Kitty hope that Aaron Burr would stay away. As the sea crashed high up the beach into the interior of Cumberland Island, Kitty gathered family, friends and servants at Dungeness. Shutters rattled and the glass windows blew in, but the dwelling, with its four feet walls, remained strong.

The winds increased in strength until a full hurricane hit them, with an alarming degree of violence. Trees were ripped to the ground before the screaming gales, and the beaches were flooded with quickly rising waters. Four ships were driven ashore on the southern tip of Cumberland, where much land was cut away and the destruction was almost complete.From one end of the island to the other, the sturdiest live oaks were twisted up by the roots; the windswept pine trees lay flat, and the fruit and cotton crops were destroyed. The storm wrecked several slave cabins and peeled the "copper off the roof" of Dungeness. Around 10 p.m. the hurricane blew all the vessels out of the water at St. Marys, and they came to rest in the marshes. Eventually all the white and black inhabitants on the island were holed up at Dungeness, along with the passengers and crews of ships driven aground on the sandbars and beaches. When the winds settled and they could go outside, everyone helped clear debris from the fields and gardens. The plantation had stood up to the hurricane better than anyone expected. Amazingly, neither slaves nor free men perished that day.

Soon another note arrived from Aaron Burr—this one from St. Marys. Kitty formulated her plan.

She wrote back to Mr. Burr that he was welcome at Dungeness as long as he wanted to stay. When she learned the time of his arrival, she sent a servant from her home to meet his boat. She and the rest of her family jumped into several two-horse phaetons, hurrying down Grand Avenue to the interior of the island, where they sought refuge at a neighbor's home for as long as Burr was on the island. He was met at Dungeness by the household servants, shown to his room and given a meal.

The answers to his questions about the whereabouts of his hostess were vague, and after a day of enduring this slight, he requested to be returned to St. Marys. Kitty awaited word of his departure before she and her family drove home. Smiling, she realized she had completed her obligation to Burr while honoring her debt to Hamilton's memory. She never saw Aaron Burr again.

FORTY SIX

1804-1808

More than a year after Phineas' death, a doctor moved to St. Marys, Georgia to practice medicine. Dr. Daniel Turner, the son of Dr. Peter Turner—a friend of Kitty and Nathanael from Valley Forge days, came down from East Greenwich, Rhode Island.

Young Dr. Turner was a frequent visitor to Cumberland Island, tending to white and black inhabitants and befriending everyone he met. He spent so much time at Dungeness that Kitty referred to him as her "personal physician." Since Phineas' passing, she had generally felt unwell. He diagnosed her recurring illness as emotional, aggravated by her grief and insecurity surrounding her hopelessly snarled financial affairs.

It seemed that Dr. Turner had many more patients on Cumberland Island than in St. Marys, so he decided to live half a month at Dungeness. Kitty's slaves required frequent ministrations and their illnesses were often difficult to diagnose. Dr. Turner did his best, and was pleased to see that those working at Dungeness had humane working hours. Beginning at sunup and finishing by noon, they were allowed the rest of the day off to attend to their own needs. Kitty and Phineas gave each family its own cornfield and new clothing every season. They were also well-fed. Dr. Turner wrote his parents in 1805 about this unusual situation, and commended Kitty and her family.

The house servants live like family. They are generally well-dressed and very indulged. I predict that the Georgia slaves will succeed in emancipating themselves within a few years.

Young Nat is an eccentric good-hearted soul. Louisa is agreeably charming and I have every reason to be pleased with Patty, Cornelia and their husbands, John Nightingale and Peyton Skipwith. Mr. Skipwith is a man of understanding and property, affable in his manners and kind to me. He is a respected judge of the county court.

I receive the most flattering attentions from Mrs. Miller. She agreeably makes her house a home to me and others. If I find myself unwell or low-spirited and at leisure, I have orders from her to come immediately to Dungeness, and to stay there as long as I please and pretty much do as I wish.

The Miller family purchased a ten-oared, thirty-passenger canoe. Rowed by the black servants, the family enjoyed trips along the inland waterway to points across the Georgia and Florida coasts. Cornelia gave a house party, and they traveled up the Crooked River by canoe, moving slowly through the salt creeks past tiny marsh islands covered in spartina grass. The tide had ebbed, laying bare miles of oyster rakes. The air exuded the marsh's sulfurous smell. Swells of water glided past, the color of darkly steeped tea. Kitty breathed it all in deeply, finding the marshland's sense of freedom irresistible.

On another occasion, her son Nat and a few others wanted to take a trip to Savannah to visit the grave of Nathanael and George Greene.

He invited Kitty to join them. "Would you like to accompany us, Mama? Louisa and I are going to pay tribute to Papa and our brother."

Kitty smiled. "No, thank you. I want to remember them as they were in life. I fear it would be too depressing for me to stand next to a vault containing their remains."

Phineas left half of his estate to Kitty, and the remainder was divided among his seven brothers and sisters. Unfortunately, a great deal of her money had been turned over to Phineas to invest, in his name, in the maligned Yazoo fraud. Ironically, just as profits were beginning to be realized in the

Miller and Whitney Company, the death of Phineas dissolved the partnership.

Kitty realized she was at the mercy of the courts and Eli Whitney to receive income from her enormous speculations in the gin company. She trusted Eli completely, and knew she would soon receive $5,000 as Phineas' share of an installment paid by South Carolina for the patent rights in that state. In the meantime, she made her living and paid her debts from the proceeds of her plantation.

The passive tranquility of Cumberland Island was broken sporadically by the effects of the war being fought by England against Spain and France. Occasionally warships of these nations met head-on in ferocious battles, observed from the sandy shores by the residents of Cumberland. There were times when the firing of cannon could be heard off the bar. On one occasion, they were told that forty British sailors, after surrendering their ship, were brutally massacred by the Creoles who boarded their vessel.

Kitty was outraged when she learned that the St. Marys' merchants dealt illicitly with the captains of Spanish and French privateers. Her island was populated by conservative former New Englanders of Federalist leanings sympathetic to the British cause. The "Crackers"—poor rural whites—sided openly with the Spanish and French. The proximity of Spanish East Florida offered an opportunity for the St. Marys' merchants to make fortunes by smuggling goods from across the border.

Kitty's solution was to shun the St. Marys' merchants, refusing to trade with them. Other islanders avoided going into St. Marys, complaining to the lawmakers about the illegal activities there.

Hoping to cheer her mother up, Patty urged her to join her on a trip to Rhode Island.

"We will have such a lovely time together. You will feel much better in the Northeast, Mama."

Kitty was not feeling well and wanted no part of ocean

travel. "Sweetie, you are pregnant. Are you certain you want to subject yourself to ocean travel now?" Her mind traveled back to the days when she, also pregnant, traveled wherever Nathanael was stationed, taking her children with her.

"I must go and John will stay here to run the plantation. I know you would be very happy with your grandchildren, but I respect your wishes."

John stayed to work *The Springs*, the name they gave their estate. Kitty checked on him and invited him for meals. When he didn't show up two nights in a row, she sent Natty over to find out why.

"He's ill, Mama. He is not eating, and he doesn't want us to be concerned. But I feel you should send Dr. Turner to see him."

After his visit, Dr. Turner concluded John had the flu. Kitty went by the next day, taking him chicken broth and tea. He felt hot to the touch, and she quickly summoned Dr. Turner back.

On September 11, 1806, Dr. Turner found John dead in his bed. Patty was in New England with the children. Kitty knew she must write the letter to her daughter. Weeping as she penned it, the letter brought back her painful losses with Nathanael's and Phineas' deaths.

Patty returned in a state of shock at the end of 1806. She found no solace within the walls of her home, and took to wandering the beaches late at night. Kitty cared for the grandchildren, keeping them at Dungeness for weeks at a time, in spite of her health problems.

In the early spring of 1808, Kitty went north to Columbia, South Carolina on plantation business. She was able to successfully negotiate a contract with live-oak contractors. With the profit, she paid back a considerable amount of money borrowed from the Greene estate. Returning, she found two English boys, ten and thirteen, on the side of the road, tossed out by the captain of their vessel. Both were trained in the blacksmith trade, but were homeless, hungry and unemployed.

"I will take you to my island, where you will both work for me," she told them. "You will be cared for and when you prove your worth, I shall pay you."

She wrote to Eli that a settlement of Nat's estate was now at hand, and he should come to Cumberland Island to conclude it. She followed up this letter with a longer one, written on April 9, 1808.

My Dear Friend,

This has been a delightful day to my having accomplished one great object of my life—a settlement with my children of the estate of General Greene. I have had great cause to fear how their characters would turn out upon a trial of Self. My pride as a Mother is highly gratified as they have done honor to their education. I believe there are few instances where a mother and children divided a large estate and everyone could trust the other to do them justice.

Leaving the four children by themselves, they settled the estate in perfect love and harmony, which I consider worth the forty thousand dollars that each has divided for themselves, leaving me double that amount. I am doomed to go on to the North where I shall have the pleasure of seeing you. Perhaps in May you can expect me in New Haven. Louisa and Natty will go with me, and Patty will leave in a few days to go by land. I will go to New York by water.

My house is full of company—all in high spirits. When will you grace my gardens? Remember me always as your old friend, for I am so on all occasions.

Kitty boarded a vessel at St. Marys for a voyage to Newport. As she stepped aboard and waved good-bye to Cornelia, she felt free of the burdens that had weighed her down for so long. Fortunately she had no idea of the enormous problems awaiting her.

FORTY SEVEN

1808–1809

The primary reason for the family's journey to Rhode Island was the wedding of Nathanael Greene, twenty-eight years of age, to Anna Marie Clarke. Kitty was not at all fond of Anna Marie's father, Ethan Clark, but her love for Natty and her admiration of Anna Marie made the bitter pill easier to swallow.

Shortly after the wedding, Eli's younger brother Josiah went to visit Kitty and claimed that the Miller estate owed Eli a large sum of money. He had handled the Cumberland Island live-oak contract with the government, and gave her the notes he claimed Phineas had not paid. Kitty immediately wrote to Eli and asked him to explain this to her. Eli's answer was swift and to the point.

> It has been painful to me that you could for a moment suppose it possible that I could treat you, the person for whom I have long cherished the most sincere friendship and esteem, with marked contempt. Our mutual friend Kollock is here with his family, and insists that the dispute between you and Josiah be concluded. Do not believe that Josiah has commenced a lawsuit. You shan't want for bail in Connecticut. I believe you both are exercising less wisdom and discretion in this than you do on most other occasions. You two must be friends again.

Kitty traveled to New Haven to see Eli and meet with Josiah. Dr. Kollock, executor of Phineas' estate, was present. No agreement was reached so they traveled to New York to meet with the judges. These issues not only involved the Miller and Whitney Company and the live-oak contract, but also the old Yazoo investments. Kitty appeared before her old friend Nat Pendleton, now a Federal judge.

"Oh Nat, I am so happy to see you," she told him, smiling broadly. "You left Georgia so quickly that I feared I would never lay eyes upon you again."

Nathanael Pendleton seemed pleased to see her also. Kitty had always been a good friend, and time away from Georgia had mellowed him. He wished her well, and wanted to help her.

"Dear Kitty, I hope I can resolve your situation to your liking. Unfortunately, I also have entered a personal claim of $10,000 against the Miller estate for legal fees, which makes it all more difficult."

Her face fell. "Then I suppose this would be a conflict of interest, am I correct? Oh dear. Perhaps you can place this matter in another court?"

The burden of the lawsuit fell on Kitty's shoulders as both Eli and Kollock left her alone in New York to do what she could. In late October, she received the shocking news that Cornelia's husband had died in Georgia. Yearning for a friend to grieve with, she penned Eli a note that evening.

Poor Skipwith was one of the untimely victims of the cruel yellow fever raging in St. Marys. His death came on October 2. The night you left me I received this sad news. I am not fortified for such an addition to my propensity to melancholy and have been confined to my room ever since. Louisa was too traumatized, and was taken with violent puking, remaining indisposed. I have no other particulars than Skipwith died at Cumberland on the 2nd of October. All communication is stopped between Savannah and St. Marys, which increases my anxiety about Cornelia.

Kitty's unease became unbearable as infrequent news reached her about the yellow fever epidemic on the Georgia coast. She mourned incessantly when she learned that one of the victims was her personal physician, Daniel Turner, who had tended to the sick and dying unassisted for many weeks. He did not know he had contracted the disease until he nursed his house servant, who died in his arms. Dr. Turner kept on working until he could no longer stand. Then he lay down on his bed and died.

Forced to stay in New York to settle Phineas' accounts, she wrote Eli several letters urging him to return. He was fighting to keep the Federal inspectors from cancelling his musket contract, and could not leave New Haven. In their letters, they expressed their personal torments, their misgivings and their outlook on life. Eli wrote that he desperately wanted a wife and children of his own. Kitty told him to take care of his health, adding: *I am keeping a room for you here. I long to see you and learn what you know.*

Her daughter Louisa, a bright and lovely young lady, was now twenty-four years old and single. Kitty worked on a plan for Louisa and Eli to become a couple, encouraging her to write him. Louisa enclosed her letters with her mother's, but saw that most of his responses were addressed to Kitty. Since Louisa conformed to the most moral standards, she remained ill-at-ease in the presence of men.

In February of 1809, Nat Pendleton visited Kitty. He was not as friendly as he had been on the previous visit and insisted on an early meeting with the referees, anxious to be awarded the $10,000. Nothing could be done until Eli returned to New York, and Kitty was weary of fighting.

"Nat, I am disappointed in your behavior concerning my late husband's estate. We have been friends for so many years. Because of that, I will sign a note to you for the face value of your claim."

Nathanael Pendleton, shaken by her words, drew up the papers. "I appreciate that, Kitty," he told her, visibly uncomfortable.

"And I would like to believe that you will not press me for payment until the referees have certified your petition as a valid debt."

She offered the same gesture of faith to Josiah, satisfying his claim in full. Believing that both men would be grateful for her selfless gesture, she waited for Eli, who had promised to come to New York by the end of January. When February ended, Kitty was angry and wrote him on March 1, 1809.

> *I certainly am endowed with more than a common share of patience, my dear Whitney, to think of you with any kindness—after the shabby trick you have played on me. The greater part of last week our bell never rang but my fancy presented you, as the kind performer of your promise. You may judge therefore how many disappointments I have suffered, and you know that I never was celebrated for bearing disappointments as I ought. You will say it's time you learned then—and I will back you—but I say; if I must learn I will not be taught by you.*
>
> *Your letter of 25th February came to my hand (filled with many pretty things) a few hours ago. One of them is that you hope to see me soon, and you might have added—I hope I can flatter her along for a month, but I tell you must come immediately. If you were not compelled to come by duty and honor, than you should come from friendship.*
>
> *I shall set off soon for dear Dungeness, but do come here and let me scold you. I shall expect you by Sunday. If you delay longer you may have something to answer for—an uneasy conscience—and which I will tell you when I see you next Sunday—not one day grace after Sunday. God bless you with more leisure and every other good prayer.*
>
> *Your friend,*
> *C. Miller*

Eli didn't make her deadline. He was ill and bedridden and said he was wounded by her suspicions of his sincerity and will to serve her. She told him she was entitled to be vexed with him.

By late March Eli was well enough to travel to New York. They fell into each other's arms and Kitty forgave him. Her tears wet his neck, and she held on tightly. All of Kitty's doubts, bitterness and frustrations were now dissolved. Even though the legal affairs could not be settled during their time together, her friendship and close bond with Eli were renewed.

Shielding herself with her cheerful laughter, she divulged her profound secret. "When I realized you and Louisa were never going to marry, I had a moment of hope that you and I could share that holy union." Then she granted him her smile: that wide, slightly goofy smile that made him laugh.

"Oh Kitty, so many times I have imagined the same thing. But we are meant to be loving friends; comrades, if you will. I cherish that allegiance." Kitty stared helplessly as he tipped her chin and touched his lips to each of her cheeks. Pressing him to her heart, she told him she concurred.

They spent the next weeks in harmonious diversions, and were able to enjoy life together for the first time that year. Those were the last weeks Kitty would spend in New York.

✧☙◉☙✧

As they prepared to leave New York for Dungeness, Louisa came down with a strange illness. When she could travel, Kitty booked a vessel to take them to Rhode Island for a reunion with the other three Greene children. Pointing out Block Island en route to Newport, a massive gale struck their boat.

Trembling with fear, Kitty drew her daughter to her. "Louisa, if we make it through this storm, I will never again travel by open sea."

They remained in East Greenwich all summer. Louisa was unwell, and Kitty's two widowed daughters needed her love. The grandchildren brought her joy, and she knew she was where she needed to be. Patty was so miserable she could hardly care for her children. Kitty was happy to do so.

After years of absence, Kitty finally went back to visit Nathanael's brothers who still lived and worked in the Potowomut home. They adored Louisa. Each afternoon she would wait for them at the forge until they finished work and then rush to their sides, kissing their grimy faces and welcoming them home. Finding this ritual amusing and compassionate, Kitty shared it in a letter to Eli on July 27, 1809.

You would laugh to see her folded in the arms of her elderly uncles. They adore her and she is all gratitude to them. They are plain country people with very good sense but little education, living in the most plentiful but plain manor. They are very rich, but work just as hard as if they were poor and feel a kind of vanity in doing so.

It occurred to Kitty that Louisa's indisposition might have to do with her unrequited feelings for Eli. While they were in New York, she realized Louisa could not help but sense the depth of Kitty's and Eli's attachment to each other. Now back in Rhode Island Louisa's questions took on a different vein.

"Mama, the letters Eli sends you are so much warmer than those he sends me," she speculated. "Yet I am the one he could marry and have children with. Why is that?"

Kitty's brows rose in concern. "Dear, you have told me you are not interested in him. Have you had a change of heart?"

Louisa shrugged. "I do not know what I feel. He needs a wife and he wants children. Possibly he could love me and get both."

Kitty looked into her eyes. "Do you love him?"

"Perhaps I could, if I had the opportunity," she answered quietly.

Louisa soon had the opportunity to test her theory. Eli came to visit them in East Greenwich, and Louisa arranged to be alone with him one evening. He courted her with flattering words and ended the evening with passionate kisses. The next day he offered her his hand in marriage, and she agreed.

Kitty gave them her full benediction. *Hopefully this will bring peace to my youngest daughter and keep Eli in our lives,* she wished. *God help them both.*

Then Eli experienced second thoughts. Uncertain about Louisa and marriage, his honor would not allow him to withdraw his proposal. Back in New Haven, he sent Louisa "nonpassionate letters," and she read his feelings between the lines. Distressed, she ran to her mother for comfort.

"This is far worse than withdrawing the proposal, Mama," she confided. "He writes me with constraint, even pain."

"Are you certain, sweetie? Are you possibly reading more into this than he wishes to say?"

Bursting into tears, Louisa described her quandary. "When I promised to marry him, my thoughts were for him. I forgot my own dignity, and at that moment I would have given my life to him."

Once again, Kitty took her child's future into her hands. Finally aware that the match she had hoped to promote was ill-fated from the start, she wrote Eli a somber letter at the end of October.

> *The tone of your letters has confirmed Louisa's fears about your sincerity. I do not believe she will ever perform her promise to you, although she continually speaks on that subject. I believe under present circumstances that she not correspond any longer with you. Both ought to forget that which will give each of you more pain than pleasure to remember. Louisa knows not that I am writing—nor would I for anything have her know what I have written.*

At long last they were ready to return to Dungeness. Kitty and Louisa went by stage to Philadelphia, while the others traveled ahead by water. In Philadelphia, Kitty bought a carriage and a pair of black horses, hired a driver, and drove southward.

FORTY EIGHT

1809–1812

K itty and Louisa enjoyed their voyage in the new carriage. Rising very early, they rode about twelve miles before breakfast, and then rested. They continued their journey until dinnertime, reading, sleeping and talking in their comfortable coach. Several days were spent in Baltimore and Washington, giving them an opportunity to see the latest public buildings sprouting up in the new capital city.

By the time they reached Raleigh, they found the city crammed with men assembling for the state legislature, and were forced to stay in a "wretched outhouse," according to Kitty's letter to Eli. Louisa was ill but Kitty got her into the carriage to continue on, unwilling to stay another night.

The following day they were delayed by a snow storm, and lost several travel days waiting it out. However, they met a young lady who had recently been to Cumberland.

"How is our dear island?" Kitty asked, yearning manifested in her eyes.

"It is indeed lovely. Beautiful weather. It seems all the inhabitants are well."

"Thank you Lord." Breathing a huge sigh of relief, Kitty continued. "We've been away for eighteen months, and that has been much too long."

It was almost Christmas by the time they reached Savannah, and both were impatient to reach Cumberland. They drove down the coastal highway to St. Marys, where Kitty sent word that the rowers be waiting at the dock. Embarking in their own canoe, they set off for Cumberland Island.

"Look Mama," pointed out Louisa breathlessly. "I can see the smoke coming out of our fireplaces in Dungeness. What a blessing!"

Kitty remembered years back when she stepped on land after rough sea voyages. She was reminded how, on several occasions, she actually bent down to kiss the ground. She felt tempted to do it again but realized it was harder now to bend. And how would the servants react?

Life returned to its peaceful island pace and Kitty felt content. There were reports that another great war with England could force them to abandon the island, but Kitty chose to ignore the information. She was back where she wanted to be: with her family on her island. She wanted to play with her grandchildren, garden, entertain, read and thoroughly enjoy her life.

When the Georgia militia was sent to garrison the island, Kitty went out to get information. "How long will you be on our island?" she asked with intent.

"As long as we are needed, Lady Miller. You are too close to Spanish East Florida for comfort. We are here to protect you."

"What good can you do if Cumberland becomes a battle-ground?"

They shook their heads and smiled at her. After a few days, when she realized they were not leaving, she went about her daily business.

Then an event took place that shattered her serenity. In October of 1810, her daughter Cornelia eloped in St. Marys with her first cousin, Ned Littlefield. Although he was Kitty's favorite brother Billy's son, Kitty believed he was a fortune-hunter, and had warned Cornelia about him. He was nine years younger than Cornelia, but Kitty had married a man eleven years her junior. In a letter to Eli on December 9, 1809, she gave free rein to her furious thoughts.

As for Cornelia, I never intend to mention her name again, or the matter of her marriage. She went in the canoe to St.

*Marys on business, she said, marching into the post office
without a soul of her own sex. The only witness to her marriage was a tavern keeper. The ceremony was performed by
that cutthroat Ross. This disgraceful transaction almost drove
me to madness—and will no doubt be the very death of me.*

Her oldest daughter Patty had also remarried in Rhode
Island, and returned with her new husband, Dr. Henry
Turner, Daniel's brother. Unexpectedly and without warning, Ned Littlefield convinced Patty and Cornelia that their
mother had been deceitful in the division of the Greene estate.
They had already agreed on a cash settlement, but there were
large tracts of land undivided. One property was Duck River
Plantation in Tennessee, a gift of the North Carolina legislature to Nathanael.

"Louisa, what is happening to us?" Kitty whimpered,
beside herself with disappointment. "How can Henry, Ethan
Clarke and now Ned drive a wedge between me and my older
daughters?"

"Mama, neither Natty nor I have succumbed to this insult-
ing defamation of your character. I shall speak with my sisters
and find out how they feel!" Her face was flushed with anger.

Kitty needed Eli's presence in Georgia in order to settle the
Miller estate. He admitted to her that he was reluctant to leave
his businesses in Connecticut, but also used his poor health as
an excuse for not traveling.

Dr. Kollock believed Eli's complaints were self-induced and
urged him to return to Georgia.

Eli knew and understood Kitty better than most people. He
wrote a letter back to Dr. Kollock.

*The truth is that Cornelia's folly has broken her mother's
heart. I sincerely wish you would do all in your power to
banish that subject from her mind. That Mrs. Miller with
all her good sense should suffer that transaction to prey upon
her mind to such a degree as wholly as to destroy her health,*

happiness and life... it is extremely wrong. If Kitty would make a vigorous and determined effort, she might, with the aid of her friends, shake it off.

A short time later she wrote Eli from Savannah, beseeching him to come to Georgia. She told him if he were worried about facing Louisa, he must not be, because she would not be problematic. She also mentioned that she was personally responsible for the estate for the $20,000 she put in the hands of Nat Pendleton and Josiah Whitney while she was in New York. These claims had still not been validated by the referees.

"Whatever will become of us?" she wearily asked her youngest, Louisa. "Your father used to tell me I could take whatever was thrown at me, but now I wonder if I am capable."

"Oh Mama, give it up to God." Her youngest smiled at her. "Only He can make sense of this."

On her return to Dungeness, Kitty found Cumberland Island occupied by state militia and the U.S. Marines. Tensions were mounting once again between America and England. The fact that British sailors were seizing former British sailors from American vessels, sailors who were now naturalized American citizens, infuriated the lawmakers in Washington, who retaliated with further embargoes.

Kitty wrote Eli that she enjoyed having the military post on the island. She had been advised to leave, but refused to be moved from her homestead. The activity of the troops around her stirred the memories of camp life so many years ago. She also mentioned that if he returned, he could help her make plans to finish the house. When he didn't respond, she had steps built in the front of the mansion, and decided to leave the rest of the building to her heirs.

Dr. Kollock was living on Cumberland and helped Kitty with her complicated legal affairs. Going through old papers of Phineas' and Eli's business, he made an insightful discovery.

"Look here, Kitty. Remember the $10,000 fee Nat Pendleton charged the Miller estate for the handling of Yazoo affairs?"

She turned to him, her large eyes questioning. "Yes, and we're still fighting that one."

"Did you know that Phineas was in partnership with him in these same ventures?"

Kitty closed her eyes, rubbing her temples. "Yes, my husband told me. How could I have forgotten?"

Then Dr. Kollock found other documents stating that Josiah Whitney had vastly overcharged Kitty in her private settlement of his claim against the Miller estate.

"I will hand deliver these papers to the judges handling the case," he offered. "Things are going to change for you, my dear. No longer will you be abused by this man."

He worried about her future and wrote Eli a letter on February 12, 1812.

> *From the view I have of Mrs. Miller's situation, I am extremely apprehensive that she will be absolutely ruined. The debts which have already fallen upon her are accumulating and will shortly be more than her property is worth. Mrs. Miller is enfeebled and is descending into the vale of years.*

When his pleas went unanswered, Dr. Kollock lost his patience and wrote another letter on May 16, expressing anger and disappointment in Eli Whitney.

> *Your incorrigible silence and obstinate perseverance in a determination not to come out to us in our distress is intolerable. I am sickened at the condition and the dreary prospect of our unfortunate friend and am truly astonished at the resolution with which she sustains this pressure of complicated evil and perplexity. Unless we can continue some alleviation, some lessening of the thick gloom that surrounds her, she must inevitably sink and lessen your and my attachment to this miserable world.*

Eli Whitney never returned to Georgia.

FORTY NINE

1812–1814

The spring of 1812 was not a peaceful time for Kitty. Four judgments, totaling $60,000, were decided against her. She had no means of satisfying the debt, unless she sold her lands and her workers. Her lawyer advised her to file a lawsuit against Eli to force him to come to Georgia to settle the accounts. Her despondent spirit was revealed in a letter she wrote to him on May 18, 1812.

> *I shrink with horror from such an idea, for to give you trouble is wounding my own heart. In your last letter you lash the villainy and ingratitude of mankind. I hope you did not mean to include me as I shall not include you when I say that I have more reasons than anyone to distrust and despise those who I have not only loved, but also cherished. Never was anyone so cheated and ill-used as I have been.*

The United States had declared war on Great Britain by the summer of 1812. Kitty was advised to leave Cumberland and again, she refused because she wanted to finalize Nat's land properties with her children. She presented the updated settlement to her children.

The estate was divided as follows: to Catharine Miller, sixty-nine slaves; to Martha (Patty) W. Nightingale, thirty-two slaves; to Cornelia L. Skipwith, thirty slaves; to Nathanael R. Greene, thirty-five slaves and to Louisa C. Greene, thirty-two slaves.

The land was divided as follows: to Catharine Miller, the tract "Dungeness" and subdivision 8 on Cumberland Island;

to Martha (Patty) W. Nightingale, the tract called *The Springs*; to Cornelia L. Skipwith, Lot 8 at Littlefield; to Nathanael R. Greene, the tract on Crooked River; to Louisa C. Greene, Lot 2 at Littlefield. The 20,000 acres on Duck River in Tennessee were divided into parts and drawn for by lot. The Catfish Islands on the St. Marys River were divided into five parts. The tract of land in Ohio was also divided into five parts.

The slaves were to remain in Kitty's possession until all debts against Nathanael's estate were paid. All the heirs signed the instrument of division, which also released Kitty from any further responsibility for the estate.

Nat and Louisa were grateful for the settlement she had drawn up. Her two oldest daughters and their husband argued behind her back and plotted against her.

"Natty, please help me understand how your sisters agreed with the land distribution in 1810 and now believe it is unfair."

He shook his head. "Neither Louisa nor I know why. We've tried to discuss it with them but they give no reasons for their odd behavior. I'm so sorry, Mama."

The most difficult decision Kitty had to make was not to break up the slave families, due to her respect for them. Patty and Cornelia and their husbands said it was a scheme to keep them for herself.

"You've never had any problem over the slave trade," hissed Cornelia. "You have held contraband slaves for your friend Robert MacKay, right here on the plantation, until he found safe places to hide them on the mainland."

Listening to her girls lashing out at her and watching their husbands' greedy faces nearly broke Kitty's heart.

Their husbands, Ned Littlefield and Henry Turner, approached her to insist on their fair share of the honors and medals of General Greene. When she said she wished to keep them, they conspired to remove them clandestinely from her room and sell them. One of the servants heard them conniving and ran to tell Kitty. It was that action, probably more than anything else, that triggered her breakdown. She disinherited her older daughters and their husbands, causing her immeasurable grief and pain.

"Through your unkind actions and words, you have left me no choice but to break off relations with you both," she told her older daughters, her voice choking on the words. "I will no longer speak to you and will refer to you in writing by your husbands' names. Regrettably, you are no longer welcome to enter through my gate." Kitty spent sleepless nights tossing in her bed, considering the different levels of heartbreak she had recently experienced, and prayed they would come to their senses and ask for forgiveness. She told herself she was prepared to spend the rest of her life without them.

～⑥～

On April 15, 1813 Cornelia Lott Greene Turner sold Tract #5, called *Great Swamp*, comprising the southern half of Cumberland, to Robert Stafford. She was ready to move to Tennessee.

In August Kitty visited Dr. Kollock and his wife in Savannah, where they now lived. Walking through one of the squares, her eyes were drawn to a wagonload of cowering slaves transported down a back street. She gasped when she recognized her daughter Cornelia and Ned driving the wagon. Instantly, she knew what had transpired. Taking advantage of her absence from Dungeness, they hand-picked several of the plantation servants belonging to Kitty, and attempted to transfer them to their new home on the Duck River Plantation in Tennessee.

Kitty was consumed with anger but went quietly about her way until she reached the courthouse. She obtained a court order restraining the family from leaving town with the slaves. Quickly returning to Cumberland, she did not have to witness Cornelia's family's arrest and detention. Several days later, bonds were signed by old family friends guaranteeing Kitty the amount of money at which the Negroes were valued.

Kitty, truly inconsolable and brokenhearted by this betrayal and the loss of two of her daughters and their children, took to her room for days. Allowing herself to fall into a deep pit, she barely touched her food, and spoke to no one. Members of her family tried vainly to pull her out of that dark hole. She lay in bed, listening to the sounds of her plantation from a distance, mourning her plight.

Louisa tried to reason with her. Her friends feared she had lost her mind.

"It is of no use, Louisa.I feel that everything that protected me has been blown apart."

"Please get up, Mama. The day is beautiful. We can ride together. Would you like that?"

Kitty shook her head and went back to sleep. She no longer cared about time.

After a long while, she sat up and read her letters. She changed her will and bequeathed Dungeness to Nat and Louisa. She also provided a large award to Lemuel Kollock, calling him her "best beloved friend." She arranged to leave generous sums to relatives, but excluded Patty and Cornelia, leaving them only a few dollars each.

One day she appeared downstairs, shocking the servants, who nervously summoned Louisa.

"Oh Mama, thank the Lord you've come to your senses. We need you so much," she cried out, sweeping her mother into her arms to comfort her, wiping away her tears.

Kitty gently touched Louisa's cheeks with her fingers and whispered softly, "I've seen the light, my child. My spirit was stunned, not broken." Their eyes locked; tears rolling down both their faces.

"Mama, there's so much for us to do together. Let us start a new beginning, shall we?"

Kitty nodded, having already determined to cast off the bitterness that seized her soul.

"Your father told me, on several occasions, that self-pity makes a sad companion." A hint of a smile flickered over her face at this memory.

During her isolation period, Kitty had finally come to accept the reality that her complex financial affairs would never be settled during her lifetime. She decided to no longer allow herself to suffer over material matters, nor would she be the instrument to cause misery to her loved ones. She would see the wider world, touching people in a way that would make them feel safe.

Natty, his wife Anna Marie and their small children came to Dungeness for a long visit. Kitty, thrilled to be surrounded again by young ones, fought her way back to a level of inner peace. When Natty told her he wanted to transfer his part of Cumberland Island to her, she accepted, knowing he wanted to prop her up financially. She smiled, understanding that he could not accept slavery and would not plant on his property, *Rayfield*, located in Cumberland's midsection. Kitty sat down again to re-write her will, leaving this land to his children.

Eli corresponded with her frequently. He teased her about "suing him," stating that if he went to Georgia, he might land up in jail. She retorted that since he had once offered to pay her bail if she were arrested in Connecticut, she would return the favor in Georgia.

In March of 1814, Louisa married James Shaw, a Scottish gentleman many years her senior, in a quiet affair with only family, held in the lovely gardens of Dungeness. James Shaw had entered into a contract with her some time before to complete the interior of Dungeness, if funds ever became available. Living at the mansion for two years and working with Louisa in several farming enterprises, they regarded each other highly. The problem was that James was a British subject, and with the war waging, they could not make a public announcement of the wedding.

"Mama, I feel so happy today. A small affair is exactly what I wanted. What a pity my cousin Phoebe Paine's nuptials are on the same day, but we will meet in Savannah in a week or so." Kitty's heart warmed seeing Louisa so joyful.

She turned to her son-in-law. "James, you know we respect, honor and love you, and because you are tender and affectionate to my daughter, you have become a most dutiful son and excellent friend to me," she told him.

Shortly after the wedding, Kitty gave James the power of attorney to act in her behalf.

FIFTY

1814

Early April of 1814 brought Kitty some excellent news. A bill was placed before Congress for an appropriation of $8,000,000 for the relief of disappointed Yazoo investors of almost twenty years before. Many of them, like Kitty and Phineas, had dropped a large amount of money into the ill-fated project. By the end of April, Kitty learned that the bill had passed.

For some strange reason, Kitty received this news with equanimity. It was as if there were other burdens on her mind, or perhaps she had truly given up the concerns over her business affairs, as she had vowed to do. She made just one casual comment to Eli about the passing of the bill: *You have seen how Yazoo has terminated so far.*

The Georgia seaboard was under looming threat of invasion. *The Savannah Republican* wrote the following on May 7, 1814: *The enemy is near at hand. Letters were received on Thursday last from St. Marys to the mayor of this city and the officer commanding the U.S. troops here, stating that a large British force was off St. Marys' bar. An attack is momentarily expected. Citizens, be on the alert!*

Kitty and Louisa watched the British men-of-war *Majestic* and *Morgiana* lying at anchor in the Cumberland Sound. When Louisa asked her mother if she were afraid, Kitty shook her head.

"No, Louisa, I am not. Whatever happens, I will stay here on my island, where I have lived some of the happiest years of my life. If I should die now, so be it."

Kitty wanted to finish up her business with Josiah Whitney and invited him to be her guest at Dungeness. He agreed, and together they worked out their financial matters respectfully and without antagonism. He left as a friend, and each concurred to finalizing the remaining details by letter. She knew this would please Eli and told him so in a letter.

In June, Natty came to Dungeness with his family. Late one afternoon Kitty asked him to ride with her to the beach. She wanted to show him one of her favorite spots, a place where she and Phineas had found solace.

The sun wasn't quite down when they set out, but the light was gray. By the time they reached the beach, the sun had set and the clouds were turning purple and blue.

"Natty, I would like to ask you something very personal, and perhaps you don't wish to answer my question," she said quietly, turning in her saddle to face him.

"What is it, Mama?"

"Are you happy? Do you have the life you envisioned all those years back, when I sent you up North to study?"

He smiled at her. "Yes, I am content, Mama. Anna Marie is a wonderful wife, and has given me beautiful children—your grandchildren—whom I dearly love."

Kitty's smile lit up her face. "That warms my heart, son. That is all a mother needs to know." The long slender arm of the breakwater curved around the marina. Fog was rolling in, bringing with it the damp cloudy smell of seaweed.

"Let's ride home," she said softly. "Thank you for coming back to spend time with me."

Kitty wrote Eli a letter on July 5, sending him news of her children and of the plantation. She ended with these words: *We have a party of eighteen to eat turtle with us tomorrow. I wish you were the nineteenth. Our fruit begins to flow in upon us—to partake of which I long for you and a few other friends to share.* This would be her last letter to her beloved friend.

More relatives and friends arrived to spend weeks at a time

at Dungeness. As always, Kitty was delighted with the diversion and took pride in her exquisite dinners and entertainment.

She found herself seeking out treasured time to spend alone, often riding or walking on the beach while her guests enjoyed their afternoon rest time. Riding down Grand Avenue on horseback, she took pleasure in passing through the patches of piney woods and hardwood trees. Occasionally, she spotted white egrets standing motionless in the fields that opened up between the forests, posing majestically on their extended legs. The great egret had always been her favorite bird.

She preferred to come when the tide was out and the gulls were fluttering—dancing at the water's edge. Making her slow descent down the dunes onto the palmetto-lined dirt path, she slipped silently through the familiar long-leaf pines, the stately hickory, and the aromatic cedars and palm trees. Kitty planned her trips to the sea when it was calm. The water surged leisurely around her. She loved the silky feel of that surge; first the lift and then the back run that pulled sand out from between her toes in small, tickling whirlpools.

She felt Phineas walking by her side, holding her hand. She missed him. She wanted him, and would have given anything if he were alive. She carried the longing like a stone in a beautiful basket. She asked him, *How does it feel to you, now that you are on the other side?*

Longing shot through her like a ripple of pain. She saw Phineas' sweet face looming before her in the ancient oaks. She felt his fingers touching her palm. Slowly, their fingers began a dance of caressing as his thumb pressed hard in the center of her palm. It was all she could do to swallow. It had been so long since she had been touched by a man.

Phineas, I feel your lips on my palm, your breath on my skin.
I know you are kissing my life line, my love line. She heard his voice responding in a soft purr.

In the beginning she only saw Phineas during her reflections.

One afternoon, completely unexpectedly, her thoughts stirred up old memories of her life with Nathanael. At first this unsettled her, but soon she embraced the sensation and accepted the comfort it offered.

As she wandered from one point of the beach to another, she spread her arms wide to the ocean and the sky, inviting everything—birds, angels, lost souls, her children, friends old and new—to join her in her celebration of life. She spoke out loud, talking to Nathanael—telling him he was the only person she knew who gave so much and never kept score.

And my darling, you taught me that kindness was more important than anything—that what you do and how you treat people is essential to living. You told me the largest part of kindness is asking for it when you need it, and giving it whenever you can.

Then she wondered: *Why are they both walking with me? What do they have to tell me?*

And then it came to her. *I have had my beautiful, poignant, soulful earth opera. I must love them all as I leave them in my slow fade to darkness. I have to touch the crazy one inside myself, the lonely one, the lost one, the wanting one, the motherless one. I must embrace the brokenness as if it were a golden ornament, using it as the key to all that needs to be unlocked, to harvest my story.*

During the last week of August Kitty's tired body was battered by one of the coastal fevers that visited the Georgia coast in the summer. During that same week, the British invaded the Federal City of Washington, D.C. It lay in ruins, burned by the British forces led by Rear Admiral Sir George Cockburn. No one told Kitty about the destruction.

Dr. Kollock came to see her. After a careful examination, he suggested she travel to Savannah.

"Kitty, the change would do you well. You can stay in my home, and of course Louisa and Natty are welcome to accompany you."

She offered him a small but loving smile. "Thank you, dearest Lemuel, for your kindness. I believe I shall stay right here, and fight this fever."

He returned her smile. She was right, of course. He feared she would never enjoy good health again.

The fever rose slowly. Nat and Louisa sat with their mother as she struggled for her life.

Kitty spent her waking time meditating on her life. She remembered the letter Martha Washington had written her shortly after George's death. *'Tis well that it is over. I shall soon follow him. I have no more trials to pass through.* And she did follow him, less than two years later, dying from the fever at age seventy. Kitty smiled at the memory, knowing she would once again see her Patsy.

"Mama, what can we do for you?" asked Louisa, hiding the rush of tears gathering in her eyes.

"Stay strong for your families. I am at peace, and I know I'll see your father, and Phineas, and your brother, as well as the Washingtons, and so many others."

"Please don't talk like that," begged Natty. "You have overcome so many obstacles in your life, Mama. You'll beat this one as well."

A strange calmness settled over her, like a soft transparent veil. "How many days have I been in bed?" she asked him.

"Six, Mama. Are you feeling the fever abating?" He reached over to place his hand on her burning forehead.

"No, but I can feel His serenity." She turned slightly, tears spiking her lashes. "I need a promise from each of you." She spoke quietly. "You must tell your sisters that I have forgiven them. And that I love them. Let them know that a mother's love can never end."

"Yes, Mama, we will tell them." Words came between sobs; hot tears stung Louisa's eyes.

"She is ready," whispered Natty, "let her sleep." They took turns at her bedside.

Her long, racking cough continued all night, but broke at

dawn. When she opened her eyes, Natty felt her love gazing at him beneath a shimmer of tears as she drifted off into an endless sleep.

The day was September 2, 1814. Kitty was fifty-nine years old. She had found her peace at last.

EPILOGUE

1818

Fifteen-year-old Phineas Nightingale was digging for crab near the landing at Dungeness. He looked up when he saw a schooner lowering a longboat. Stepping onto the landing to watch, he saw the captain and a mate helping an old man gingerly step ashore. The mate hefted the visitor's baggage—a battered trunk and a case of Madeira wine—and followed.

When Phineas approached them, the captain recognized him and introduced the feeble elderly gentleman.

"Son, please welcome Colonel Henry Lee, known as 'Light-Horse Harry.' This dear friend of your grandfather seeks temporary shelter with the family of his comrade, General Greene."

"It is an honor to meet you, Colonel Lee. I will help you with your belongings. Welcome to our island." As Colonel Lee embraced the boy, tears streamed down his hollow cheeks.

"I have come here to spend my last days with Lady Greene," he declared, his voice hoarse.

Phineas, after explaining that his grandmother had died four years previously, warmly welcomed Colonel Lee to stay as long as he wished. The gentleman was too weak to walk from the wharf to the house, so Phineas ran ahead to ask his Aunt Louisa to send a carriage. It wasn't long before she alighted from the carriage.

"Captain, what do I owe you for his expenses?" asked Louisa, after introducing herself.

"Not a thing, my lady. It has been a rare pleasure and privilege to minister to the comfort, and respond to the wishes, of such a distinguished hero of the Revolution," he answered.

Within a few days Light-Horse Harry had recovered some of his strength, due to the loving care he received from the family and staff at Dungeness. Soon he was able to join them at supper and regale them with stories of the war and his family.

"In 1790 the love of my life and a cousin of mine, Matilda Lee, passed away and left me with three children. After that, my life crumbled as I faced one tragedy after another." The colonel continued with a loud sigh.

"I married again, this time to an heiress named Anne Hill Carter, and we have five children. My youngest son, Robert E., was born in 1807, so he would be several years younger than you, Phineas. Yet you remind me a great deal of him," he said with a nostalgic grin.

"Sir, what tragedies are you speaking of?" asked the inquisitive Phineas.

"There are too many to tell, my son. I lost a great deal in land speculation, fell deeply into debt and spent time in the debtors' prison, transferring the deed for my home to my son Henry. Four years ago I became embroiled in a political riot in Baltimore, while defending a friend and the freedom of the press. This caused permanent injuries and painful wounds. I became a penniless invalid."

"Dear Lord," murmured Louisa. "So what did you do?"

"My dear friends, Madison and Monroe, raised the funds to send me to the West Indies in the hopes of finding a cure."

"What about your family?" asked Louisa gently.

He gazed at her, sorrow etched across his face. "I left them in Alexandria."

Wiping away a tear, he went on. "I wandered from island to island for several years without finding a cure, so I sailed from Nassau on a schooner bound for Boston, planning to return to Virginia and my beloved family."

Henry paused to clear his throat. He picked up again, his voice thin with weariness. "But I was failing fast, my body visibly withering away; I knew my time was limited so I asked the captain to set me ashore on Cumberland Island, thinking the wife of my old comrade-in-arms General Greene would allow me to die there."

Looking gravely at each of them he added, "I am very sorry I was too late to tell her goodbye."

One week later, Light-Horse Harry was able to walk around the garden, leaning on young Phineas' shoulder. He also received visits from old comrades living in the area.

He wasn't isolated at Dungeness. An American fleet had anchored in Cumberland to negotiate the transfer of Florida from Spanish to American control. As soon as the top officers learned that Light-Horse Harry was ill at Dungeness, they came by to pay their respects.

"It is such an honor to meet you, sir," the army commander said. "I have heard that you wrote and gave the eulogy for President George Washington."

Smiling, Colonel Lee nodded. "First in war, first in peace and first in the hearts of his countrymen...second to none in the humble and endearing scenes of private life."

Another officer spoke up. "Did you write *Memoirs of the War in the Southern Department of the United States* soon after that?

Colonel Lee smiled widely. "Have you read it?" His brow furrowed under the weight of memories and he looked directly into the young officer's eyes. "Actually, sir, I wrote that in a 12-by-14 foot prison cell."

Two navy physicians were sent to the mansion to remain at his beside day and night, checking his condition and keeping him company.

Two months after arriving at Cumberland Island, Colonel Henry Lee died. He was sixty-two years old and still sheltered by the fond memories of his beloved commander. His body was escorted to the burial ground half a mile away—to the same plot where Kitty's body lay.

Colonel Henry Lee was given a full military funeral on the

little island of Cumberland. A deployment of Marines fired thirteen salvos from the *John Adams,* the proper sendoff for a major war hero. The boom of artillery followed.

Thus the Southern Revolutionary hero was buried in Georgia soil. In 1870 his son Robert E. Lee visited the cemetery. The commander of the Army of Northern Virginia solemnly placed a wreath on his father's grave. Robert E. Lee followed in his father's footsteps, and was later recognized as one of the greatest generals in American history.

AFTERWORD

Catharine Littlefield Greene Miller was buried in a little tabby-walled cemetery among her favorite oak trees, close to the tranquil tidal creek that twisted through the marshland next to Dungeness, a place she and Phineas had shared.

Her simple tombstone reads: *She possessed great talents and exalted virtue.*

Nathanael Greene, a singularly capable and resourceful general, was like other prominent generals on the American side, a self-trained soldier. Second only to Washington among American generals in his military ability, he was also the only one other than Washington and Henry Knox to serve the entire eight years of the war. Humane and kindly towards his British counterparts, Nathanael also defended the often treacherous Horatio Gates against criticism of his Southern campaign.

The Greene Brothers returned to work their mills again after the Revolutionary War. Although now prosperous after years of hard work, they continued to live simple and modest lives. The family homestead in Potowomut remains privately owned by Thomas Casey Greene, Nathanael Greene's great-great-great-great nephew. Nathanael's "Spell Hall"—built as his future wife's home—stands on a small hill in Coventry and is open to the public. It is maintained by the General Nathanael Greene Society.

Eli Whitney's contribution to the Southern prosperity was the cotton gin. But his contribution to the country is the foundation of its great industrial expansion as creator of a mass production system. The concept of interchangeable parts revolutionized the manufacturing industry, ultimately contributing to the North's victory in the Civil War and making the United States a world leader. When he died of prostate cancer in 1825, a worn-out mechanical genius, he left behind his wife, Henrietta Edwards, and four children. His sons continued his business by securing government contracts to make muskets.

General Anthony Wayne enjoyed serving as General George Washington's commander-in-chief in the first American frontier. Leading his men to a decisive victory at the Battle of Fallen Timbers in 1794, he seized the defeated Indian tribes' extensive territory, including much of Ohio, as part of the 1795 Treaty of Greenville. Loved by his men and respected by his foes, he effectively brought peace to the area, earning the respectful title of "The Chief who Never Sleeps" among Northwest tribes. Yet the hardships of the army weakened his body; on December 15, 1796 a flare-up of gout claimed his life.

Thirteen years later his son, Isaac Wayne, rode in a one-horse sulky to Erie, Pennsylvania to retrieve Anthony Wayne's remains. Upon opening the grave, they discovered his body was in an almost perfect state of preservation so it could not be transported in the sulky. An army surgeon recommended boiling the body, then separating the flesh from the bones. Although horrified at the idea, Isaac ultimately agreed. The bones of General Anthony Wayne were transported home to his family plot at St. David's Church, Radnor, Pennsylvania, while the flesh was reinterred in his gravesite in Erie. General Wayne remains buried in two places.

Martha and George Washington are fondly remembered as "The Father and Mother of America." A letter written by Nathanael Greene to Kitty illustrates the love they shared. He wrote, *Mrs. Washington is excessively fond of the General and he of her. They are happy in each other.* Sadly, but in an effort to protect their privacy, Martha destroyed all correspondence between them before her death.

The deep fondness shared by George Washington and his devoted subordinate Nathanael Greene has been well-documented in their personal writings. General Washington often ended letters to General Greene with *Love... George Washington,* rather than the customary *Your most affectionate and humble servant.* His comments regarding Nathanael's death, written to the Marquis de Lafayette a year later, illustrate his depth of feeling. *I can scarce persuade myself to touch upon it.*

The Marquis de Lafayette returned to his native France and found it on the brink of revolution. The twenty-four-year-old major general of the Continental Army became a member of the National Assembly in 1789 and assumed a leading role in the French Revolution. He wrote France's Bill of Rights, basing it on America's *Declaration of Independence.* Advocating the need for nonviolent change, he worked between the Crown and representatives of the people, but was seen as the enemy of both. Fleeing to northern France, he was captured and imprisoned.

Due to his military rank, he was treated respectfully until an attempt to rescue him was thwarted and he was thrown into a rat-infested dungeon cell, held in solitary confinement. Eventually his reading material was confiscated; receiving no news of his family, he believed them dead.

But his wife Adrienne du Motier had managed to get their son George out of France and eventually to America under George Washington's guardianship. When political extremists came to arrest Adrienne, she gave thanks to God that her daughters would be allowed to remain in the custody of their tutor.

After a year in solitary confinement, with only one smuggled message of his family's well-being, Lafayette was speechless when his cell door opened to admit Adrienne and his daughters.

Falling into each other's arms, they shared the emotions of any couple married twenty years.

After two more years in cruel captivity the family was exiled to Holland, per orders of France's first consul, Napoleon Bonaparte, who considered the Marquis' popularity a threat. When Lafayette boldly returned to France with his family—declaring that if France were free, then so was he—Napoleon ignored him. But Lafayette wasn't allowed to attend a national memorial service for George Washington. After Napoleon's downfall Lafayette served in the Chamber of Deputies as a vocal critic of corruption, social inequality, and religious intolerance.

Ten years after their release from prison, Adrienne passed away, dealing Lafayette his most serious setback. His doleful comment—*Up to now you have found me stronger than my circumstances; today the circumstance is stronger than I*—expresses his great love for a beloved wife of thirty-four years.

In 1824 President James Monroe invited Lafayette and his son George to visit every state in the Union. Thousands turned out to greet this Revolutionary War hero and honor him with dinners, formal balls and official functions everywhere. Spending time with former revolutionaries and ex-presidents, they saw John Adams, Thomas Jefferson, James Madison, James Monroe, and the newly-elected President, John Quincy Adams. The Marquis wept openly at George and Martha Washington's tombs, poignantly mourning his friends.

Longing to be buried beneath American soil, he nevertheless made the decision to lie beside his beloved wife in France. At a Masonic ceremony to lay the cornerstone for the Bunker Hill Monument, Lafayette gathered up enough American soil to take back to France for his gravesite. In France he rejoined the Chamber of Deputies and served as commander of the National Guard during the Revolution of 1830. The Marquis de Lafayette died at the age of seventy-six, grasping a medallion holding Adrienne's portrait. He was quietly laid to rest under the American soil he'd brought back with him. A period of national mourning was observed by Americans in tribute.

Benedict Arnold was commissioned brigadier general in the King's Army and served his post conscientiously before heartlessly leading the British troops in the burning and pillaging of towns in Virginia and even his own Connecticut. He later admitted to treasonable correspondence with British General Clinton while serving as military governor of Philadelphia. Benedict Arnold died at the age of sixty in 1801, never completely trusted by the Americans or the British. His last request was to be buried in the uniform he wore as a Continental Army general.

Mulberry Grove, an active plantation from 1736 until the end of the Civil War, was destroyed in December, 1864 by Union General William T. Sherman, during his march to the sea. Sherman's famous telegram to U.S. President Abraham Lincoln, presenting "the City of Savannah, as a Christmas gift, with 150 heavy guns and plenty of ammunition, and also about 25,000 bales of cotton" is still well-known.

Despite this illustrious history, today the plantation is only a deserted wilderness on a riverbank. Long marsh grasses crowd the rice stalks of the dead plantation era. Empty rice canals are covered with brambles and bushes. Only the foundations remain of the magnificent dwelling house, and even the slave cabins have long disappeared except for a row or two of crumbling chimney bricks.

Dungeness was abandoned during the U.S. Civil War. Slavery ended after the war and like many plantation owners, Greene descendents found that it was no longer profitable to pay wages and were forced to move out. Dungeness burned to the ground in 1866. This, unfortunately, would not be the last time that this fate would befall a house built on this spot.

In 1884, Thomas and Lucy Carnegie bought the land to construct a new mansion, also named Dungeness and inspired by Scottish castles, on the spot where the original house was built. Thomas, like Nathanael, died before the house was finished. Lucy Carnegie lived there happily for many years with her nine children. The mansion boasted fifty-nine rooms, a swimming pool, golf course, casino, stables and many other small buildings for 200 servants. In 1929, one of Lucy's daughters was married at Dungeness.

Although the Great Depression brought the Carnegie era to an end and they moved away and left it vacant, they continued to own the mansion. One night in 1959 a disgruntled poacher, shot in the leg by the housekeeper for trespassing, purportedly burned the house to the ground. Since then the mansion and surrounding buildings have slowly deteriorated. Its ruins stand as a grand testament to a long and colorful history. Descendents of the original families still live on the island or vacation there, but Dungeness—littered with misfortune—is no more.

Colonel Light-Horse Harry Lee was buried on Cumberland Island with full military honors provided by an American fleet stationed near St. Marys, GA. In 1913 his remains were removed to the Lee family crypt at Lee Chapel, on the campus of Washington & Lee University in Lexington, Virginia.

A Last Thought and Tribute to Kitty: Women have been inventors since the dawn of civilization. Many anthropologists believe that women made civilization possible, by inventing the basics of clothing, housekeeping, and agriculture. In the modern era, women have had more difficulty gaining credit for their inventions than they have had inventing.

The classic example is Catharine Littlefield Greene Miller, an unknown woman to the general public. Experts on invention agree that Eli Whitney could not have developed the cotton gin—the quintessential American invention—without Kitty's advice. In fact, some even believe that Whitney stole the credit for what was essentially Greene's invention. This is well-documented in the following website from the Massachusetts Institute of Technology: www.mit.edu/invent/iow/whml.html.

CAMDEN COUNTY

WILL BOOK A., PP. 122-128

Last Will and Testament of Catharine Miller

Dungeness, Cumberland Island, State of Georgia

In the name of God, Amen.

"I, Catharine Miller of Cumberland Island in the State of Georgia, do make this my last Will and Testament.

"As my much beloved son Nathanael Ray Greene has inherited a considerable Estate by the Will of his honored and Illustrious Father, General Nathanael Greene, which he can dispose of according to his own wishes, I am more solicitous that the property which I intended for him should descend to his lawful children. I therefore make this my last will in the following manner—In the first place I do give, devise and bequeath my plantation on Cumberland Island known by the name of Rayfield, together with a number of Negroes, land, plates, books, to the lawful children of my son, Nathanael Ray Greene, who shall forever manage the property so bequeathed to his children as he see fit—reserving all the rents and profits thereof for his own use during his lifetime and that his last will shall determine what proportion each child shall possess of my bequest. But I positively forbid any sale or exchange of this property during the lifetime of my son, Nathanael R. Greene.

"And I humbly hope that my grandchildren may consider this property I now give them as a sacred deposit in their hands for their children. But in the case of the death of my son before his children become of lawful age, then I appoint my Executors to take possession of and manage this property for the sole use of those children.

"In the second place and upon the above conditions I give, devise and bequeath to the lawful children of my son, fourteen silver wine cups, and a silver Tankard together with half of the silver spoons marked N.G., and thirty Negroes whose names are as follows, with all their future issue: Big Nell, Elie, Warren, Juda, Nutta, Cuffy, Amy, May, Phebe, Dorothy, Nelly, Mary, Warrin, Step, Tom, Cate, Polly, Stephen, Die, Pricilla, Clerysa, Mary, Die, Ellen, Peggy, Lucy, Stepney, Mana, Amonetta.

"And one half of the books belonging to the Honorable Nathanael Greene, I do give, devise and bequeath to the lawful children of my son Nathanael R. Greene to their Heirs and Executors forever.

"In the third place I do give, devise and bequeath to my Excellent and dutiful Daughter, Louisa Catharine Greene and to her Heirs, Executors and assigns forever my plantation on Cumberland Island called Dungeness, be the same more or less, together with all my household furniture, which I have not already disposed of, namely the articles of Plate mention above—with one half of the Books belonging to her honored father, General Nathanael Greene, my carriage and horses and my Boat called Nonpareil with all my Books belonging to Phineas Miller Esq. (his miniature picture set in gold and a Brest pin of the hair of General George Washington which he presented to me). I also give my daughter Louisa Catharine during her life time to descend to her children who survive her, otherwise it is my will that the above named picture and pin shall descend at her death to my Godson, Phineas Miller Killock of Savannah. I also give, devise, and bequeath to my beloved daughter, Louisa Catharine Greene, thirty-seven Negroes, whose names are as follows: Ashton, Raina, Billy, Billa, Sarah, Abbo, Bob, Hannah, Dick, Oscar, Isaac, Stephen, Frank, Liberty, Feby, Hilly, Jenny, Daniel, Peter, Hager, Smith, Isaac, Peggy, Eliza, Butler, Will, Driver Billy, Nancy, Jacob, Jonny, Die, Clarinda, Cenda, Andrew, Jude, Sail and Will with all their natural Issue.

"As my beloved nephew Ray Sands is considered rich and without a family, I only give him my favorite little boy Charly, as a testimony of my affection for him.

"I also give, devise and bequeath to my beloved and dutiful niece Phebe R. Paine the one half of my right in an undivided tract of land situated on Catfish creek on St. Marys River, be the same more or less to her Heirs, Executors, and assigns forever, and I also give her three Negroes named Polly, Betty and Jack, with one thousand dollars to be paid her by my daughter, Louisa Catharine, within eighteen months after my death.

"And it is further my will to hereby give, devise and bequest to my Godson, Phineas Miller Kollock, and to my best beloved friend Doctor Lemuel Kollock, five hundred acres of my portion of an undivided tract of land situated on Duck River in the State of Tennessee. In case (upon the settlement of Mr. Miller's Estate there shall be more property than will pay the debts and defray the expenses of settlement) then I do give to my beloved Godson, Phineas Miller Kollock, the one half of whatever I may fall Heir to from that estate to him, his Heirs and forever. To the same Godson I give a pair of pistols, which belonged to my beloved and ever-lamented husband Phineas Miller, Esq.

"And it is further my will I hereby direct my Executors to sell all the rest of my Estate and after paying my debts if there should remain ten thousand dollars, then I command my Executors to pay to Captain William Littlefield of Rhode Island, my only and most beloved Brother, the sum of one thousand dollars, and to my equally beloved sister, Phebe Sands of Block Island, the sum of one thousand and all my wearing apparel.

"I also give to my grandson Phineas Miller Nightingale the sum of one thousand dollars, and to my granddaughter, Catharine Nightingale five hundred dollars, and to my grandson Joseph Nightingale five hundred dollars.

"And it is further my will that fifteen hundred dollars be equally divided between my three other grandchildren: George W. Skipwith, Paten Skipwith and Gray Skipwith.

"I do give my daughters, Mrs. Martha W. Turner of Est. Greenwich, and Mrs. Cornelia D. Skipwith Littlefield, the sum of fifty dollars each.

"To Dr. Lemuel Kollock, who to me has been a friend indeed, I give one thousand dollars, and to my beloved friend Russel Goodrich, I give five hundred dollars as a small testimony of my affection.

"The residue of my property, if any there should be, I give to my son Nathanael Ray Greene, my daughter Louisa C. Greene and my niece Phebe R. Paine to share and share alike.

"But in case I should not die possessed of as much property as I have given in legacies, then it is my will that my Estate or rather my proportion of the Tennessee lands be sold to the best advantage and the proceeds divided among my Legatees in the same proportion that I have devised to them in my will: namely Phebe Paine, Phineas M. Kollock, Captain William Littlefield, Phebe Sands, Phineas M. Nightingale, Joseph Nightingale, George, Payton and Gray Skipwith.

"I appoint my beloved daughter Louisa C. Greene, and my dear friends Lemuel Kollock of Savannah and Russel Goodrich of Augusta, Executrix and Executor, investing them with full power, and I hereby invest and command that their Judgment shall decide everything relating thereto. It is further my will that no Court interfere with any part of my property.

"In witness whereof I have set my hand and seal the *10th of March in the year of our Lord Eighteen Hundred and Thirteen*. Catharine Miller" (seal). Signed, sealed, published and declared by the testatrix as and for herself her Last Will and Testament in the presence of us who in her presence of each other have put our names as witnesses hereto.

N.S. Bayard

Samuel B. Parkman

James Shaw

Will recorded and examined the 12th Day of April 1815 by ISAAC CREWS, Clerk.

ACKNOWLEDGMENTS

It seems that each book I write becomes a little more difficult than the last, perhaps because the subject matter hits closer to my heart or because I learn more about writing itself. But first and foremost, I offer my deepest thanks to God, who has given me the words to share, and has woven my life and art into a beautiful tapestry.

Secondly, thank you, Mike Mueller—my beloved husband. I admire your generous spirit, your prayers and encouragement, and your patience to work with me and make sure we get it right. Thank you for lying with me in the trenches, keeping your sense of humor, and employing your culinary skills when I'm "on a roll." You and my family mean everything to me, and I cherish the moments we work together. Thank you for understanding that my writing is part of my purpose here on Earth. May I always support you in the same way.

I am indebted to the knowledgeable staffs of the many libraries and historical societies I visited. I would like to single out Katherine Chansky, Special Collection Reference Librarian at the Historical Society Library in Providence, Rhode Island, for taking the extra step and having all my resources ready when I arrived.

I cannot imagine having written this book without the loving community of friends who offered me wisdom and encouragement. There are too many to name, but you know who you are. Thank you, Suzi Hassel, my *forever* friend and former next-door neighbor, for riding the train with me all the way to Rhode Island so I could find Kitty's heart and character. You, my wonderful "advance scout," located the next work sites while I was researching at historical societies and libraries.

Together we visited sources, laughing our way through each new adventure, including out-running Hurricane Sandy on Interstate 95 in a small rental car. You and I will always giggle over the indelible memory of lunch with Nathanael's nephew Tom Casey Greene and his dog Adina—a story only the three of us can appreciate.

I am deeply indebted and grateful to Tom Casey Greene, Nathanael's great-great-great-great nephew, who opened up his home to us, showing us where Nathanael grew up. Tom Greene lives in the same home where General Nathanael Greene was born. After inviting Suzi and me to spend the day with him, we wandered through the Greene cemetery behind the house, meeting other family members through their grave markers. Tom shared family momentos, photos and stories about Nathanael, Kitty and the rest of the family as we sat inside the family homestead, dating back to 1684. What a joy to meet Nathanael's descendant and hear his story firsthand. Tom, thank you so much for your generosity!

David Procaccini heads up the General Nathanael Greene Society in Coventry, and spent several hours touring us through the home Nathanael built for his future wife—Spell Hall at Coventry. David's amazing knowledge of Nathanael's and Kitty's story came to life as he guided us through the rooms, now restored to their original setting. David, thank you so much for taking the time to assist me on Nathanael's journey.

A huge thank you to my precious team, friends and partners who have journeyed with me through every book from frenzied inception to ragged completion. Pam Pollack, my brilliant editor whose magnificent insight always polishes my final product, you have my deepest thanks. Patty Osborne, my genius friend who takes the manuscript and cover and transforms them into beautiful books: this could not happen without you. Fellow author and talented friend Carey (Trip) Giudici, thank you for working through my stumbling words and making them better. Sharon Castlen, my publicist and friend, thanks for your insight and assistance! Bob Whalen, history teacher and role-player colleague, I am grateful to you for reading the manuscript through your historical vision and pointing out the mistakes.

Tom Casey and David Procaccini, I also want to thank both of you for reading the first draft of my manuscript to ensure historical accuracy. How fitting that you two, residing in the area where they grew up, were available to walk me through their early lives.

As always, I am grateful and indebted to my cover artist and dear friend, Gini Steele, who magically takes black and white historical photos and hand tints them to perfection. This time, Gini also found the cover image for me. You are amazing!

A heartfelt thank you to Buddy Sullivan, Coastal Georgia historian, fellow author and friend, for recommending I read about Kitty Greene as a possible story option. Three years passed before I found her, and now I'm deeply grateful you led me to her world.

Proof readers are always invaluable to an author. Huge *shout outs* go to Cassandra Coveney, Suzi Hassel and Cathy McLain for meticulously screening the final manuscript. Your sharp eyes saved me from aggravating "writing bloopers."

Nancy Thomason, thank you for advice on cover font and back cover wording. As a bookshop owner, and one of the first who believed in my talent, you certainly have the discerning eye in books!

The title of the book was changed several times, but we decided on *Lady Unveiled* after my friend Chris Belis joined in a conversation with other role-player friends and came up with "the winning" name. As Kitty was "Lady Greene" to many, and I definitely "unveiled" her, *Lady Unveiled* seemed to be the perfect call.

BOOK GROUP DISCUSSION QUESTIONS

1. The bond between a mother and a child can be one of the strongest forces in nature. How could Kitty have broken all ties with two of her daughters, when she lived a close yet complicated relationship with them for so many years? What drove her to this decision?

2. Kitty's beauty plays a major role in this story. What do you think accompanied that endowment: blessings or curses? How did this serve Kitty as a woman?

3. Kitty felt a deep-seated need to spend the winters with her husband Nathanael during the war. Can you sympathize with this? Was it self-serving, patriotic or something else?

4. What were Kitty's motivations as a young girl? Did they change when she reached womanhood?

5. This novel touches on adolescence and how defining that period of our lives is. How important was family to Kitty and Nathanael? What impact did their families have on their lives?

6. Kitty had a dream—a house and her family—that constantly shifted during her years with Nathanael. How did this form her character and their relationship?

7. There are times when Kitty and Nathanael's circumstances pushed them into places they didn't want to go.

How do you think God uses such times in our lives? Does Kitty's relationship with God change over the course of the novel?

8. During the course of the story, Kitty slowly becomes involved in unhealthy relationships with several men. Could you sympathize with her changing feelings toward Phineas Miller, Anthony Wayne and several others? How do you think you would have responded in her situation?

9. Several of the characters in this novel suffered because of decisions they made. Discuss the themes of guilt, grief, and redemption in this story.

10. Eli Whitney seemed to move in and out of Kitty's life. How did they shape each other's experiences? Would their lives have been the same had they not come together?

11. How does Kitty grow and change as a character through the book? How does she stay the same?

12. Kitty broke the bonds of tradition during her lifetime. Was she concerned with other people's opinions? How was she able to cope with the consequences of living an unconventional life?

RESOURCES

Primary Sources

Brady, Patricia, *Martha Washington: An American Life*, New York, NY. Viking Penguin, 2005.

Seabrook, Charles, *Cumberland Island: Strong Women, Wild Horses*, Winston-Salem, N.C. John F. Blair, 2002.

Stegeman, John F. and Janet A., *Caty: A Biography of Catharine Littlefield Greene*, Athens, GA. The University of Georgia Press, 1977.

Thane, Elswyth, *The Fighting Quaker: Nathanael Greene,* New York, NY. Hawthorn Books, Inc., 1972.

Secondary Sources

Bullard, Mary R., *Black Liberation on Cumberland Island in 1815,* Savannah, GA, Wormsloe Foundation Publications, 2005.

Bullard, Mary R., *Cumberland Island: A History,* Athens, GA, University of Georgia Press, 2003.

Bullard, Mary R., *Cumberland Island: Robert Stafford of Cumberland Island: Growth of a Planter*, Athens, GA, University of Georgia Press, 1995.

Eller, Elisabeth Fries, *The Queens of American Society,* Philadelphia, PA, Henry T. Coates & Co., 1867.

Fraser, Walter J., *Low Country Hurricanes: Three Centuries of Storms at Sea and Ashore*, Athens, GA, University of Georgia Press, 2006.

Gage, Matilda Joslyn, *Woman As An Inventor*, Fayetteville, NY, The Matilda Joslyn Gage Foundation, 2004.

Golway, Terry, *Washington's General: Nathanael Greene and the Triumph of the American Revolution,* New York, NY. Henry Hold and Company, 2006.

Granger, Mary, *Savannah River Plantations,* Savannah, GA, The Oglethorpe Press, Inc., 1997.

Kerber, Linda K., *Women of the Republic: Intellect and Ideology in Revolutionary America*, Chapel Hill,N.C., University of North Carolina Press, 1980.

Norton, Mary Beth, *Liberty's Daughters: The Revolutionary Experience of American Women, 1750-1800,* Ithaca, NY, Cornell University Press, 1980.

Roberts, Cokie, *Founding Mothers: The Women Who Raised Our Nation,* New York, NY. Perennial, 2005.

Rutherfurd, Edward, *New York: The Novel*, New York, Ballantine Books, 2009.

Showman, Richard K., *The Papers of General Nathanael Greene:* Vol II, (January 1777-October 1778) and Vol. V (November 1779-May 1780), Chapel Hill, N.C., University of N.C. Press, 1980.

Torres, Louis, *Cumberland Island National Seashore,* Denver, CO, National Park Service, 1977.

Uhlar, Janet, *Freedom's Cost: The Story of Nathanael Greene,* Indianapolis, IN. Dog Ear Publishing, 2011.

Ulrich, Laurel Thatcher, *Good Wives: Image and Reality in the Lives of Women in Northern New England 1650-1750,* New York, NR. Alfred A. Knopf, Inc. 1982.

Waldrup, Carole Chandler, *More Colonial Women: 25 Pioneers of Early America,* Jefferson, N.C. McFarland & Company, Inc. 2004.

INTERNET ARTICLES

"About Catharine (Littlefield) Greene (1754-1814)", www.nathanaelgreenehomestead.org/caty.htm

"American Revolutionary War General Nathanael Greene", http://en.wikipedia.org/wiki/Nathanael_Greene

"Battle of Ft. Washington", http://en.wikipedia.org/wiki/Battle_of_Fort_Washington

"Catharine Littlefield Greene", http://en.wikipedia.org/wiki/Catharine_Littlefield_Greene

"Catherine Littlefield Greene", www.answers.com/topic/catherine-littlefield-greene

"Clothing of 18th Century England-1770 to 1800", www.americanrevolution.org/clothing/clothing4.html

"Dungeness Island, Georgia", www.wikipedia.org/wiki/Dungeness_(Cumberland_Island,Georgia)

"General Nathanael Greene (1742-1786)", www.minerdescent.com/2010/07/27/nathanael-greene

"Henry 'White-Horse Harry' Lee, Revolutionary War Officer", http://en.wikipedia.org/wiki/Henry_Lee_III

"Inventor of the Week", www.web.mit.edu/invent/iow/whitney.html

"Major Nathanael Greene Collection", www.rihs.org/mssinv/Mss464.html

"Mulberry Grove Plantation", www.en.wikipedia.org/wiki/Mulberry_Grove_Plantation

"U.S. History/Military Ranks in the American Revolution", http://en.allexperts.com/q/U-S-History-672/2009/7/Military-Ranks-American

"Washington's Earnest Prayer", http://www.ushistory.org/valleyforge/washington/earnestprayer.html

"Who Served Here? General Nathanael Greene", www.ushistory.org/valleyforge/served/greene.html

"1775-1795 in Fashion", http:/en.wikipedia.org/wiki/1775-1795_in_fashion

NEWSPAPER AND MAGAZINE ARTICLES

Arnold, James N., *Vital Record of Rhode Island, 1636-1850: First Series: births, marriages and deaths: a family register for the people,* Providence, R.I., Narragansett Historical Publishing Company, 1891.

Barnes, Edna S., "Nathanael Greene's Rhode Island Home", Savannah, GA, *Savannah Morning News Magazine*, 03/22/1959.

Boisfeuillet Floyd, Dolores, "Mulberry Grove Plantation Near Savannah", Savannah, GA, *Collections of the Georgia Historical Society,* 1936.

Conrad, Dennis, "Nathanael Greene: Rhode Island's Forgotten Hero", The Lively Experiment, Alexandria, VA, September 2007.

"Eli Whitney's Cotton Gin", Savannah, GA, *Savannah Evening Press,* October 7, 1946.

Ford, Elizabeth Austin, "Catherine Greene—Godmother to the Cotton Gin", *Daughters of the American Revolution,* 2012.

Lawrence, Alexander A., "By Direct Male", Savannah, GA, *Savannah Morning News*, April 12, 1959.

Schlick, Stephanie A., "The Lively Experiment", Alexandria, VA, September, 2007.

Sewell, Cliff, "Eli Whitney: The Birth of the Cotton Gin, September 11, 1793", *Savannah News Press Magazine,* September 7, 1969.

Stokes, Thomas L., "Rivers of America", Savannah, GA, *The Savannah,* 1951.

Stegeman, John F. and Janet A., "The Search", Savannah, GA, *The Atlanta Journal and Constitution*, 1976.

"The Sea Islands," *Harpers New Monthly Magazine 57, No. 342,* 1878.

Winn, William W., "Cumberland Island and How Modern Times At Last Have Reached It", *American Heritage Magazine,* April 1972.

ABOUT THE ARTIST

Combining her mutual love of photography and history, Gini Steele and her husband Richard have created an extensive collection of photographic images of times long gone by. Throughout their work with historical societies, archivists and researchers they realized that there was a need to restore and reproduce these historic images and make them available before they are lost forever.

Staying true to the genre Ms. Steele used traditional photographic processes to both restore and reproduce the collection of old glass plates, negatives and photographs.

She enjoys the challenge of interpreting the old negatives in her darkroom and prints the silver gelatin photographs by hand one at a time. Once the photographs are printed, they are tinted by hand. Once the hand-tinting is accomplished, Gini uses digital technology to complete the image, creating a unique piece of art.

Gini resides in Beaufort, SC with her husband Richard and her two cats Bailey and Penelope Butterbeans.